What Every SENIOR Should Know

1,267 Secrets to Living Well on a Fixed Income

Publisher's Note

This book is intended for general information only. It does not constitute medical, legal, or financial advice or practice. The editors of FC&A have taken careful measures to ensure the accuracy and usefulness of the information in this book. While every attempt has been made to assure accuracy, errors may occur. Some websites, addresses, and telephone numbers may have changed since printing. We cannot guarantee the safety or effectiveness of any advice or treatments mentioned. Readers are urged to consult with their professional financial advisors, lawyers, and health care professionals before making any changes.

Any health information in this book is for information only and is not intended to be a medical guide for self-treatment. It does not constitute medical advice and should not be construed as such or used in place of your doctor's medical advice. Readers are urged to consult with their health care professionals before undertaking therapies suggested by the information in this book, keeping in mind that errors in the text may occur as in all publications and that new findings may supersede older information.

The publisher and editors disclaim all liability (including any injuries, damages, or losses) resulting from the use of the information in this book.

Wealth and honor come from you; you are the ruler of all things. In your hands are strength and power to exalt and give strength to all.
— 1 Chronicles 29:12

FC&A Publishing®
103 Clover Green
Peachtree City, GA 30269

Produced by the staff of FC&A
ISBN 978-1-935574-32-3

Table of Contents

Home Budget

Simple steps to debt-free living

Best basic budget for a fixed income

If you sometimes get to the end of your money before you get to the end of the month, you know how difficult it is to make ends meet on a fixed income. Having bill collectors hounding you for money can make the situation even worse. You may be tempted to pay the bill that comes with the biggest threat.

Paying bills based on fear rather than prioritizing them is a money mistake almost everyone makes. But the reason credit card companies get so good at making you afraid not to pay on time is they have to.

This kind of debt is an unsecured debt, meaning that unlike a secured debt, such as a mortgage, the credit card companies have less power to get their money. It's possible a credit card debt could be wiped out in bankruptcy court, while some other debts will follow you forever.

When it gets right down to it, certain expenses have to come first so you can survive to budget another month. Use limited funds to pay bills in this order.

Shop for groceries. Buy the food you need to survive. This doesn't mean loading up on gourmet nonessentials at the supermarket, of course, but you have to eat.

Be sure you have transportation. Pay your car note and purchase gas. If you use public transportation, be sure you have train or bus fare. After all, you need to be able to get to work, or at least get to job interviews if you're in a really tough situation.

Keep a roof over your head. Pay the rent or the mortgage note.

Satisfy your creditors. Last on the list are those other bills, whether they're from a credit card company, a jewelry store, or a doctor's office.

It's true that leaving some bills unpaid can harm your credit. But if you're in such a bad situation that you can't cover all your expenses, maintaining a high credit score may be the least of your worries. Get through each month and work toward improving your situation.

Pay bills on time and save $35 every month

You may prefer to keep money in your own hands as long as possible. The utilities or credit card company will get the money eventually, right? But habitually paying bills late can add up — to the tune of around $35 wasted each month if you pay one bill late. That could cost you $105 annually if you're late just three times.

Use this trick to avoid late fees. When a bill arrives in the mail, immediately place the return portion of the statement in an envelope, address and stamp it, then write the due date on the corner of the envelope.

Make two piles — bills to be mailed on the first of the month, and those going out on the 15th. Then, on the first and 15th days of the month, write checks and send out all bills in that pile.

Plan ahead for worry-free spending

Following a budget may seem limiting. But without a map of where you will spend your money, you're likely to go off course and run out of funds for what you really need. Do yourself a favor and create a budget — call it a personal spending plan, if you like — that provides the freedom to be free of money worries.

The secret of this six-step plan is you design it yourself. Here's how.

- Write down your total monthly income. Include take-home pay and any regular income from pensions and the like.

- Total up essential fixed monthly expenses, including rent, insurance, and so on. These amounts will stay the same each month.

- Add up essential variable monthly expenses. Items like your phone bill, groceries, and gas vary each month, but you can figure good estimates based on the past.

- Decide on reasonable estimates for nonessential expenses, including eating out and entertainment. Look back at your check register and credit card statements to remind yourself of items like Christmas gifts, vacations, or dog grooming. For expenses that don't occur every month, determine the annual cost and divide it by 12 months.

- Add up your expenses. If the total comes to less than your monthly income, you're golden. You can stop fretting over the state of your finances. But if expenses are higher than your income, you have found an opportunity.

- Choose what to cut. That's right — you decide what nonessential expenses to reduce. Do you want to keep your gym membership but cut back on golf outings? Great — as long as you stick to your plan.

Now you can feel good knowing you're not overspending. It's a budget you design to fit your personal needs.

Keep control by limiting automatic bank drafts

If you look closely at your bank statement and notice money has been taken out without your approval, you may be the victim of an unauthorized automatic bank draft.

Businesses like to receive payment by Automated Clearing House (ACH) debit, which you can approve to pay monthly bills to the utility company, your cellphone provider, or any other company. According to government figures, more than two-thirds of non-cash payments are made using ACH and other forms of electronic payments, as people write fewer and fewer checks.

ACH payments are convenient, but they're a problem when a business continues making debits from your account after you end the business relationship. When you cancel your gym membership, for example, monthly payments should end. If money is still deducted from your account, it's up to you to track down the error. That can cost you time and frustration.

Stop your losses. After you end the ACH payments in writing by contacting the offending business, you can set your mind at rest with a letter to your bank. In this letter, instruct the bank to stop allowing automatic withdrawals from your checking account to the business you list by name, as of a certain date. Also include the fact that you've canceled your account with that business. Federal law says the bank must then stop these payments.

Negotiate a different payment method. A business may try to push you into allowing automatic drafts, but you can sometimes avoid it. When Jenny H. went to sign up at a new fitness club in her area, the manager pulled out a contract detailing how the monthly membership fees would be deducted straight from her checking account. Jenny was able to avoid this option by paying by check for six months of membership in advance, even getting the seventh month free. No ACH agreement means she doesn't need to worry about inappropriate charges.

Get control over online payments. But sometimes you have to find a way to pay bills online if you want to do business with a company. In those cases, set up electronic bill payment through your bank. You can still enjoy the convenience of paying bills without having to write a check or buy envelopes and stamps, but you are in control of each payment. Then you can stop them at any time.

Get electronic help managing your finances

Paper and pencil are out, and electronic tools are in. That's how you make a budget these days, and the good part is you'll never have to do another math problem.

Computer programs that manage your money, such as QuickBooks and Quicken, have been available for years. Now you can also use programs that you access through the Internet, letting you see your financial information even when you're away from your home computer. At the store debating a large purchase? Call up your account on a smartphone and see what you've spent so far this month.

Check out these features. The service Mint.com is a free web-based tool that helps you stick to a budget and manage your money. Just imagine having a free online tool that offers these great features.

- Get email or text alerts if you overspend in a certain area.

- Receive alerts that a bill is due or you're about to incur a late fee.

- See a weekly summary of your spending and accounts by email.

- Track large purchases and rate changes.

Be smart about security. Some people are concerned that you must input your bank and investment account numbers and passwords to link accounts to Mint.com. Without doing that, the account-management and budgeting tools won't have up-to-date information to work properly.

Experts say the service is safe, since appropriate security steps are taken and your personal information is not linked. In addition, no money can be moved, or changes made to your accounts, through Mint.com.

Music educator David H. found Mint.com through an Internet search. After a year of using the service, including its smartphone app,

David is most pleased with the monthly budget features. He says he's not too concerned with security of Mint.com and has his online accounts linked.

"I feel pretty safe with Mint's security level," David says. "I think that is in part because it is a read-only service and you can't move funds with Mint. They say it has the same security as any financial institution, and I figure that if I just regularly change my passwords I should be fine."

But if you're concerned about security, there are alternatives to Mint.com.

Consider your options. Other sites offer similar features, sometimes without requiring that you link your accounts to the money-planning tools.

- ClearCheckbook.com. This web-based tool offers features similar to Mint.com, and it's also free for a basic membership.

- Yodlee.com. The Money Center tool available at Yodlee.com helps you track your accounts and budget, including meeting a set savings goal. It also gives you the option to share limited information with certain people, such as an accountant or spouse.

- HelloWallet. The app is free to download to your computer or smartphone, but an account costs $100 a year. It can help plan wise spending and track your online accounts. One special feature of HelloWallet is its ability to offer advice based on the good choices of other members — kind of like crowd-sourcing money management.

5 tricks to fool yourself into spending less

Researchers have discovered that people trying to watch what they eat can suffer from decision-making overload. After a long day of tough choices about diet and exercise, they find it difficult to make the best decision when it comes to a late-night snack.

It's the same thing with money. You can only tell yourself "no" to those little spending splurges for so long before you're ready to hear a "yes." That's why sticking to a budget may be easy in the short term, but it can be challenging in the long run.

Trick yourself into living within your means by making saving easy and spending difficult.

- Set up an automatic savings or investment deposit from your paycheck each month. If you never see the extra money, you won't be tempted to spend it.

- Take cash out of your bank account only once a week, and make that money last.

- Wait at least 24 hours before making any large, non-essential purchase.

- After you pay off a debt like a car note, continue to deposit that amount into a savings account every month.

- Every time you skip that $4 cappuccino, put four bucks into a cash jar. You can enjoy seeing the savings add up.

Find help when you're in debt over your head

When your best efforts at budgeting go awry, you may need help. You don't have to pull yourself out of debt alone. Take steps to get your head above water.

Get some counseling. This may be your first time in serious financial difficulties, but you can get help from people who know the ropes. Contact the National Foundation for Credit Counseling for advice about the best options for your situation. This network of nonprofit, community-based credit counseling agencies is available at *www.debtadvice.org*, or call 800-388-2227.

Voice your complaint. You can file a complaint related to a car loan, credit card company, mortgage, or student loan with the Consumer Financial Protection Bureau. Find this government agency on the Internet at *www.consumerfinance.gov*, or call 855-411-2372.

Ferret out information. The National Consumer Law Center (NCLC) offers a guide to surviving debt. From the NCLC website at *www.nclc.org*, click on the link to "Surviving Debt." This publication offers advice from legal experts on how to deal with debt collectors, strategies for paying down debt, refinancing, and many other issues.

Find personal help. Debtors Anonymous (DA) is a nonprofit organization that uses a 12-step program to help people who are out of control with spending and getting into debt. Check the organization's website, *www.debtorsanonymous.org*, to find a group near you or to take a brief questionnaire that may indicate whether you need help. You can also contact the national headquarters at 800-421-2383.

WARNING

Beware debt assistance with too high a price

Be careful of for-profit debt negotiation firms that offer to deal with your debts for a price. You may be paying someone else to do what you could do yourself, which is costly enough. Even worse, many debt negotiators are simply scams.

The Federal Trade Commission warns that many companies offering to have your debts discounted end up charging high fees for the help. They may also make promises they can't keep or even take your money and disappear.

A legitimate debt advisor will look at your situation and help design a debt-management plan (DMP), possibly even negotiating lower rates from your creditors and disbursing payments each month. If an advisor claims to be able to settle your debts for a fee without counseling or creating a DMP, find help elsewhere.

Keys to clearing out-of-control debt

A recent survey found that people 65 years and older have an average credit card debt of nearly $9,300, more than any other age group. But carrying credit card debt means you're paying heavy interest charges every month. You can pay off out-of-control debt and put more money in your pocket by keeping three key things in mind.

Use available cash. Don't let money sit in a checking account or low-interest savings account while you keep a balance on a credit card. You're probably paying much more in interest for the credit card debt than you're earning in a savings account.

But it's not a good idea to use a cash advance from one credit card to pay off another card, since you'll end up paying even higher interest and probably also a fee.

Pay off debts before you apply for a loan. At least 45 to 60 days before you plan to apply for a car loan or other loan, pay off all consumer debt. Making this change will lower your credit-use ratio so that your credit score goes up, likely qualifying you for the best financing deal possible.

Save money on interest charges. Paying 16 or 18 percent interest on your credit card debt is painful. That's why you'll want to pay off the card fast.

But if your only available cash is a small emergency fund, it may be too risky to use that money to pay off the card. Only do that if you have another source of emergency funds, such as borrowing from a retirement fund.

And don't think it's a good bet to put money into an investment rather than paying off debts first. You'd have to earn a ridiculously high profit — say, a pretax return of at least 21 percent — to justify making the investment rather than paying the debt.

Save $630 by paying off credit card fast

You know vaguely that the $3,500 balance on your credit card is costing you money. It's probably worse than you think.

The problem is you likely pay a high rate of interest on the balance, and paying it off will take a long time if you make

only minimum monthly payments. That's true even if you stop using the card.

Find some money to pay off a $3,500 balance, and you'll save $630 in interest that you would have paid over the next year. That's assuming your card carries an 18 percent interest rate.

And that's just for the first year. If you took longer to pay off the debt, you'd pay even more interest.

So what do you want to do with your $630? Surely you can think of something better than making a credit card company rich.

3 risky credit card habits

Credit cards can make shopping more convenient, but they can also wreak havoc on your carefully crafted household budget. To avoid having to dig yourself out of credit card debt, make sure you never get caught in that trap. Avoid these bad credit card habits.

Getting emotional with your spending. You have a budget — now stick to it. That means avoiding the ease of quick purchases that credit cards can allow.

Just a couple impulse buys funded by plastic can devastate your budget. Take time to think about a large purchase, such as a new set of golf clubs or a high-end vacation package. If you still want the item in a day or two — and if it fits into your budget — then buy it.

Making online checkout too easy. You can save money shopping on the Internet, but the process is almost too easy. Online stores like to have you save your credit card information in their online shopping cart, and doing so makes it easier to make a purchase quickly.

But it's better to make online checkout just a bit more difficult by forcing yourself to dig out your credit card and type in that information for each purchase. Doing this gives you another opportunity to stop and think about whether you really need to buy the item.

Becoming comfortable with carrying a balance. If you pay off your credit card every month and never carry a balance, you don't pay interest. That's a huge savings. But if you get in the habit of allowing a balance to carry over, then you can quickly get comfortable with an expensive situation.

One survey found about half of people with credit cards don't pay off the balance each month. That means you will spend the next 24 years making minimum monthly payments on a balance of $2,000. It's just not worth it.

Smart ways to get out of debt quickly

Paying off credit cards may be the simplest, fastest way to maximize your income and minimize your debt. You'll be amazed by how much money is left over at the end of the month once you don't have to send checks to all those credit card companies.

When you carry a balance on more than one card, you may need to decide which card to pay off first. It's usually not the best choice to pay a little extra money toward each debt, doling out dollars equally. That method would drag out all the debts for too long.

Financial expert and author Dave Ramsey discusses "snowballing" your debts. This involves making minimum payments on all but one debt, and sending all the extra cash you can to the debt you want to pay off most quickly. Like a snowball rolling downhill, gathering momentum as it grows, you then focus your extra cash toward paying off another debt once the first one is done.

Depending on your personality, you have several options of how to create your snowball.

Get some powerful motivation. Ramsey's advice is to first focus on paying off the debt with the lowest balance, regardless of the interest rate you're paying. That way you can quickly have one debt paid off, giving yourself success that will motivate you to continue.

If you've had trouble staying on track with your finances in the past, this bit of extra incentive may be just what you need to keep the snowball rolling.

Pay the least interest over time. Do the math, and you'll find that putting extra cash toward the debt that carries the highest interest rate will save you money. That means you can simply check the interest rates on your credit cards and see which is higher. You'll have to decide whether you need the psychological boost that comes with paying off a debt quickly, or whether you feel more comfortable knowing you're saving the most money.

Try using a comparison calculator, such as the Snowball Calculator available at *www.whatsthecost.com/snowball.aspx*, to find out just how much you can save by paying off the highest-interest debt sooner.

Increase your available cash. You also have the option of first paying off the debt that requires the highest monthly payment. This choice will create more available cash each month, since that higher payment will be erased quickly. Of course, ideally you would then put that extra cash toward a remaining debt.

But there are times when you may need to make a different choice about which card to pay off first, such as when your focus is on raising your credit score. For more information, see *Raise credit score with right payment plan* later in this chapter.

Save $213 by snowballing the right way

You want to pay off your credit card debts fast. Putting extra cash toward the debt that carries the highest interest rate will save you money in the long run. Here's how.

Let's say you have balances on two credit cards. You owe $2,000 on your Bank A card, and you owe $3,000 on your Bank B card. You pay minimum balances of $25 on each card every month, plus you have $100 extra to put toward one of the debts. The Bank A card charges 12 percent interest, while the Bank B card charges 16 percent interest.

Do the calculations, and you'll find that in this case you could save $213 in interest just by choosing to pay off the credit card with the highest interest rate first. Send your extra money to the Bank B card.

Keep money in your pocket during a divorce

When you go through a divorce, you probably want to get things over with quickly — including dealing with joint debts like credit card bills. The temptation to be finished fast can cause you to pay bills you don't need to pay. Know your rights and avoid losing money to your ex's credit card debts.

Deal with debt the right way. Pay off and close any joint credit card accounts, in part to avoid having your soon-to-be ex running up bills in your name. But here's where it can get tricky.

Some people assume they are responsible for a spouse's credit card debt, but that's not always the case. You may not be responsible for credit card debt your spouse incurred before your marriage.

Debt taken out during the marriage can be even more complicated, depending on several factors.

- Is the credit card in both your names?

- Do you live in a community property state or a common law state?

- What does your divorce decree say?

Your divorce decree can rule who is responsible for paying off which credit card. However, if you cosigned on that account, the credit card company may come after you for an unpaid debt — even if your ex was held responsible for the debt in the decree. You may need to contact the lender to ask about having the debt put in your ex's name only.

Keep tabs on your credit future. Take two important steps to make sure your ex doesn't leave you holding a bag of credit card bills in the future.

First, splurge for a credit-monitoring service beginning with the date of separation. No matter how congenial your divorce seems to be, remember that people can do some crazy, selfish things when emotions take over. For about $100 per year, your peace of mind is well worth the cost of a credit-monitoring service.

Then, place a fraud alert on your credit report immediately after your divorce. That way you will know if your angry ex has tried to open an account in your name. He could open an account in your name with statements sent to his address, then skip out on payments. If he runs up a balance, that could ruin your credit.

5 ways to stay on the good-credit road

You've reached the finish line — your credit card debt is paid off. Now what? Stay out of debt and on the road to good credit by taking these next steps.

Pay yourself. Continue making the same payment every month, but put the money in your savings account instead of sending it to your credit card company. You'll never miss it, since you've been doing without it as you worked to pay off your debt.

Try a charge card. Unlike a credit card, a charge card must be paid off in full every month. Knowing this, you'll be less likely to run up a bill. Companies like American Express and Diners Club offer charge card options.

Consider a prepaid option. You want the convenience of paying at the gas pump rather than going inside the store, and you may also want to shop online. Get a prepaid card and you can still have this freedom — without the worry of going into debt again. Check the fees when you pick a card.

Stay at a safe level. Using a credit card responsibly is important in keeping your credit score high. But there's a limit to how much you should charge.

Financial experts say a well-planned household budget includes no more than 4 percent of monthly pretax income for consumer debt payments. That category includes credit card and personal loan payments, but not mortgage or car loans.

Here's an example. If your annual salary is $50,000, you should have monthly loan and/or credit card payments of no more than $167. That's $50,000 divided by 12 months, times 4 percent. Keep your payments in this safe zone, and you can avoid trouble down the road.

Keep your card, but make it manageable. After you pay off a credit card balance, don't close that account. Keep it open and in good standing, so the amount of available credit can help boost your credit score.

But you don't want to keep paying monthly fees. See if you can downgrade your account to a lesser card offered by that bank to avoid paying the fees of a higher card. Even if you no longer get the rewards of a higher-level card, that's probably fine. You're saving money and boosting your credit score.

Top 5 tricks to boost your credit score

Your credit score, or FICO score, is an important number — between 330 and 850 for most people — that indicates whether or not you're a good credit risk. A high score will get you the best rates for a car loan, for example, while a low score can even keep you from being hired for certain jobs.

The details of how your score is calculated are kept secret, but five factors figure into its calculation. You can raise your score by making changes in each area.

Don't apply for credit you don't need. Ten percent of the score is based on recent applications for credit. Improve your score by staying conservative. Skip that shiny new credit card from your favorite department store — even if it means you don't get the one-time 10-percent discount being offered.

Add variety to your credit. Having various types of credit makes up 10 percent of your score. This factor is about the basic types of credit — installment credit such as a student loan, revolving credit like a credit card, and consumer finance such as a bank loan. Add a small personal loan, for example, if you don't have any installment loan history. Be sure to pay it back on time.

Pay with an older credit card. Length of credit history counts for 15 percent. Improve this factor by pulling out an old, dusty credit card you haven't used lately to add more weight to the longevity of your history with that lender.

Reduce your debts. Some 30 percent of your score comes from how much of your available credit is used. You can gauge the ratio of your credit debt to total available credit by looking at how close your credit card balance is to its limit. Pay down the balance to less than 30 percent of your limit — below 10 percent, if you can.

Ask for forgiveness. The largest portion of the score, 35 percent, comes from whether you've paid your bills on time. You may be able to get a "goodwill adjustment" — a one-time forgiveness of a late payment — if you haven't paid late before. You can also try for a goodwill deletion of a late payment that's made it onto your credit report. Call the lender and ask.

Amazingly, a single late payment damages a high score more than it affects a low score, potentially dropping a score of 700 by 100 points.

Nab $200 discount with high credit score

Next time you move and need to have utilities connected at your new address, you may be able to get it done for free. If your credit score is high enough, some utility companies will waive the security deposit. That can easily mean $100 to $200 that stays in your pocket just because you've shown yourself to be a good credit risk. Your high credit score may also nab you a better deal on expenses like cellphone plans.

Check your credit identity for free

There's more to good credit than just your score. That number is based on your history as a buyer and borrower, and it's all contained in your personal credit report. If your score is not so hot, you need to see your credit report to find out what's behind the low number.

Find and fix errors. Even if you've done everything right, your report may have errors that make you look bad. One survey found 79 percent of consumer credit reports in the United States contained at least one error. Many were harmless, like listing an old address, but around 30 percent of the errors showed open balances on accounts that had been closed.

You can dispute errors on your report with the credit reporting agencies, either by letter or at their websites. By law they must respond within 30 days. If they can't verify the negative information about your credit history, they must remove it from your report.

Another reason to check your credit report is to be sure it contains all the good information possible. If your report does not include an account where you have a history of on-time payments, you can ask to have it added. This is common with utility bills, like your phone or cable bill, which typically don't appear on a report unless you are delinquent.

And contrary to what you may have heard, your credit score won't be hurt when you request a copy of your own credit report. This is considered a "soft pull" rather than a "hard pull," which is what occurs when you apply for a loan. A lender's hard pull can lower your credit score, and it stays on your report for six months.

Never pay for a report. Three major credit-reporting agencies exist in the United States — Experian, Equifax, and TransUnion. Get your report from all three, since they may be different.

By law you can get a copy of your reports free once a year through a single source, AnnualCreditReport.com. If you prefer, you can call 877-322-8228 toll free. You can also get a copy for free if information in the report results in negative action against you, such as being denied a loan.

But while the report is free, you'll pay around $6 to $8 to see your credit score.

Since you can get your report for free, there's no need to pay $14.95 to get it from a company like TrueCredit.com. And skip offers from companies such as FreeCreditReport.com. Your report may be free, but you'll automatically get signed up and billed $200 annually for a credit-monitoring service.

Save $15,000 by keeping your FICO score high

A high credit score does more than make you feel good about yourself. It can save you money when you finance a large purchase.

That's because your rate of interest for a car loan or mortgage is determined largely by your credit score. If a lender offers the best rates only to borrowers with a score of 700 or higher, and your score is 698, you're out thousands of dollars in interest.

Look at it this way. According to finance experts, the difference between these two scores means the interest rate you'll pay will be about one-third of a percentage point higher. If you want to get a 30-year fixed-rate mortgage of $180,000, that one-third of a point will cost you $15,001 in added interest charges. That's assuming 5 percent is the lowest rate available.

Raise credit score with right payment plan

More than one-third of your credit score is based on your history of paying bills. That makes it an important area to focus on as you work to raise your score. Fine-tune your method with these tricks.

Focus on recent debts first. Experts say it's better to pay off newer debts first rather than trying to pay off older debts and defaults, which are probably the ones eating at your conscience. If your debt is so old that it's gone to collections, the amount you owe doesn't really matter. The current debts will affect your credit score more.

Don't ignore these side items. Recent changes in credit reporting mean certain elements that didn't affect your score in the past are now being followed. The big one is rent payment history. In fact, Experian, one of the three major credit bureaus, has acquired a new unit to track rent behavior — Experian RentBureau.

Other types of debts, including payday loans and child-support payments, are also now being tracked by some credit agencies.

Pay credit card bill extra fast. Even if you pay your credit card bill as soon as it arrives, that may not be fast enough. The statement balance could still be recorded on your credit report. That's a big problem if you have a card with a revolving credit limit, since the difference between your monthly limit and what you've charged during the month can make it appear that your account is over the limit.

Avoid that problem by paying your bill even before the statement arrives. You can pay online, which is convenient and saves the cost of a postage stamp. But even an online payment may take two or three days to clear. The absolute fastest way to pay is to go to the bank that issued your card and pay at the window. You can also pay your bill for a store credit card at the store itself.

Pay off card that boosts credit ratio. If you have balances on more than one credit card, put extra money toward paying off the one that represents the highest percentage of credit available.

For example, let's say you have two credit cards, each with $1,000 outstanding balances, but card A has a $2,000 limit and card B has a $4,000 limit. Pay off card A first. Doing this — rather than choosing based on how high the balance is — will boost your score by raising your credit-to-debt ratio the most.

WARNING

Sweat the small stuff to save your hide

Even an unpaid library fine can lower your FICO score. Roughly 35 percent of your credit score is based on payment history, which includes small items like parking tickets, speeding tickets, and library fines. Ignore these little debts, and your score can suffer.

How much can it hurt? One financial expert warns an unpaid library fine can lower a credit score by up to 100 points. That can mean the difference between a 750 score, giving you access to loan rates better than the prime rate, and a 650, with subprime financing.

Various library systems have different policies about using collections agencies, but it's best to return books on time and pay fines promptly. Generally speaking, if you pay up before an overdue fine is turned over to a collections agency, you should be able to avoid a credit-score mess.

Surprising effect of bad credit

If you're single and dating, you may find yourself asked a really big question as early as a first date — but it may not be the one you're thinking of.

How about "what's your credit score?"

Savvy singles of all ages are paying close attention to the credit history of people they date, rating money-management skills equal to looks in romantic relationships. In fact, a survey of 1,000 adults found 75 percent of women and 57 percent of men said credit scores play into their dating decisions.

A healthy concern for money-handling skills makes sense, since finances can greatly affect a long-term relationship. A person's credit history may be especially important to older adults who are dating again and want to protect their finances.

If you're reluctant to bring up the subject, you can limit your partners by looking for love through websites that do the vetting for you. CreditScoreDating.com factors your credit score into the matchmaking process, helping you find a partner with a similar score. But credit scores are self-reported, so it's an honor system.

If you really want peace of mind, you may want to do a background check instead. Criminal records, driving records, bankruptcy, and liens can all be discovered through a background check. Although credit records are not usually part of the search, they can be accessed depending on how much you want to pay. Check the laws and regulations in your state to see whether certain information may be restricted from your report.

Investments

Wise ways to grow your nest egg

Pensions and IRAs

5 critical ways to judge a lump-sum offer

"Take your entire pension in this lump sum, instead of monthly payments for life," suggests the letter from your pension plan. The giant dollar figure the letter displays may make you feel like a lottery winner, but your choice may influence your financial status for decades — so don't be fooled. Consult with a financial professional, and use these five basic questions to help you make this incredibly important decision.

How long will your retirement be? If your life expectancy is low, you may do better taking the lump sum, but the longer you live, the more you benefit from monthly payments. One expert even recommends turning down the lump sum unless you can cover all vital retirement expenses without touching your pension.

Can you invest the lump sum to make more money than your pension would? If you choose the lump sum, you must make it last the rest of your life. To start, estimate the length of your retirement in months, and multiply that number by your monthly pension amount. For example, 360 months (30 years) times a monthly payment of $2,500 equals a lifetime payment total of $900,000. Calculate your own lifetime payment total, and compare it to your lump sum.

If your lump sum is less than your lifetime payment total, you must expertly invest the lump sum so it grows enough to cover all monthly pension payments until retirement ends. If you're not sure how to do that, either take the monthly payments, or seek help from a financial professional.

Have you planned for the bite of fees, commissions, and inflation? If you choose monthly payments, your pension plan pays low institutional fees and commissions on its investments. But if you invest the lump sum, higher consumer investment fees and commissions reduce the money your investments can make. Hiring a financial professional to invest for you may take an even bigger bite from returns.

On the other hand, prices rise every year, but most pension payments never increase. People who invest the lump sum have better odds of keeping pace with rising prices. Just remember, if you take that lump sum, you must roll the lump sum into an IRA or 401(k) instead of receiving it directly. Otherwise, you must pay taxes on the entire amount.

How will you manage withdrawals so money is left for your spouse or heirs? Your pension may offer to pay your spouse a benefit after you die, but only if you take the monthly payments. Lump sum recipients must determine which withdrawal amounts will make the money last long enough to pay a benefit to a spouse or an inheritance to heirs. Unexpected expenses make sticking with a withdrawal amount tough. In fact, research suggests that cashing out a retirement account is one reason why many widows are poor.

Will your pension still pay full benefits years from now? Pension benefits paid by business employers can't be reduced after you retire. Even if your employer goes bankrupt, the Pension Benefit Guaranty Corporation insures most pension payments up to certain limits. Visit *www.pbgc.gov* to see if your pension is covered.

WARNING

Watch out for pension deception

Be careful when choosing between taking your pension as a lump-sum or taking it as monthly payments. Examine the lump-sum offer and the pension information carefully because some employers strip out early retirement subsidies worth thousands before they make a lump-sum offer.

Find out whether subsidies or subsidized benefits are available with the monthly payment option — or with an early retirement offer — and learn how much you stand to gain.

Boost pension with other savings

You may have noticed that the price of a movie ticket or gallon of gasoline was cheaper during your 20s — and so were many other things. This gradual rise in prices over decades is called inflation, and it can put a surprisingly big dent in anyone's retirement. But inflation may be particularly important to workers and retirees depending heavily on a pension for retirement. Here's why.

Cost of Inflation

Year	Expenses	Monthly	Annual
Year 1:	2,500.00		
Year 2:	2,575.00	75.00	900.00
Year 3:	2,652.25	152.25	1,827.00
Year 4:	2,731.82	231.82	2,781.81
Year 5:	2,813.77	313.77	3,765.26
Year 6:	2,898.19	398.19	4,778.22
Year 7:	2,985.13	485.13	5,821.57
Year 8:	3,074.68	574.68	6,896.22
Total lost buying power:			$26,770.08

Most pension plans don't adjust for inflation, so you get the same payment in year 30 of retirement as you did in year one. The average rate of inflation over recent decades has been about 3 percent, meaning prices rise roughly 3 percent each year. At that rate, $2,500 in monthly living expenses in your first year of retirement will cost you $5,000 by year 24, but you will feel the bite long before then — as this table shows.

Your Social Security payment may help make up some ground because it rises with inflation. But Social Security only replaces one-third of the income most people received before retirement. On the other hand, your living expenses may not rise as much if you have a fixed mortgage payment.

You can see how each person's financial situation can be different, so check with a financial professional to determine whether your after-tax retirement income can meet your expenses throughout retirement.

You may find you need other savings and investments in addition to your pension to cover part or all of your future expenses.

WARNING

Don't lose your nest egg to inflation

If inflation is 3 percent and you keep your nest egg in a bank account or CD that earns 1 percent, your money will gradually lose its power to cover your retirement expenses.

That's why experts recommend you put part of your retirement savings into accounts or investments that earn a higher rate of return than the rate of inflation. A financial professional can help you figure out how much of your nest egg to move and which investments will work best.

Score free money for your retirement

Are you throwing away free money? Don't make this crucial mistake. Here's why.

If your employer offers a 401(k) plan, you can choose to contribute a portion of your before-tax salary to your personal 401(k) account to save for retirement. Unfortunately, the IRS limits the amount you can contribute, but some employers match part or all of your contribution. Find out how to qualify for your employer's 401(k) match, and make sure you meet those requirements because that money can add up to thousands over time.

If that sounds unlikely, consider this. Camille H. did not enroll in her 401(k) when she started her job. If Camille starts contributing

6 percent of her $50,000 salary 10 years before retirement, her contribution will total $3,000 each year. Her company matches each dollar she contributes up to 6 percent of her salary, so that adds another $3,000 to Camille's 401(k) every year for a total of $6,000 a year.

Without the company match, Camille would only contribute $30,000 before retirement. But remember, most 401(k) plans offer investment choices to help retirement money grow. Assuming Camille's money grew around 8 percent each year, she would accumulate $46,936 in her 401(k) by her retirement date. But the company match gives her $30,000 in free money over that same 10 years, doubling her total to $93,872.

As good as this sounds, your 401(k) also has pitfalls you should plan for.

- You must pay the standard income tax on money withdrawn from your 401(k) during retirement. Your retirement tax rate may or may not be higher than your current rate.

- Your retirement money from the 401(k) depends entirely on how well or poorly your investments perform.

- You must wait until age 59 1/2 to withdraw money from your 401(k) or pay penalties. To learn about exceptions to this rule, see *Little-known 401(k) danger* and *No-penalty way to tap retirement accounts* later in this chapter.

Fortunately, your 401(k) also offers extra advantages to make up for these pitfalls:

- If you put money into a taxable investment account, you'd have to pay taxes on every dividend and every sale of a stock or mutual fund, but that doesn't happen with investments in your 401(k). That money grows tax free until you withdraw it.

- Your contribution comes from pretax money, meaning you pay no income tax on your 401(k) contribution before retirement. Here's how that saves money if you normally pay a 25 percent income tax rate. Before you can invest $2,400 outside your 401(k), you must pay $600 in income tax on that money. But you can contribute $3,000 of pretax money to your 401K — both the $2,400 and the $600 you would have paid in taxes — all without paying taxes or spending a penny more.

- If you are in a lower income tax bracket during retirement, you may pay a lower tax rate on money withdrawn from your 401(k) than you'd pay on that money today.

WARNING

Beware of costly penalties

"Cash out" or withdraw money from your 401(k) before turning age 59 1/2, and you can lose thousands to income tax and the 10-percent early withdrawal penalty.

For example, if you're in the 25 percent federal tax bracket and pay 4 percent in state income tax, receiving a 401(k) check for $10,000 costs $2,500 in federal tax, $400 in state tax, and $1,000 in penalties. You lose $3,900 or 39 percent, leaving only $6,100. Your actual losses may be higher or lower depending on your federal tax bracket and state income tax rate.

If you must cash out, avoid all taxes and penalties by requesting a "trustee-to-trustee" direct rollover into an IRA. If you can't do that, talk to a tax professional or visit *www.irs.gov* to determine whether you qualify for exceptions that may reduce penalty costs.

Forgotten tax credit rewards low-income savers

The saver's tax credit is so hush-hush that four out of five folks who qualify don't even know it exists. Find out what you may have been missing.

Cut your taxes. The Saver's Credit, also called the Retirement Savings Contributions Credit, can help lower-wage earners save for retirement.

"The Saver's Credit is particularly great because it offers many workers an added incentive to save for their future retirement, while potentially lowering their tax bill today," said Catherine Collinson, president of the Transamerica Center for Retirement Studies.

According to the IRS, you may qualify for a credit up to $1,000 — or $2,000 if married and filing jointly — which could mean a dollar for dollar cut in taxes. The actual credit amount depends on your income, filing status, and how much you put into retirement plans.

You may be eligible for this tax break if you have contributed to a traditional or Roth IRA, 401(k), or other qualified plans. This tax credit is nonrefundable, so it cannot boost your refund, but it could reduce your taxes to zero.

Claim your credit. To qualify, you must be age 18 or older, but you cannot be a full-time student or be claimed as a dependent on anyone else's tax return. In addition, the Adjusted Gross Income (AGI) on your tax return can be no higher than prescribed income limits. For example, in 2013, your AGI could not be more than $29,500 for single filers or $59,000 for those married, filing jointly. You also cannot claim this credit if you file form 1040EZ.

For more information or the current year's requirements, visit *www.irs.gov* or call toll-free 800-829-3676 to order Publication 590.

Leave more money for those you love

Want to hold on to your money longer or leave your loved ones an inheritance? Put as much as you can into a Roth IRA.

Your traditional IRA or 401(k) requires you to start taking withdrawals by age 70 1/2, whether you want to or not. And because you pay taxes on it, it you'll receive less money to live on or to leave to your spouse and children. Roth IRAs have no required minimum withdrawals, so you can withdraw all the money tax free, or leave it there to benefit your heirs.

Rescue your retirement with a Roth IRA

You may be surprised at the big bite taxes take from 401(k) or traditional IRA withdrawals during retirement, especially if tax rates rise, as some experts predict. Remember, you must pay income taxes on withdrawals, so taxes may eliminate up to 39 percent of withdrawal dollars, depending on your tax bracket. Your withdrawals could even raise your income enough for Social Security payments to be taxed. Fortunately, a Roth IRA may help, and it could be cheaper than you expect.

What a Roth IRA can do for you. The Roth IRA comes with these advantages.

- A Roth IRA resembles a traditional IRA, but you pay taxes on your contributions now so you can withdraw money tax-free during retirement. This may not seem important. But if you supplement Social Security income and traditional IRA withdrawals by working in retirement — or if tax rates rise — you may be in a higher tax bracket. Your taxable income will be lower if your IRA withdrawals come from a Roth IRA, because Roth IRA withdrawals are not taxable.

- You can contribute to a Roth IRA while contributing to a 401(k).

- You can make tax-free withdrawals from a Roth IRA at age 59 1/2.

- In the past, a few companies let you open a Roth IRA account with $100 or less. To check whether Fidelity, Vanguard, Schwab, or T. Rowe Price offers a low-minimum Roth IRA account now, visit their websites or call their toll-free numbers. Reach Fidelity at *www.fidelity.com* or 800-343-3548; Schwab at *www.schwab.com* or 866-855-5636; T. Rowe Price at *www.troweprice.com* or 866-224-3759; or Vanguard at *www.vanguard.com* or 800-551-8631.

Remember these restrictions. Roth IRAs may not be right for everyone, and here's why.

- Your contributions are capped. For example, you could contribute up to $5,500 in 2013 if you were under age 50, or $6,500 if you were age 50 or older.

- The IRA reduces your maximum allowed Roth IRA contribution by the amount contributed to your traditional IRA that year. So if the maximum is $5,500, and you contributed $4,000 to your traditional IRA, you can only contribute $1,500 to your Roth IRA.

- Your allowable Roth IRA contributions are reduced or banned if the Adjusted Gross Income (AGI) on your tax return is too high. In 2013, for example, you could not make a full contribution if you were a single filer with an AGI above $112,000 or married, filing jointly with an AGI above $178,000.

- Roth IRA contributions can't be deducted from taxes, but traditional IRA contributions can. If tax rates rise or you are in a higher tax bracket during retirement, you will be glad you paid the lower tax rate on your Roth IRA contributions. But if retirement puts you in a lower tax bracket, you would have been better off contributing to a traditional IRA to take the tax deduction when your tax bracket was higher.

Little-known 401(k) danger

With no credit check and a competitive interest rate, borrowing from your 401(k) may sound like a great idea. But you won't just pay back the loan with interest — you'll pay in other ways, too.

- You pay income tax on every penny you use to pay back your 401(k) loan, but you also pay income tax on that money again when you withdraw it from your 401(k) during retirement.

- Leaving your employer or being let go causes the entire loan to become due within 60 days.

- You must start paying off the loan during your next pay period or within a couple of months, and the loan must be paid off completely within five years. You may be allowed more time if you borrow the money to help buy your main home.

- If you cannot pay back the loan by the five-year deadline, a deadline set by your plan, or soon after leaving your employer, it becomes a withdrawal, and you must pay income tax on it. If you are under age 59 1/2, you must also pay a 10 percent early withdrawal penalty.

- Your retirement nest egg may end up smaller. Research by Fidelity corporation found that people contribute less to a 401(k) while repaying a 401(k) loan, and continue to contribute less than usual for a couple of years after the loan is repaid. Meanwhile, the money that has been loaned cannot grow if it is not invested, so your 401(k) either shrinks or fails to grow as fast as it would without the loan.

- You may not be allowed to borrow enough to meet your needs. Borrowing from your 401(k) is limited to half your vested contribution or to $50,000, whichever is less.

Mutual funds

Make more money on mutual funds

Just as termites can eat away at the wood in your house, small things can eat away at your returns from mutual funds. Check any new funds you consider to make sure your returns are not smaller than they should be.

Reconsider actively managed funds. Your mutual fund's portfolio and investments can be chosen by a manager, or the portfolio may be set up to match and keep pace with an established group of investments called a market index.

For example, the S&P 500 index is a market index. Funds based on indexes are called index funds, while funds that depend on managers are actively managed funds. Both kinds of funds charge an expense ratio, the fee that covers the fund's operating costs.

Subtract the expense ratio from the advertised return on investment to find out the real return. If the advertised return is 5 percent and the expense ratio is 1.5 percent, the real return is 3.5 percent.

On average, actively managed funds charge expense ratios 1 percent higher than index funds. If you invest $25,000 in an actively managed fund that makes 4 percent yearly, that extra 1 percent reduces returns by $250 or more every year. Without that extra 1 percent, you'd be $1,400 richer after five years. Here's why.

"The less investors pay in expenses, the more of their returns they can keep, and that can compound over time," said Tim Buckley, managing director and head of Vanguard's Retail Investor Group.

That compounding means each year's savings earn additional money in the years that follow. But that's not all. Statistics suggest index funds are more likely to deliver higher returns. So review the returns and fees in actively managed funds to help decide whether index funds should play a larger role in your investments.

Think twice before buying a target date fund. A target date retirement fund (TDF) is a mutual fund named for the approximate year you retire, such as Target Retirement 2025. The TDF manager chooses a mix of investments and gradually shifts that mix to more conservative investments as your retirement year looms closer. But the average expense ratio for a TDF in 2012 was 0.91, close to 1 percent.

Before you buy a TDF, shop around, research each fund thoroughly, and check the expense ratio. Sign up for a free membership at *www.morningstar.com*, and use their basic fund screener to find highly rated TDFs with low expense ratios.

Save up to $600 when you buy a mutual fund

Many mutual funds charge a 4 to 6 percent sales commission or load when you buy them. That would cost you $120 to $180 if you spend $3,000 on mutual fund shares or $400 to $600 if you spend $10,000.

But no-load funds that charge no commission perform just as well as funds with loads. To help find good no-load funds, visit *www.morningstar.com*.

Don't be surprised if many of your results come from the leading no-load fund families at Vanguard, Fidelity, and T. Rowe Price. But no-load does not always mean low cost, so check the expense ratio of no-load funds before you buy.

Annuities

Enjoy retirement and a steady income

Retirement today may mean worrying more about outliving your savings and seeing less in monthly income. Social Security may not cover your living expenses, and fewer people have pensions, so consider whether steady income from an annuity should be part of your retirement.

Discover the truth about annuities. When you buy an annuity from an insurance company, you pay a lump sum. In return, the seller agrees to send monthly payments for the rest of your life or a period of years. Several kinds of annuities are available, including the variable annuity you have been warned about because of high fees.

But experts suggest the simpler immediate fixed annuity is a more legitimate option for retirees. Unlike a deferred annuity, an immediate fixed annuity starts paying you soon after you buy it. And it differs from a variable annuity because all payments are set at one fixed amount.

Learn the fixed immediate annuity basics. Receiving payments for the rest of your life slashes your odds of outliving your savings. What's more, these payments make you less vulnerable to plummets in stocks or other investments.

If you are a conservative investor, you may even get a bigger monthly payment from your annuity than you could from regular 4-percent withdrawals from your nest egg. Here's why.

Buying a fixed immediate annuity is like buying a dishwasher. Once you pay for the annuity, you no longer have access to the money you used to buy it. That money goes into a pool of dollars paid by other annuity buyers.

Statistics show some annuity holders die younger than average, leaving extra money in the pool. The extra money is spread among the remaining people in the pool, giving you a higher payment.

Your payment amount depends on your age when you start receiving payments, your life expectancy, and current interest rates. The older you are on your first payout date, the higher the fixed payment.

But the lower interest rates are when you buy, the smaller your payment. For example, during the low interest rates of 2013, a $100,000 annuity paid $573 a month to a 65-year old man or $545 to a 65-year old woman.

Turn lemons into lemonade. A plain fixed immediate annuity may not pay your spouse or heirs after you die, and all payments are fixed at one amount rather than adjusted for inflation.

Fortunately, you can buy payout options or riders to solve these problems. To make sure your spouse gets money after you die, buy a Joint and Survivor Life Annuity. To see that your heirs get money, purchase a death benefit or return-of-premium rider.

Inflation or cost-of living protection ensures your payment will rise with inflation. Buying any payout option reduces your monthly payout, so ask for quotes both with and without each option to see the difference.

WARNING

Avoid this devastating annuity mistake

Don't put your entire nest egg into an annuity. Reserve some money for emergencies, long-term medical expenses, and investments that help keep inflation at bay.

Smart way to buy a fixed immediate annuity

Buying a fixed immediate annuity is complicated, and mistakes can cost you both now and later. Discover these expert-recommended tips to help you buy an annuity wisely and protect your retirement finances.

Get more for your money. Don't put all your eggs in one annuity. Instead, ladder your annuities. Experts suggest buying two to five annuities, but allow at least two years between purchases.

The first annuity will have the lowest payments. You will be older when you buy the next annuity, so your payment will be higher. If you buy a third annuity when you are even older, those payments will be the highest yet. After you buy the last annuity, your total monthly payment will probably be higher than if you had bought one large annuity when retirement began — assuming interest rates stay the same across purchases.

Another reason to ladder annuities is that low interest rates keep payments low. Remember, interest rates are part of the equation that determines your monthly payment. If interest rates are low when you purchase, but are expected to rise, your payments from future annuities should be even higher than they would be if based on age alone.

Become a savvy consumer. To help prevent problems with your annuity, follow this advice.

- Discover the single biggest factor that determines whether you'll actually see any money from an annuity — yet very few people even know to check. That factor is the financial strength of the insurance company paying your annuity. After all, you want to make sure that company will survive long enough to make all your payouts. Check ratings of the company's financial strength by visiting *www.weisswatchdog.com*, or look up the company in the A.M. Best or Standard & Poor's guide in your local library.

- Be aware that your state guaranty association pays part or all of your annuity if the insurance company goes bankrupt. Call your state's department of insurance, or visit their website to find out how much of your annuity the association covers. Check the rules for coverage, too, especially if you are retiring to another state. Buy annuities from several companies if your total annuity amount is higher than the amount your state guaranty association covers.

- Comparison shop. Visit *www.immediateannuities.com* for free quotes from many large insurance companies.

- Ask each seller for multiple quotes, even when shopping on the Web. Request one quote for the annuity alone. For each rider you consider, ask for one quote with just the annuity and that rider.

- Ask for details about the annuity's commissions and fees.

Stocks and Bonds

Survive the next stock market crash

Don't let a market "correction" decimate your retirement portfolio. Combine these key investment strategies to help protect your nest egg.

Rebalance regularly. When stocks rise sharply, your percentage of nest egg money in stocks jumps, too. Rebalancing means you sell off enough "expensive" winning stock shares and buy enough bonds or other investments to return to your original percentage of stocks.

This also locks in profits before a market crash can erase them. When stocks fall sharply, you sell other investments and buy the suddenly cheaper stocks. You can do this every year after sharp rises or falls in stocks or other investments. Some experts suggest rebalancing in late April and October, or use automated rebalancing options available from online brokers.

Own some blue chip dividend payers. Some stocks recover from market drops better than others, especially large, famous companies that carry little debt and consistently pay healthy dividends. This particularly applies to consumer staple stocks — companies that make food, shampoo, and other products people don't stop using, even during bad economic times.

Blue chip stocks are familiar names from the Dow Jones Industrial Average such as 3M, Johnson & Johnson, McDonald's, Coca-Cola, Exxon Mobil, Procter & Gamble, General Electric, Home Depot, and Wal-Mart.

Take advantage of dollar cost averaging. This means you contribute a fixed dollar amount every month or quarter to buy shares of a broad stock index fund or mix of stocks. Consequently, you buy more when shares are cheap and less when they are expensive.

"Over a longer time horizon, this strategy offers the potential to accumulate more shares of a company or units of a fund at a lower cost per share than if invested as a one-time, lump sum," said Viki Lazaris, President and CEO of BMO InvestorLine.

The dollar amount need not be large, and you can often automate the process through an online broker or your IRA or 401(k) custodian.

Practice diversification. Rather than putting all your money in one stock, invest in a mix of bonds, American and international stocks from various industries, and other investments like money market funds. While this may not save you in every market crash, it helps during company and industry slumps and will cut the long-term chances of all your investments collapsing at once.

Keep panic at bay. Risk tolerance means how you react to drops in the prices of your investments while waiting for those prices to rise. Some people weather a large drop below their purchase prices, while others lose sleep over small changes. The more you trade, the lower your returns. Determine your level of risk tolerance, and choose a mix of investments that matches the level of risk you are comfortable with.

WARNING

Stop panic selling with an emergency fund

If stocks or other investments serve as your emergency fund or your main source for debt repayment, you may be forced to sell those investments at a loss when emergencies happen or debts come due.

Keep a separate emergency fund instead of depending on investments, and seek ways to reduce debt without touching your nest egg.

Hedge your bets with a bond ladder

The trouble with bonds is they tie up your money for a long time, and you may miss chances to get higher interest payments as interest rates rise. A bond ladder can help.

Meet the bond ladder. Instead of buying one big bond that matures years from now, build a ladder of smaller bonds staggered to mature at different times. To construct a five-year bond ladder, you'd buy five bonds — one that matures in a year, another maturing in two years, a third in three years, and so on. As each bond matures, reinvest the money in a new five-year bond to keep the ladder going.

A bond maturing each year offers access to most of your money sooner than if you had bought a single five-year bond. You are also paid interest on the bonds until they mature. What's more, a bond ladder eases the effects of interest rates. When rates fall, bonds that have not matured continue paying higher rates. When rates rise, reinvesting as each bond matures brings you higher rates and interest payments sooner.

Know your options. You can tailor a bond ladder to your needs by:

- forming a longer bond ladder with more years or more bonds than five.

- selecting bonds that mature more often than once a year for more frequent access to your money.

- choosing a wider array of bonds including treasury bonds, corporate bonds, and more.

If interest rates are expected to rise for a long time, you can also reinvest in bonds with shorter maturities so you reinvest more often and get higher rates even earlier.

Ladder wisely. Fidelity offers a tool to help form a bond ladder at *www.fidelity.com*, but consider these points before you start.

- Avoid callable bonds that can be redeemed early.

- Invest in treasury bonds or highly rated corporate bonds to lower your risk of losses from default.

- Don't ladder bonds unless you have enough money to form a $10,000 bond ladder. Be sure to invest in stocks, too, to diversify your investments, and keep an emergency fund. If you don't have enough money to do all three, consider investing your bond money in a bond fund instead of laddering.

Managing investments

Top ways to retire with more money

Investing for retirement can be confusing, but it doesn't have to be. Just consider your age.

Think stocks during the early years. During your 30s, you don't have enough money in your nest egg, and you want it to grow. Like you, the dollars in your nest egg have a long way to go.

Every dollar has 30 years before you'll use it to pay retirement expenses. Because stocks are better at growing than fixed income investments like bonds, you put most of your money in stocks to help grow your nest egg.

Although stocks have more risk of losing money than bonds, your stock dollars will have decades to recover from stock losses before you need them for retirement. So you invest mostly in stocks, but keep some money in bonds and other fixed income investments to help your nest egg recover from stock losses.

Aim for balance as years pass. As you age, the day when nest egg dollars must pay retirement expenses gets closer. But you won't use all your nest egg during the first decade. That means some nest egg dollars are running out of time to grow, but others have decades of growth ahead.

To protect dollars that will fund your early years of retirement from a stock market crash, gradually move that money into fixed income investments like bonds. Experts recommend keeping the remaining dollars in stocks for three reasons:

- That money has as much time to recover from stock losses as dollars you contributed in your 30s did because you won't use it until your 70s, 80s, or 90s.

- Stocks have better odds of beating inflation than bonds, so they could help you cut the risk of outliving your nest egg.

- You may not have saved enough for retirement yet.

Even after retirement, keep some money in stocks to fight inflation and defend against possible bond losses.

Get the right mix. Knowing how much to invest in stocks is easy. This simple formula tells you how much and where to invest every year — no financial advisor needed.

Percentage of nest egg to invest in stocks = 110 - age

Using this formula, you would have 75 percent of your money in stocks at age 35 because 110 - 35 = 75. By age 65, only 45 percent of your nest egg would be in stocks.

For best results, experts suggest you invest in a stock market index fund that covers a broad array of stocks. Check your nest egg every four years to make sure your mix of stocks and fixed income investments matches up with the formula. If not, rebalance to the right amounts.

WARNING

5 biggest money mistakes as you near retirement

You may not have reached retirement yet, but you can see it from here. To keep your retirement dreams alive, fix or avoid these mistakes.

- not paying off credit card and other debts before retirement
- forgetting to rebalance your nest egg into less risky investments as you age
- not choosing a distribution strategy for your nest egg
- taking Social Security too early
- not taking advantage of a 401(k) match

Stop your 'bulletproof' nest egg from shattering

This "safe" investment, popular among retirees, can slip away over time if you go all in. Research suggests a couple who retires at age 65 with a $1 million all-bonds nest egg faces a 72 percent chance of running out of money during retirement if they withdraw 4 percent from the nest egg each year. Find out the important information you need to prevent this.

Beware of falling payments. Hold an individual bond to maturity, and you get a fixed interest payment during the life of the bond. However, inflation eats into those payments. If inflation is just 3 percent, a $50 interest payment today will only be worth $37.20 10 years from now. That is like taking $37.20 instead of your usual $50 to the supermarket. It won't buy as much, so you must get by on less.

Fight inflation and losses. If you had invested 25 percent of money in stocks and 75 percent in bonds in 1987, and maintained that balance until 2002, you would have had less danger of losses than someone who only invested in bonds. This happens because bond prices fall when interest rates rise.

That is why you might lose money if an emergency forces you to suddenly sell shares of an all-bond mutual fund or sell individual bonds before they mature.

"Investors have long relied on such traditional investments as Treasury bond funds as a safe way to protect and grow their money. For 30 years it worked, with Treasuries delivering annual returns of up to 8 percent," said Frank Porcelli, Managing Director and Head of BlackRock's US Wealth Advisory Business.

"However, if interest rates rise or inflation picks up, the traditional bond funds investors once thought were risk-free could lose money," Porcelli added. "The fact is that trying to 'play it safe' with traditional government bond funds is actually much more risky than many investors realize," he said.

What's more, stocks are better at beating inflation, so consider including them in your nest egg. This doesn't mean you should replace all your bonds with stocks. Instead, see *Top ways to retire with more money* earlier in this chapter, or talk to a financial professional.

10 questions to ask before hiring a financial advisor

A financial advisor may seem friendly and trustworthy, but he might be paid a commission to sell you particular investments or might not offer services you want. Research your potential advisor before meeting him, and ask smart interview questions to help decide whether to hire him.

Before you contact a financial advisor, learn whether he has ever been disciplined by a state regulator, the Securities and Exchange Commission, or another professional organization. Your state securities regulator can help you get this information. For the contact details of your state securities regulator, visit *www.nasaa.org*. If you are considering a Certified Financial Planner, verify his certification at *www.cfp.net* or call toll-free 800-487-1497.

When you meet with your prospective financial advisor, ask these questions.

- What experience and qualifications do you have?

- How are you paid — by flat fee, commission, amount of assets managed, hourly fee, or another method?

- Which services do you provide?

- What kind of clients do you typically work with?

- Describe your process for working with clients.

- What is your investment approach or philosophy?

- How much do you charge?

- Are you a fiduciary? This means he is required to disclose fees and potential conflicts of interest.

- Can anyone else benefit from your recommendations to me?

- Have you or this company ever been involved in arbitration? What happened? Arbitration helps settle disputes between financial advisors and clients.

WARNING

Get it in writing for better answers

Ask for information in writing about the financial advisor's services and how they will be provided. "You'll get better answers because verbal information can be a sales pitch, and it's too easy to deny later on," says Jack Waymire, author of *Who's Watching Your Money: The 17 Paladin Principles for Selecting a Financial Advisor.*

Find your retirement 'sweet spot'

What is the retirement "sweet spot," and how do you get there? The sweet spot is the amount of money you need in retirement accounts so you can live through retirement without running out of money. To figure out how to get there, see if you are saving enough now.

Get organized. Gather these numbers to get started.

- Find out your expected Social Security payment by visiting *www.ssa.gov.*

- Check how much money is in your retirement accounts and other retirement savings, and determine how much you add each month or year.

- Find out how much money you can expect monthly or yearly from your pension or other regularly paid sources of income.

- Decide what percentage of your current household income you will need during retirement.

Once you have these numbers, you can choose one of two ways to find your sweet spot.

Put the Web to work. This is the place to find free retirement calculators that let you plan your future without all that pencil work. Use one of these calculators — or better yet — try all of them for estimates of how much you need to save for retirement from now on. For best results, visit these websites and search for "retirement calculator."

- *www.troweprice.com*
- *www.financialmentor.com*
- *money.msn.com*
- *www.schwab.com*

Use the experts' rule of thumb. Some experts suggest the total nest egg required to fund your retirement should be equal to 33 times the income you expect to need during your first year of retirement. But those experts also point out that part of that income will come from Social Security instead of your savings.

Here's how to do the calculation correctly. Estimate the first-year income you will need, and then subtract the first year of Social Security payments. Multiply your result by 33 to get the total amount you need to save.

For example, if your first year income should be $30,000 and your Social Security payments total $12,000, $30,000 - 12,000 = $18,000. Then you would multiply $18,000 by 33 for a result of $594,000.

Don't panic. This is not necessarily the amount you must save between now and retirement. To determine that number, use this formula:

(Total Nest Egg) - (Current Retirement Savings) = Total Left to Save

For example, if you already have $250,000 in your IRAs and 401(k), $594,000 - $250,000 = $344,000. Use Web calculators or talk to a financial advisor to determine how much money must come from your paycheck and how much can be earned by investments.

WARNING

Avoid these retirement planning mistakes

The retirement calculator you choose may make assumptions about future tax rates, investment returns, inflation, or how long you will live.

Yet, if even one of those assumptions turns out to be wrong, the calculator will be wrong about the amount you need to save. To work around this problem, experts suggest you try several retirement calculators, and compare their results.

For an even better retirement plan, assume a worst case scenario with a life expectancy of 100, high expenses, inflation above 3 percent, poor investment returns, and higher taxes. That can help make sure that you save enough money to get through a long retirement, no matter what happens.

Hedge your bets with the 4 percent rule

Your retirement dream can turn into a nightmare if you withdraw too much money from your nest egg during the early years of retirement. A few experts have recommended withdrawing 8 percent of your nest egg each year, but that could reduce a $500,000 portfolio to $50,000 in just 12 years. Try this instead.

Research by retirement experts and investment companies suggest this rule can slash your odds of running out of money. The rule assumes half your nest egg is invested in stocks and half in bonds.

Day one. On your first day of retirement, divide the total dollar amount of your nest egg by 25 to get 4 percent. For example, $500,000 divided by 25 equals $20,000. Withdraw the result of your calculation — $20,000 — to cover your first year of expenses.

The following years. To calculate your withdrawal during each of the following years, use these steps:

- Find the current inflation rate. Watch or read the business news, or find the 12-month inflation rate at the Bureau of Labor Statistics' website — *www.bls.gov.*

- To figure your inflation factor, add the inflation rate to 1. For example, a 3 percent inflation rate would equal 0.03, so 1 + 0.03 would be 1.03.

- To calculate this year's withdrawal amount, multiply the amount you withdrew the previous year by your inflation factor. If you withdrew $20,000 last year and inflation is 3 percent, 20,000 x 1.03 equals $20,600.

This rule may not be perfect for everyone, especially if you have a small nest egg or very little retirement income from other sources. For best results, talk to a financial advisor to find the right withdrawal strategy for you.

Enjoy a long life without outliving your money

Withdrawing 4 percent from your nest egg during each year of retirement may not seem like a good idea when the stocks in your nest egg have plunged like they did in 2008.

Now experts suggest two different approaches that may help your money last as long as you do.

Keep withdrawals under investment returns. When choosing what percentage of your nest egg to withdraw during your first year of retirement, consider how much investments in your nest egg are likely to earn. If they are only likely to earn 4 percent, one expert suggests you should withdraw less than 4 percent of your nest egg.

But if your investment return is so small that it pushes withdrawal income below an amount you can live on, you may need a different strategy.

Try a flexible "floor-to-ceiling" strategy. Retirement withdrawal expert William Bengen studied a more flexible strategy. For a nest egg with 37 percent invested bonds and 63 percent in stocks of large companies, he suggested a retiree could calculate a first-year withdrawal of 5 percent and use that dollar figure as a base for future years.

In years when stocks fall, the retiree would only withdraw 90 percent of that dollar amount. In years when stocks rise, the retiree could withdraw up to 125 percent of the amount.

His calculations suggest retirees using this strategy would have less than a 10 percent chance of running out of money during a 30-year retirement.

Test a flexible strategy in the real world

Imagine you retired with a $900,000 nest egg just before 2001, invested Bengen's recommended amounts in stocks and bonds, and calculated your 5 percent withdrawal. If you had withdrawn 5 percent from your nest egg every year until 2013, you would have withdrawn $45,000 each year — even during the five years the stock market lost money.

To use Bengen's flexible strategy, you would have invested the same way and calculated a first-year withdrawal of $45,000. If you kept withdrawals between 90 and 110 percent of $45,000, you would have withdrawn:

- $40,500 after each year of stock market losses
- $49,500 after years the stock market grew 10 percent or more
- $45,000 after other years

Although you would have withdrawn a total of $4,500 less using Bengen's flexible strategy during the 12 years, your "flexible strategy" nest egg would be $11,260 richer than the 5 percent nest egg, thanks to lower withdrawals after bad stock market years.

Retirement hazard every woman should know about

Living on a fixed income is different for women than it is for men — because women must survive on that fixed income for longer, even though prices will keep rising. Here's what women and married couples must plan for.

On average, women who turned 65 in 2011 could expect to live another 20 years, but men who turned 65 that same year were only likely to live another 18 years. That is a two year difference.

What's more, almost 70 percent of all Social Security beneficiaries 85 or older are women. But even with Social Security, 28 percent of all older, single women live on incomes near or below the poverty line. That is why single women and married couples should plan and save for a longer-than-average retirement.

This means you should give extra attention to planning the last half of your retirement. You may also need to make adjustments like these.

- Working longer to be sure you get the highest possible benefit from Social Security. Remember, Social Security is based on your highest 35 years of earnings.

- Saving more or withdrawing less to spread your nest egg over more years.

- Investigating long-term care insurance or life insurance policies that include it.

- Contributing to a spousal IRA if you are married, but don't work.

- Taking Social Security later to create larger payments. This may include talking with the higher-earning spouse about taking Social Security later to boost the spousal benefit. Otherwise, the surviving spouse may face a drastic cut in income.

- Considering joint-and-survivor options if you or your spouse have a pension. Skipping these options means crucial pension income will end when the surviving spouse may need it most.

Remember these tips for a secure retirement

Make sure you don't forget what you have learned.

Avoid the three biggest 401(k) mistakes:
- not qualifying for an employer match
- withdrawing too much too fast during retirement
- borrowing from your 401(k)

Start working on the two smartest retirement moves you can make.
- redistribute risk as you age
- open a Roth IRA

No-penalty way to tap retirement accounts

Every year, nearly 40 percent of retirees are forced to retire earlier than planned due to health problems, layoffs, or other causes beyond their control.

If early retirement or an emergency happens, you need to know when it's OK to withdraw money from your 401(k) or other retirement accounts without the 10-percent tax penalty. These general guidelines can help.

Withdrawals are penalty-free if they come from one of these accounts:

- Traditional IRA or 401(k), and you are age 59 1/2 or older.

- 401(k) when you are age 55 or older and you lose or leave your job.

- 401(k) or traditional IRA, and you have become permanently disabled. Withdrawals may also be penalty-free if you use them to pay unreimbursed, tax-deductible medical expenses that exceed 10 percent of your adjustable gross income (AGI) — even if you do not have a job. Through 2016, people age 65 and older can make penalty-free withdrawals if they have tax-deductible medical expenses exceeding 7.5 percent of AGI. Talk to your tax advisor to determine when the disability or medical expense exception may also apply to Roth IRA withdrawals.

- Traditional IRA, and the $10,000 withdrawal helps pay for the purchase of a first home.

- Traditional IRA, and the withdrawals pay for a college education for you or a close relative during the same tax year. Withdrawals are also penalty-free if you use them to pay medical insurance premiums while you are paid unemployment benefits. Talk to a tax advisor to find out when these exceptions also apply to Roth IRA withdrawals.

Although all these are penalty-free, you may still have to pay income taxes on the amount withdrawn. But withdrawals from a Roth IRA are both tax- and penalty- free if at least five years have passed since you first contributed to your Roth IRA, and you meet one of these qualifications:

- You are at least 59 1/2 years old.

- You are permanently disabled.

- You use a withdrawal of $10,000 or less to buy, build, or rebuild your first home.

Just remember, the tax laws for retirement accounts may have changed in recent months or years. So before you make withdrawals, check the tax rules to see if the withdrawal is still penalty-free and whether you must pay taxes on it.

Banking

Insider secrets that pay off big

How to get truly free checking

It's getting harder and harder to find free checking. According to MoneyRates.com, only about one in three accounts is actually free. And the average monthly maintenance fee keeps going up. In 2013, it topped $12.26. That's a whopping $147.12 a year.

Tired of your bank treating you like a fee machine while they hold onto your cash? All is not lost. Here's how to beat banks at their own game.

Read the fine print on "free" checking. Some accounts claim to be free but aren't. In reality, you may get hit with a fee every time you use your debit card or the ATM machine.

Ask the bank representative exactly what you must do to keep your checking free. You may need to have your Social Security or pay-checks deposited directly into your account, for instance. Also ask about special accounts for seniors. Some banks offer these for free.

Get a waiver. If you get socked with an unexpected fee, don't be shy about asking the bank to remove it. The same goes for routine charges like maintenance fees. Many institutions will waive them if you bother to ask.

Ditch high-yields with high fees. Interest-bearing checking accounts sound great, but you're better off without one if it charges a fee. That's particularly true for accounts with high minimum-balance requirements and hefty penalties. Expect to pay far more in fees than you ever earn in interest.

Move to a credit union. Try this switch and get treated like a shareholder instead of a cash cow. Credit unions generally charge lower fees than big banks because they answer to members, not investors looking for a profit.

Credit unions aren't as exclusive as they once were. Chances are, you're eligible to join one based on where you live, work, or go to church. Find one using the National Credit Union Administration's online search tool at *www.mycreditunion.gov/Pages/mcu-map.aspx*.

Keep in mind not all of them deliver great deals. Read their list of fees and disclosures before opening an account, and keep an eye out for increases if you already bank there.

Say "no" to overdraft protection. What happens when you try to buy groceries with your debit card but there's not enough money in your account to pay for them? It depends on whether you signed up for overdraft protection.

- If so, the bank will let the transaction go through, then charge you an average of $30 for the privilege.

- If not, your card will be declined, you'll pay for your items another way, and avoid that hefty fee.

Banks make big money off overdraft protection — so, of course, they try to sell you on it. Tell them "no thanks." Carry spare cash as a backup, instead.

Link to your savings. Opting out of overdraft protection won't prevent overdraft fees on bounced checks or automatic payments, however.

You can guard against these by linking your checking account to a savings account at the same bank. If your checking is overdrawn, the bank will automatically transfer money from your savings account. You may pay $10 per transfer, but that's cheaper than an overdraft fee.

Cut the cost of buying checks

Pay half price for your next box of checks by ordering from an independent company instead of the bank. You could pay as little as 10 cents per check and get free shipping. Order from a big, national bank, however, and you could pay 23 cents per check, plus shipping.

Look for deals from check ordering companies in your coupon circulars. Or find a company on the Internet, such as Check-Works at *www.checkworks.com* or Checks In The Mail at *www.checksinthemail.com*.

Because checks contain so much important personal information, verify any company you consider using with your local Better Business Bureau.

Save $240 a year with online banks

Stop settling for high fees and inferior service at too-big-to-fail, brick-and-mortar banks. Online banks offer the same services for less. Since they don't have physical branches, they have lower overhead. They pass those savings along to you.

Say you have a checking account with a $500 balance and a savings account with a $5,000 balance, both at the same bank. At Bank of America, you could potentially pay:

- $15 a month in maintenance fees on your checking account.

- $5 a month on your savings.

At the online-only bank Ally, on the other hand, you would pay no maintenance fees on either your checking or savings account. You would actually earn a little money, since even a basic Ally checking account bears interest. That's a potential savings of $240 a year. Checks from Ally are also free.

Both banks charge for overdrawing your accounts, placing stop payments, and wiring money, but those fees are drastically different, too. For instance, you'd pay $35 for each overdraft at Bank of America — but only $9 at Ally.

You're right to be skeptical. After all, if a bank has no branches, how do you deposit checks, take out cash, or ask questions?

- Have your paychecks and social security checks deposited directly into your bank account. For paper checks, simply take a photograph of the check with your cellphone or camera and email it to the bank. The bank will deposit the funds into your account.

- Online banks have partnerships with national ATM networks around the country. You can use these for cash without facing a service charge.

- Customer service representatives can answer questions by phone, sometimes 24 hours a day.

If you still visit your bank's branch regularly, then online-only banks may not be for you. But if you rarely use them, the savings are substantial.

Put your savings account to work

Don't let your savings just sit there. Accounts that pay a decent interest rate have become harder to find, but they still exist. You simply have to know where to look.

Ask about rewards. Credit unions and smaller, local banks may offer accounts that pay a higher interest rate if you agree to do things like use your debit card every month or enroll in direct deposit.

Go online. High-yield savings accounts are alive and well at online-only banks. These businesses have no brick-and-mortar branches for you to visit. Instead, you do your banking using a computer and an Internet connection. Because they don't pay for expensive buildings, online banks can offer higher interest rates. Compare rates at different banks at *www.bankrate.com*, *www.money-rates.com*, and *www.nerdwallet.com*.

Make a match. Price-matching isn't just for big-box stores at Christmas. Banks do it, too, if you know to ask. First, do your homework and find a higher-paying account. Get the interest rate in writing. Take this documentation to your current bank and challenge them to match that rate.

Pump up your checking. Find high-yield checking accounts online through Kasasa. This service connects people looking for higher interest rates and rewards with community banks and credit unions that offer them. Visit *www.kasasa.com* and search by ZIP code for participating banks near you. Remember to read the fine print of any agreement before opening an account.

Consider other options. A money-market account may serve you better than a traditional savings account. It typically pays more interest in exchange for more restrictions, like withdrawal limits or a higher minimum balance.

Whatever you do, continue to check rates at other banks and credit unions regularly to be sure you're still getting the best deal. And make certain an institution is insured before opening an account there.

- Check a bank by calling the Federal Deposit Insurance Corporation at 877-ASK-FDIC. Or look up the bank online at *http://research.fdic.gov/bankfind*.

- Check a credit union by contacting the National Credit Union Association. Call 800-755-1030 or visit the website *http://researchcu.ncua.gov/Views/FindCreditUnions.aspx*.

Amp up the interest on your CDs

Forget what the bank advertises. The interest rate you're earning on your Certificate of Deposit (CD) isn't the real rate. It's much less. Subtract the inflation rate from the CD's yield. If you earn 3 percent interest from your CD, and inflation sits at 2.5 percent, then you're only earning 0.5 percent interest on your investment. Pretty puny.

This depressing math makes it even more important to maximize your yield. Try these hidden tricks to squeeze the most interest out of bank CDs.

Become a new customer. Banks lure new customers with hot deals, including higher rates on CDs. You might earn:

- twice the average yield on a three-year CD.

- three times the average yield on a CD that matures in less than a year.

This second option is especially appealing when yields are low. Tying up your money for shorter periods of time gives you more freedom to nab a good rate when they rise again.

Go long but limit fees. Long-term CDs may make you nervous when yields are low. After all, what if you tie up your money for 10 years, only to watch rates double during that time? Hedge your bets. Look for long-term CDs with small early-withdrawal penalties. If rates rise significantly, you can cash out early and reinvest.

Read the fine print carefully before buying a long-term CD. Some banks charge big fees for early withdrawals, and the penalties could eat up any extra money you stand to make.

Think outside the big-box banks. National banks offer some of the worst rates on CDs. Local banks, credit unions, and online banks may do better. Compare rates easily at websites like *www.nerdwallet.com* and *www.bankrate.com*.

Climb the ladder. Building a CD ladder is still the best way to maximize your return over time. Purchase a one-, two-, three-, four-, and five-year CD. When one matures, reinvest the money in another five-year CD. You'll always have one coming due and always have a five-year CD with a better interest rate. It also gives you more flexibility to nab a better deal as interest rates rise.

5 tips to find the best credit card

Credit card companies must give you 45 days notice before they raise your interest rate or tack on new fees. That means you have 45 days to shop around for a better card. So get going.

Start by asking yourself how you plan to use it. Do you:

- tend to carry a balance from month to month? Look for a card with a low interest rate.

- use your cards to buy everyday items like groceries, and do you pay the balance in full each month? Hunt for a generous rewards card that gives you cash back or points.

- use it only in emergencies? Shop for a bare-bones card with a low interest rate and no annual fee.

Leave corporate cards to the pros. Banks like to push credit cards designed for professionals and small businesses, but don't buy in. These cards are a bad deal for regular people. They aren't protected by federal laws the way normal cards are, leaving you vulnerable to sneaky fees and surprise spikes in interest rates.

Shop around online. Why pay high interest and hidden fees? Find low-interest credit cards, no-fee cards, cash-back cards, gas reward cards, and more, including the best cards for transferring those high-interest balances. Several websites offer free services that too few folks know about. Answer the questions at *www.creditcardtuneup.com* or *www.nerdwallet.com* to get a list of cards that may fit your lifestyle.

Ask for the lowest rate. You might think a solid credit score and steady income would net you a card with a low interest rate. Wrong. Banks try to shunt responsible people like you into cards with higher rates and more fees, because they know you'll pay.

When you call, be sure to ask about cards with low interest rates and no annual fees.

Think about the future. About to buy something expensive? Look for a card that offers a 0-percent introductory interest rate on new purchases. "Honeymoon" periods like this typically last between six and 18 months. Try to pay off your purchase before the introductory period ends and interest begins to accrue.

Check out balance transfer fees. Are you carrying a hefty balance on a high-interest card? Then transferring that balance to a 0 percent-interest card could help. Look for one with an interest-free introductory period on balance transfers. And ask the card company if they'll waive the transfer fee, usually 3 percent of the total amount of money you're moving. Do your absolute best to pay off the balance before the interest-free period expires.

Save big by slashing interest

Believe it or not, you can cut interest payments on your credit cards simply by calling your card company and asking for a lower rate.

Do your homework to find a different credit card with lower rates. Then call your current company. Be polite, but tell them you are thinking about switching to another company. Ask if they can match their competitor. That's only the beginning. Try these tricks to save even more on interest.

Pay early. Don't wait to pay your credit card on the due date. Pay it on the day you get the statement, especially if you're carrying a balance.

Say you racked up $2,000 in charges at an 18 percent interest rate, and you put $350 a month toward paying it off. You would save $3.97 a month by making that payment on Day 2 of the cycle rather than Day 25. It would take seven months to pay off the debt at that rate, and you'd save nearly $28 in interest by paying early.

The savings are even more significant if your credit card doesn't offer a grace period. If you rang up $1,000 in charges on your card, you'd save $11.34 paying on Day 2 compared to Day 25.

Pay extra. Paying as little as $10 more than the minimum amount due each month can chip away at credit card debt faster and slash interest payments over time.

Maybe you owe $2,000 on a card at 18 percent interest, and your minimum monthly payment is $50. At that rate, it would take you more than 15 years to pay off the debt, and you'd spend $2,423 on interest alone. Pay just $10 more each month, or $60, and you'd pay it off in less than four years and spend $793 on interest — a savings of $1,630.

Pay on time. Late payments can send your interest rate skyrocketing. So can payments that bounce. Stay on top of due dates and your bank account balance to avoid big hikes.

Don't use cards for cash. You can pull cash from most credit cards when an emergency strikes, but that convenience will cost you. Card companies charge much higher interest on cash advances. You might pay 18 percent on purchases but 25 percent on a cash advance. That's one expensive loan.

Keep an eye on introductory offers. Lots of cards come with teaser rates of 0 percent interest to lure you in. When the introductory period ends, your interest could shoot as high as 35 percent.

Read the card agreement carefully before you sign up. Know what the true cost of the card will be once the honeymoon period ends.

WARNING

Guard against fraudulent charges

Don't sign up for a new credit card without asking the company what steps they take to protect you from credit card theft.

Ernie Farr's card company did a much better job than did his friend's. "I have a friend whose card was used by ID thieves all over Europe before he knew anything about it," he recounts. "On the other hand, when my card got pinged for $1 in Poland and Russia one day, my card company called me immediately and issued me a new card after talking to me."

That level of protection can cause a few headaches, but Farr says it's worth it. The card company sometimes blocks large purchases, or those made out of state. "I've learned I can call them in advance and get clearance," however. All in all, he says, "I'd rather have a card company looking out for me than get a slightly lower interest rate and have no one minding the store."

Repair or replace broken items for free

Credit cards these days are packed with hidden perks, such as free extended warranties. Tim Anders found out exactly how valuable that benefit could be.

His $1,200 television broke shortly after the warranty expired. Fortunately, he had paid for it with his American Express card, which automatically adds another year of warranty coverage to any purchase.

Anders contacted the card company and sent them a copy of his original receipt. "They needed to know the date the TV was purchased, and the amount." American Express checked it against their records and contacted him two weeks later. They told him to get an estimate for the repair. Based on the cost, they would either repair or replace it.

Anders hired a local repair service to come to his house and give him an estimate. Then he sent the information to American Express. Two weeks later, the card company credited his account for the cost of the initial estimate — $92 — and the planned repair work of $538.

Extended warranties like this cover less expensive items, too, such as eyeglasses and small appliances. Stop missing out. Check your credit card's list of benefits, and be sure to ask about benefits when picking a new card.

Apps earn you even more rewards

Ever wonder which rewards card to use at which store to maximize the benefits? New cellphone apps will do the thinking for you.

- Tell Wallaby which credit cards you have, then choose a merchant from its list. The app will tell you which card will nab you the most rewards or the biggest discount at that store.

- The Glyph does much the same thing, but it also alerts you to rewards cards you don't have that could save you money.

Neither app asks for your personal information, only for the names of the credit cards you use.

Make money with the right rewards card

Play your credit cards right, and you could reap big rewards —
cash, airline miles, shopping discounts, and more. But betting
against the banks is risky business. They're experts at outsmarting
consumers and getting more of your money than you get of theirs.
Turn the tables. Start by choosing the right type of rewards card
for your lifestyle.

Cash back. Bill and Deborah Lausman have discovered a way to
make money off the bank. These active seniors have only one credit
card, a "cash back" rewards card with no annual fee. Each time they
use it, the issuer gives them a small percentage of money back. "We
charge almost everything," the Lausmans explain. "Even when it is
just as convenient to pay by check, we put it on the card whenever
the vendor accepts it."

A cash back rewards card won't make you rich. Most return as little
as $1 for every $100 spent. It adds up, though. "We charge $1,000
or more a month," say the Lausmans. They get back around $150
every year. "Not enough to buy a new car, but it's $150 we wouldn't
have otherwise."

Airline miles. Other cards offer airline miles, instead, perhaps one
mile for every dollar you charge. Some promise thousands of bonus
miles just for signing up.

Avoid a card branded with a particular airline's name. A general bank
card that gives you miles is more likely to let you redeem them with
any airline you choose. You may also face fewer blackout dates and a
lower threshold for redeeming your miles.

Gasoline discounts. Oil companies tout credit cards that give you
future discounts on their gas. If you always buy the same brand of

gasoline, then they might be worthwhile. But keep your eyes open — oil company cards may charge much higher interest rates than other rewards cards.

Now you know what rewards are out there. Here's the skinny on how to maximize them.

- Pay the card off every month. "Keep your charges down to what you can pay when the monthly bill comes in," advise the Lausmans. "Never, never carry a balance to the next billing period." Otherwise, the interest payments will outweigh any rewards you earn.

- Look for a card that gives you the most rewards for the things you already spend the most money on. For example, don't pick a travel rewards card if you only fly a few times a year. Get a cash-back card, instead.

- "Select a card that doesn't charge an annual fee," the Lausmans warn. An annual fee could offset the value of your rewards.

- Avoid cards that make it hard to redeem your rewards. Some cards carry so many restrictions the rewards are almost useless.

- Watch out for hidden caps on how much cash or how many points you can earn, as well as cards where rewards don't start to accrue until you've spent several thousand dollars.

- Limit the number of rewards cards you have. Focus on building up big rebates on just one or two.

- Look for cards backed by banks. Points earned on these tend not to expire as quickly as those backed by airlines and hotels.

- Read the fine print before redeeming points for cash. They may be worth less as cash than if you use them as travel miles or other rewards.

3 tricks to never miss a payment

Credit cards can be useful, and some can even save you money — but only if you pay them on time. Pay late, and you'll be slapped with hefty fees and a higher interest rate that could erase any benefits you've earned.

Do it in person. That's right. You can still walk into a brick-and-mortar building to pay your credit card. If your card is issued by a bank, like Wells Fargo or Chase, simply pay at a branch in your area. If it's a retail store card, like Target or Macy's, pay at the store itself.

Go online. Schedule your payments using the credit card company's website. That's how Melanie Dewalt pays. "I used to have to remember to mail my payments a full week before they were due," she says. "If I forgot, I would have to pay a fortune to overnight a check to the credit card company to avoid a late fee. Not anymore."

Now she goes to the credit card issuer's website as soon as she receives her monthly statement. "I tell the company how much money I want to pay toward the balance and which day I want to pay it." Then she sets it and forgets it. "They deduct it automatically from my checking account on the day I choose. It's so easy, and, best of all, no more late fees."

At the very least, have the company deduct the minimum amount due from your bank account each month. Call your card company to get help setting up your online account.

Set reminders. Go old-school and write a note on your calendar or in your scheduling book on the day you should mail your payment. You can also set electronic reminders. Type the note on your cellphone's or computer's built-in calendar.

How to dodge hidden fees

High interest rates aren't the only downside for credit cards. Some carry surprise fees, and some merchants charge extra for paying by credit instead of cash. Learn how to dodge these sneaky charges.

Higher fees for better rewards. That generous rewards card packed with perks may have a surprise for you. Companies often charge an annual fee for their more generous cards but waive it for the first year. They're probably hoping you'll forget about it. Then the next year, without warning, a hefty fee will appear on your statement.

You may not have to pay it. Call the card company and ask them to waive the annual fee for another year. You may get at least 12 more months of free usage.

Penalties for paying with plastic. Visa and MasterCard charge merchants a fee every time you pay with a credit card. That fee typically ranges from 1.5 to 3 percent of the total purchase price. Thanks to a lawsuit, retailers can now pass those fees along to you. Some do — just ask Elizabeth Morton.

"There is a wonderful seasonal produce market where I buy much of my summer produce," she explains. "After I had made several purchases, I saw a small sign on the wall behind the cashier stating that they add a 3 percent service fee for credit card sales." Other than that sign, no one at the store had warned her when she checked out. "I told them if they had informed me of their policy when I had previously presented my card, I would have planned to pay in cash to avoid the surcharge."

Retailers must post a sign on their door and by the cash register if they add a fee to credit purchases, as well as list it on your receipt. Take Morton's advice and be proactive. "When I shop at a store for the first time, I ask them if they charge a fee for using my credit card. That way, I have a choice and am not taken by surprise." Carry a little backup cash, just in case.

Fines for arguing a charge. Federal law gives you the right to dispute charges that appear on your credit card, but be aware that the retailer you are disputing may penalize you for it. They may charge you a "research fee" to investigate the dispute, or add your name to a blacklist of chargeback abusers. Online retailers, including eBay sellers, are more likely to levy these fees.

If you have a problem with something you bought, don't automatically call your credit card company to dispute the charge. Contact the seller first and try to work it out. Shopping online? Read the terms and conditions on the seller's website before you buy to see if they levy chargeback penalties.

Should you get slapped with such a fee, complain to the Federal Trade Commission and your state's attorney general. These sellers may be breaking the law.

WARNING

Don't pay debit card swipe fees

Merchants are allowed to charge you a fee for using a credit card, but not a debit card. Some stores may not distinguish between the two and try to charge you extra for paying with any type of plastic. File a complaint with the MasterCard or Visa company if you've been improperly charged a checkout fee.

Boost savings with smart card use

Debit cards come with fewer perks than credit cards, but that doesn't mean they're duds. Learn how to stretch your debit for bigger savings and better value.

Sign up for special savings. Ask your bank about special programs that transfer money into your savings account each time you use your debit card.

For instance, Wells Fargo's Way2Save transfers $1 from your checking into a savings account each time you pay with a debit card. "The Way2Save account is nice because the more I spend, the more I save," says Renee Wetli. "In the last year, about $500 was transferred to my Way2Save account. The transfers are so small, I hardly notice them, but they add up quickly."

Keep in mind that the money going into your savings actually comes from your checking. Include the transferred amount in your check register each time you make a purchase. Otherwise, you could accidentally overdraw your checking.

Some banks charge a fee for this type of program but will waive it if you sign up for direct deposit or keep a minimum balance. Ask how to get this benefit for free.

Get around ATM fees. Each time you use an ATM machine that's not in your bank's network, you get slapped with a fee ranging from $2 to $5. Stop paying it.

Walk into your local grocery or convenience store and take out cash for free. Make a small purchase and pay with your debit card. At the register, tell the clerk you want cash back. He'll ring up your purchase and add on the amount of money you request. Swipe your debit card, and he'll hand you the cash. The cash comes directly out of your checking account, so be sure to note it in your check register.

Think twice about returns. Don't pay with your debit card if you think you may need to return the item later. Pay with cash or credit. It can take up to a week to get the money from a debit return deposited back into your account, leaving you stuck in the meantime.

WARNING

Beware the fees with prepaid cards

Prepaid debit cards give you another spending option. Instead of drawing on your checking account, like a normal debit card, you load them with cash in advance and use them until the money runs out.

Unfortunately, they often carry exorbitant fees. Prepaid cards may charge several dollars the first time you use them, along with monthly maintenance fees, transaction fees, reloading fees, and ATM fees. They also offer you fewer legal protections against fraud than credit or regular debit cards.

Still, if you don't feel safe carrying cash or you're trying to stick to a budget, then a prepaid debit card could be for you. Look for one that charges as few fees as possible, the lower the better. Read the fine print carefully for hidden charges.

Dodge the trap of payday loans

Payday lenders aren't the only loan sharks out there. Your own bank is getting in on the act, offering paycheck advances at hidden, triple-digit interest rates.

Of course, banks don't call them payday loans. They use names like "Direct Deposit Advance," "Early Access," or "Ready Advance." They'll offer to give you a loan against your next Social Security or paycheck, to tide you over for a couple of weeks. But according to the Consumer Financial Protection Bureau, these loans are actually payday loans because:

- the loans are for small amounts of money.

- they must be repaid quickly.

- you must give the bank permission to withdraw money directly from your account when the loan comes due.

The banks advertise low interest rates on these advances, but the fine print says otherwise. A two-week loan that charges $15 to $20 for each $100 borrowed actually boasts an interest rate between 391 and 521 percent.

The insane interest rates and short payback period make it easy to fall into a cycle of debt. "Payday loans are marketed as an appealing short-term option, but that does not reflect reality," says Nick Bourke, an expert on small-dollar loans at the Pew Charitable Trusts. "The loans initially provide relief, but they become a hardship."

The average loan is for $375, according to the Pew's research. Unfortunately, most people are unable to pay it off when the loan comes due two weeks later. So they borrow again. Pew found that the average payday borrower stays in debt for five months and spends a whopping $520 in interest on the initial $375 loan. Worse, one in four people who take out a payday loan is a senior on Social Security.

Loans aren't your only option when cash is tight.

- Seniors may qualify for assistance with food, rent, mortgage, and utility bills — help that does not need to be repaid. Find services near you through the Eldercare Locator at 800-677-1116.

- Get financial counseling and debt help by calling the National Foundation for Credit Counseling at 800-388-2227.

They will put you in touch with a reputable nonprofit agency that will help you get your finances back on track.

Exercise extreme caution when weighing any product that looks like a payday loan, no matter what it's called. Don't get an advance from the same bank that handles your Social Security benefits or other direct deposits. The bank could end up garnishing your Social Security checks if you fail to repay it.

Stop ATM thieves from stealing your money

Ever wonder if that automatic teller machine (ATM) you just used is safe? Crooks sometimes tamper with them to steal your debit card and bank account information. Be wary of machines that:

- are privately owned. Try to use only ATMs owned by your bank.

- have parts on their front that look loose, crooked, or broken. Crooks may have tampered with them.

- look dirty or beaten up.

- give you unusual instructions, like asking you to enter your PIN number twice.

- are outdoors. Indoor machines are harder to tamper with. The more bustling the location, the better.

Guard against debit card fraud

Criminals are going high-tech and getting even more sneaky. Fortunately, a few simple tips can help stop someone from stealing your debit card information and draining your bank accounts.

Beware where you swipe. Sometimes, it's safer to pay with cash or a credit card than debit. If a thief steals your credit card information, you're legally only liable for $50 in losses. But if they steal your debit card info, you could be out thousands. Don't pay by debit at gas station pumps, restaurants, or when shopping online.

Set up alerts. Have your bank send you an email, text message, or phone call when certain types of debit purchases are made. Ask for an alert, for instance, when someone uses it outside the country or makes a large purchase.

Keep tabs on your account. Check your balance and account activity every few days over the phone or on the bank's website, and look over your statements when they arrive. Tell your bank immediately if you notice anything suspicious. The sooner you catch fraudulent activity on your account, the better. The amount you're liable for depends on how quickly you alert the bank.

Emergency aid for identity theft

Don't wait for a thief to run up your charge card or drain your bank account. Act fast if your wallet, social security card, or other personal information has been stolen.

Sound the alarm. Contact one of the credit reporting agencies, tell them your identity has been stolen, and ask them to place a fraud alert on your credit file. This makes it harder for a thief to open new accounts in your name. Make sure they have the right contact information for you.

Call Equifax at 800-525-6285, Experian at 888-397-3742, or TransUnion at 800-680-7289. You only need to place an alert with one agency. It will notify the other two.

Check your report. Placing a fraud alert entitles you to a free copy of your credit report. Call all three credit reporting agencies at the phone numbers above. Tell them you placed a fraud alert, and request a free copy of your report. Read through them carefully for accounts you didn't open or debts you didn't run up. Scour your bank, credit card, and other financial statements, too.

Leap into action. See something fishy? It's time to take these next steps.

- Report the identity theft to the Federal Trade Commission (FTC). Fill out the form online at *www.ftc.gov/complaint* or call 877-438-4338.

- Print a copy of the complaint you filled out online, or ask the FTC representative on the phone to send you a copy. This is your official Identity Theft Affidavit.

- Take this Affidavit to the police and file a separate police report. Get a copy of the police report or the report number. Staple it together with the Affidavit to create an official Identity Theft Report.

- Place a freeze on your credit file to block thieves from opening any more accounts in your name. Call all three credit reporting agencies again, tell them you're a victim of identity theft, and request a freeze. Placing one is free in some states but not all. Your state's Attorney General's office can tell you the cost.

- Contact all the businesses where a thief has used your identity to make purchases. For instance, if the crook rang up lots of long-distance charges, call your telephone company.

- Get in touch with any financial institution that houses one of your hijacked accounts. Close those accounts, place a stop-payment on any checks written from them, and get a new debit card and personal identification number (PIN).

- Does the fraud involve stolen or forged checks? Alert check verification companies to the theft. Call TeleCheck at 800-710-9898 and Certegy at 800-437-5120. Have them tell businesses to refuse those checks.

Learn more about your rights and how to handle all types of identity theft in the FTC pamphlet *Taking Charge: What to do if your identity is stolen*. Download it for free online at *www.consumer.ftc.gov/articles/0274-immediate-steps-repair-identity-theft*.

WARNING

Fight back against hackers

Another big company had its customer information stolen by computer hackers — and you're one of their customers. What do you do now?

- Immediately change all your passwords, especially those for financial and banking websites.

- Be wary of emails you receive that appear to be from the hacked company. It could be from the scammers trying to get more personal information from you.

- Double-check any link in these emails before clicking on it. Hover your cursor over the link to see where it will take you. The address should pop up beside the cursor or in the bottom left corner of the window. If the destination is not the business's website, or if it doesn't look familiar, don't click on it.

Taxes

Keep the government out of your pocket

Save hundreds on taxes every year

Pay less in taxes from now on — without any trouble from the IRS. Up to 2 million people overpay their taxes by an average of $610 every year because they don't try this simple strategy.

Dare to compare. The standard deduction for 2013 for a married couple, filing jointly, was $12,200. If both spouses were over age 65, they could also deduct an extra $2,400 for a final standard deduction of $14,600. But the average total of itemized deductions for a married couple, even back in 2009, was nearly $32,000.

Increasing your deductions by just $1,000 may lower your taxes between $100 and $396, depending on your tax bracket. So increasing deductions from the $14,600 standard deduction to $32,000 in itemized deductions may reduce a married couple's tax bill by $1,500, and possibly much more.

For single filers in 2009, the average itemized deduction was $19,000, and for head of household, it was $20,000. Both figures may double the standard deduction you normally take. To lower your taxes, try itemizing deductions, and compare your total itemized deductions to your standard deduction. If your itemized deductions are higher than the standard deduction, take the itemized deductions.

Get the most from itemizing. Experts say you are most likely to benefit from itemizing if you:

- paid mortgage interest and taxes on your home.

- contributed to charities.

- experienced large, uninsured casualty or theft losses.

- paid ample unreimbursed job expenses.

- had high, uninsured medical and dental expenses.

- paid deductible investment expenses.

And if that doesn't seem like enough, you can also deduct either the state income tax or state sales tax you've paid. Some people may also find that moving part of next year's charity donations to this year may help boost their itemized deductions.

Come up with a game plan. To start itemizing, you must file your taxes using Form 1040, and report your deductions on Schedule A. Keep receipts and bills rather than depending on canceled checks or credit card statements alone to prove you qualify for a deduction.

Now that you know the basics, get more details to help you itemize properly. For additional information about the standard and itemized deductions, use your phone or computer to get explanations from the IRS itself.

Visit *www.irs.gov* to find tax information for individuals. You can even download free tax forms and publications. For example, consider publications like Publication 17: *Your Federal Income Tax (For Individuals)* or Publication 910: *The IRS Guide to Free Tax Services*, which provides a complete list of available IRS publications.

If you don't have a computer, see *4 sources of free tax help* later in this chapter. You'll find information about ordering publications by phone and details on using the toll-free IRS TeleTax phone service to become more familiar with various tax topics. For best results, consult with your tax professional.

3 deduction rules you must know

The choice between itemizing and taking the standard deduction usually depends on which deduction amount is higher, but IRS rules like these may change the amounts you can claim or even dictate which choice you must make.

- If you choose married filing separately as your tax status, and your spouse itemizes deductions, you are legally required to itemize deductions, too.

- If your Adjusted Gross Income is above a certain level, the tax laws may reduce or eliminate some of your itemized deductions.

- You cannot take the extra standard deduction for being age 65 or older if you itemize your deductions.

Beat the new minimum for medical deductions

Your medical expenses must be even higher to qualify for the medical deduction starting in 2013. Learn how the new rules work, and how you can work around them to claim your money-saving deduction.

As in the past, you must itemize deductions on your tax return to take this deduction. Also, only unreimbursed medical expenses that aren't paid for by insurance or government programs can qualify.

Unfortunately, you may be out of luck if your medical expenses are only high enough to equal 7.5 percent of the Adjusted Gross Income (AGI) on your tax return. For most people, that's no longer enough to qualify for the medical deduction. Starting with 2013 tax returns, total medical expenses for the year must equal more than 10 percent of your AGI if you're under age 65.

What's more, only expenses above the 10 percent level are eligible for deduction. So if your AGI is $45,000, 10 percent of the AGI is $4,500, and eligible medical expenses total $5,000, subtract $4,500 from your $5,000 in medical expenses to get the $500 you can deduct.

But here's some good news. If you or your spouse is age 65 or turns 65 during the tax year, your total medical expenses must only be higher than 7.5 percent of your AGI to qualify for the deduction. Keep in mind this only lasts until December 31, 2016.

Starting with 2017 tax returns, even people age 65 and older must meet the 10-percent-of-AGI minimum. These tactics can help.

Focus on family. Include medical expenses for your spouse and dependents in your deductible medical expenses. In fact, a person may qualify as a dependent for this particular deduction even if he can't qualify as a dependent on your overall tax return. Eligible people include parents, children, or adult children whose medical expenses you pay, but only if you pay over half the person's support for the year. Play it safe and make sure you've met all the requirements.

To do that and to get more information, talk to your tax advisor, or read IRS Publication 502: *Medical and Dental Expenses*. See *4 sources of free tax help* later in this chapter to learn how to order or download IRS publications.

Count long-term care insurance. Part of your long-term care insurance premiums qualifies as medical expenses. Your age determines how much you can include.

For the correct amounts and information about which long-term care insurance policies qualify for the medical deduction, check IRS Publication 502.

Schedule elective expenses smartly. Ask your doctor which medical expenses are optional. When a surgery or another medical expense is elective or can safely be delayed for months or years, consider scheduling it during a year when you already have — or expect — other medical expenses. This may mean you can take the deduction every second or third year instead of failing to qualify for it every year.

Forgotten expenses you can deduct

You may think you've tallied up all your medical expenses, but don't forget these supplies and services.

- oxygen or oxygen equipment to ease breathing problems caused by a medical condition
- dental cleanings, fillings, and other services
- acupuncture
- laboratory tests
- Braille books and magazines
- prescription medicine and insulin
- chiropractor, psychologist, and registered nurse services
- eyeglasses, contact lenses, hearing aids, and hearing aid batteries

You can also deduct a portion of the cost of making changes to your home for medical purposes. For example, you might widen a door for wheelchair access. To calculate the amount you can deduct, figure out how much value the change adds to your home, and subtract that amount from the total cost.

For more information on which expenses count toward the medical deduction and what rules apply, see IRS Publication 502.

4 costly charitable deduction mistakes

Mr. Roberts donated cash and more than 400 items of used clothing and household goods during the year, so he documented and claimed thousands of dollars in charity deductions. But the United States Tax Court took away those deductions because he hadn't followed the rules for deductions closely enough. To avoid losing your deduction, remember these "Don'ts."

Don't fully deduct donations that give you something. If you buy a ticket to a charity barbecue, you can't deduct the entire cost of the ticket. Instead, you need the dinner's fair market value (FMV), which is the price the dinner typically costs in restaurants. To figure how much you can deduct, subtract FMV from your ticket price.

Rules like these apply to any charity donation that provides a product, service, or benefit in return. For more details, see IRS Publication 526: *Charitable Contributions*.

Don't expect deductions from donating to an individual. The IRS won't let you deduct donations made directly to individuals, no matter how deserving they are. You can still donate to the individual, but you can't deduct the donation. Yet, if you donate to an IRS-qualified charity that's helping the individual, you can deduct your donation.

Don't forget to document donations. For donations of less than $250 in cash or property, get a dated receipt from the charity with its name, address, and a reasonably detailed description of what you donated. For cash donations, a canceled check, credit card statement, or bank copy of both sides of a canceled check may serve as a substitute.

For cash donations worth at least $75 but less than $250, make sure the charity also provides a disclosure statement that describes any benefits or items you received and estimates their value.

As the amount or value of your donation increases, the IRS requires extra documents and more details. Watch out for the small stuff.

For example, if you receive a thank you note or other acknowledgment for a donation, but you didn't get any benefits or products in return, make sure the acknowledgment states that no gifts or services were exchanged.

To learn more about IRS rules for charity deductions, including special rules for vehicle donations, talk to your tax advisor or see IRS Publication 526.

Don't overvalue used clothing donations. Irene plans to deduct $100 for a recently donated dress she paid $100 for five years ago, but that could mean trouble if she's audited. For donations of used clothing and household items like furniture, linens, and furnishings, you can only deduct the fair market value. Fair market value for these items is often not your purchase price, but it's more likely to equal what you'd pay for a similar item in a thrift shop.

If you have Web access, get free estimates of typical values of used items by visiting *www.itsdeductible.com* or checking the value guide at *www.salvationarmyusa.org*. Also, remember, your deduction won't count unless the item is in good condition or better, or it has been appraised for a value of over $500.

WARNING

Contributions you can't deduct

You might think every school and hospital counts as a deductible charity, but donations to schools and hospitals that are run for profit don't qualify for the deduction. Neither do donations to political action committees, political candidates, chambers of commerce, civic leagues, or labor unions.

Surprising way to save $300 or more

Use your tax refund to pay down debt, and you could save hundreds in interest charges. For example, if you have a $2,500 balance on a credit card that charges 18 percent interest and requires a $100 minimum payment, you will pay $657 in interest payments by the time you pay off the debt more than two years from now.

But if you use your tax refund to pay off the debt this year, you can save at least $300 in interest charges — and probably much more.

Get wise to troublesome tax scams

There is a new scam in town and the IRS wants you to know about it.

Someone claiming to be from the IRS calls and says you owe taxes. The scammer demands you pay the taxes immediately with a pre-loaded debit card or wire transfer — or face serious consequences.

"Rest assured, we do not and will not ask for credit card numbers over the phone, nor request a prepaid debit card or wire transfer," says IRS Acting Commissioner Danny Werfel. "If someone unexpectedly calls claiming to be from the IRS and threatens police arrest, deportation, or license revocation if you don't pay immediately, that is a sign that it really isn't the IRS calling."

Pinpoint the scam. Be alert to these details.

- The IRS usually contacts you by regular mail first.

- Don't be fooled, even if your caller ID shows the IRS toll-free help number. This can be faked.

- Scammers may give you a badge number or know personal information like your address or part of your Social Security number. It's still a scam.

If you get one of these scam calls and think you might owe taxes, call the IRS at 800-829-1040 to find out. If you don't owe taxes, report the call to the Treasury Inspector General for Tax Administration by calling 800-366-4484.

Beware of other cons. This isn't the only scheme you should know about. Watch out for other tax-related scams like these.

- Someone may steal personal information, like your Social Security number, use it to file a false tax return, and get the refund money.

- You may receive an email claiming to be from the IRS or the Electronic Federal Tax Payment System (EFTPS) attempting to trick you into revealing personal information.

- A flyer or ad may falsely claim you can file a tax return with very little paperwork or documentation, and still get a nice refund — even if your income is so low you almost never pay taxes. These notices often turn up at churches.

- After a major disaster, scammers may pose as a fake charity and contact you for donations. They may even remind you that charitable donations are tax deductible.

Foil and frustrate scammers. Protect yourself with these tips.

- If you receive an email, tweet, text message, or other communication claiming to be from the IRS, remember they won't initially contact you this way, and never for personal or financial information. The IRS also won't ask for your PIN, password, or other private details used to access your credit card or other financial accounts.

- Before donating to a charity, search for it on the IRS database of qualified, legitimate charities at *http://apps.irs.gov/app/eos*.

- Don't give personal financial information like Social Security numbers or financial account numbers and passwords to anyone who asks for a charitable contribution.

- Use your credit card or a check to contribute to a charity — never cash.

Get your tax refund sooner

You could get part of your tax refund up to 15 months early, and it's completely legal. Here's what you need to do.

Learn the secrets. Imagine a program where $500 is deducted from your paycheck each month to pay for groceries. If you buy more than $500 worth of groceries in a month, you pay what you owe. But if you buy less than $500, you can't get your unspent money back until the end of the year.

This may sound crazy, but that's how tax refunds work. Money is deducted from each of your paychecks. The amount deducted is based on your income and the way you filled out your W-4 form when you were hired. If your year's deductions add up to less than the taxes you owe, you must pay the difference and possibly a penalty.

But if the deductions add up to more than you owe, the government sends the money back to you as a tax refund. That means extra money deducted in January may stay with the government up to 15 months.

If you could put that extra money back into your paycheck each month, you would start getting your tax refund up to 15 months earlier than usual.

That early refund could be helping you every month by:

- ending the need to carry a credit card balance and pay interest.

- beefing up your retirement savings.

- earning interest in a high-yield savings account.

- paying down existing debts.

- covering expenses during an emergency.

Talk with your tax advisor. If you regularly get a big refund, you can change your W-4 form so your total yearly withholding is closer to the amount of taxes you owe. That gives you a bigger paycheck and a smaller tax refund. For example, if your annual refund is near the national average of $2,800, and you reduce it to $1,000, your paycheck could be $150 richer each month.

This won't be right for everyone every year, so talk with your tax advisor before you take the plunge. If you're married and you both work, coordinate with your spouse, too.

Fill out a form. Ask your human resources representative for a blank W-4 form, or download it from *www.irs.gov*.

For help filling out your W-4 properly, work with your tax advisor, or use these:

- TurboTax software

- the IRS withholding calculator at *www.irs.gov*

- IRS Publication 505: *Tax Withholding and Estimated Tax* and Publication 919: *How Do I Adjust My Tax Withholding*.

Reviewing last year's tax forms and your latest pay stub may also help. Make sure you don't reduce your withholding too much, or you might owe a big tax bill in April and be charged a penalty. Also, remember to file your new W-4 with your employer, not the IRS.

Tax laws change, so review your W-4 yearly, or whenever major life changes occur, to check whether updates are needed.

WARNING

Stay on top of changes

Tax laws change constantly — and sometimes very suddenly — so check with your tax advisor, visit *www.irs.gov*, or call the IRS tax assistance line toll-free at 800-829-1040 to be sure the rules described in this book still apply.

E-file for free with Free File

File your federal taxes fast, free, and safely. That's the claim of the Free File Alliance, a nonprofit group of private tax software companies partnered with the IRS to provide free electronic tax services.

You are eligible for Free File if your 2013 Adjusted Gross Income (AGI) is $58,000 or less — that's about 70 percent of all taxpayers — and if you are willing to file completely via the Internet. In addition, you must meet certain criteria set by the individual software companies offering this service.

Since this program began in 2003, more than 36 million people have used it to file their returns — and 98 percent say they would recommend it to others.

Your first step is choosing commercial online software to use. All your options come with the latest encryption to protect your privacy. Go to *www.irs.gov* and click on the Free File logo. You must access Free File this way in order for the service to be free. Either let the system help you find a Free File company that's right for you, or browse the list of Free File companies to choose your own.

Then, you simply start answering questions posed by the software. No need to download forms or do the math. The software selects the correct form for you and completes your return. It will even automatically find any tax credits and deductions you are entitled to. When you're finished and your return is filed, you'll receive an electronic receipt.

Through Free File you can also:

- file an extension.

- pay federal taxes you owe.

- file jointly as long as your combined income is less than $58,000.

- select direct deposit to receive your refund fast.

State taxpayers have Free File option

Twenty-two states participate in the State Free File Program that allows you to prepare and e-file your state taxes for free — if you qualify.

Arkansas	Michigan	Oklahoma
Arizona	Minnesota	Oregon
Georgia	Missouri	Rhode Island
Idaho	Mississippi	South Carolina
Indiana	New York	Vermont
Iowa	North Dakota	Virginia
Kentucky	North Carolina	West Virginia
District of Columbia		

For more information go online to *www.freefile.irs.gov* and click on "Get Ready."

Save $246 and e-file with ease

Gone are the days of preparing your taxes surrounded by stacks of paperwork and stumpy pencils, dumping boxes of receipts on your accountant, and meticulously filling in endless forms. Electronic filing — or e-filing — is here to stay. Out of more than 134 million filed tax returns in 2013, almost 85 percent were e-filed. Over a third of those were done by people just like you.

In most cases, forgoing paper forms and filing electronically is cheaper than hiring a professional tax preparer, and it can be just as accurate. The National Society of Accountants reports the average cost of a professionally filed return is $246. Don't forget extra fees if you require more than a basic return, need an extension, or must have your return pushed through quickly.

On the other hand, e-filing a federal return yourself is cheap — even free. So why not save some money and let technology help you.

Commercial software. You can buy tax preparation software either as a CD you run from your computer, or as a download from a website. Prices for highly rated online options can range from just under $10 for TaxSlayer to over $40 for H&R Block. But take note — the mid-priced TurboTax and TaxACT, at around $20 each, got higher marks by independent reviewers. The lesson here is you don't have to spend more to get more.

If you select a well-reviewed product, it should be accurate, up-to-date, easy to use, and come with good customer support. The best choices will also do the math for you and catch simple entry errors.

Free File Fillable Forms. Just as Free File is a smart choice for people earning less than $58,000 a year, Free File Fillable Forms is for those earning more. Basically, it is the electronic equivalent of IRS paper forms and instructions. Consider it if:

- you are comfortable filling out tax forms without guidance from a software program.

- you can follow IRS instructions on your own to complete your return.

- you take responsibility for the accuracy of the information you input.

There are none of the extra bells and whistles you'll find with commercial software, but Free File Fillable Forms is free.

To access this program, go online to *www.irs.gov/Filing*, then click on "Fillable Forms." You'll continue to a page where you must create an account with a user ID and password. In addition, you'll need an email address, a high-speed Internet connection, and certain computer settings you can read about in the General FAQs. There is also an online tutorial that will walk you through every step. Keep in mind, you cannot use Fillable Forms for your state income tax return.

Tax apps for tablets and smartphones. Today's life is on the go. And preparing your taxes doesn't have to be any different. Most of the big names in tax preparation software have a version suitable for your tablet or smartphone.

Phone versions are best for simple returns — tap, swipe, and you're done in 10 minutes. Many even come with jazzy little features. For instance, take a picture of your W-2 with your phone and the data automatically moves to the correct blanks in the IRS form.

Tax apps for the iPad and Android tablets can do almost anything a full desktop computer version can, including more complicated returns.

Mobile apps like these range from free to inexpensive, and while some provide free filing, most charge a fee to file.

4 sources of free tax help

It's tough to keep up with an ever-changing federal tax code. Throw into the mix new legislation — like the American Taxpayer

Relief Act — and no wonder filing your taxes is one gigantic headache. If only you had somewhere to go for sound, free advice. Well, you do.

Get personal IRS help. Sometimes you just need to sit down with a professional for some one-on-one time.

- Taxpayer Assistance Centers (TAC) offer help explaining issues that may not be handled well over the phone. Locate a TAC online at *www.irs.gov/localcontacts* or look in the phone book under "United States Government, Internal Revenue Service." Then call for an appointment.

- The Volunteer Income Tax Assistance (VITA) Program gives specific help preparing your tax return if you make $51,000 or less. The IRS-certified volunteers are particularly knowledgeable on special tax credits. Find a VITA site by using the locator tool online at *www.irs.gov/Individuals/Find-a-Location-for-Free-Tax-Prep* or calling 800-906-9887. They are usually located in libraries, schools, community centers, and shopping malls.

Visit the government online. The official IRS website at *www.irs.gov* is a wealth of free information and assistance. From the home page, you'll find links to all these resources.

- Download free forms and IRS publications including those that explain tax laws.

- Find phone numbers for live telephone assistance, like the tax question hotline at 800-829-1040 or, if you have a hearing impairment, 800-829-4059.

- Read short explanations of close to 150 tax topics for individuals and businesses.

- Let the Interactive Tax Assistant (ITA) walk you through a series of questions and answers on tax law.

- Get tax tips and information specific to seniors and retirees at *www.irs.gov/Individuals/Seniors-&-Retirees*.

Find guidance for seniors. The AARP Foundation Tax-Aide program partners with the Internal Revenue Service's Tax Counseling for the Elderly (TCE) to offer free tax preparation and counseling to households with low to moderate incomes, giving special attention to those over age 60. You can find trained and certified volunteers at an AARP Tax-Aide site near you by checking online at *www.aarp.org* or calling 888-227-7669.

Call TeleTax. Recorded tax information is available from the IRS 24 hours a day, seven days a week. Simply call 800-829-4477 and use your touch-tone phone to listen to prerecorded messages covering various tax topics. Topic 123 gives you a directory to the more than 100 available subjects.

Or download Publication 910, the *IRS Guide to Free Tax Services*, from *www.irs.gov*, which has an index of the topics.

Avoid common filing errors

The IRS has seen it all, but here's their list of the most common filing mistakes made by taxpayers over age 65.

- Many seniors fail to take the higher, age-related standard deduction they are entitled to.

- Sometimes Social Security income is taxable. Understand the factors that make a difference, such as income from other sources and your filing status.

- If you receive income from qualified dividends, it is usually taxed at a lower rate.

- It is frighteningly easy to enter your Social Security number incorrectly.

Other common blunders include forgetting to sign your forms, making a mistake in the math, entering bank routing numbers incorrectly, and missing the deadline.

Pick the right tax pro

You might be surprised to learn that the official definition of a tax preparer is "any person who receives compensation for the preparation of all or a substantial portion of any tax return for another individual." That's it. You pay someone and they instantly become a tax preparer — no obligatory education, no professional requirements.

Since you could spend about $250 to have your taxes prepared by someone else, you'll want to make sure this is money well-spent.

Make sense of titles. There are several types of tax preparers, offering different levels of expertise for a variety of fees. Here's a list, from those with generally the least amount of tax training to the most tax-proficient. Take into account how complex your tax situation is and what you can afford to pay, then choose accordingly.

- preparers hired by national or local tax services
- enrolled agents
- accredited tax preparers
- certified public accountants (CPAs)
- tax attorneys

Do your research. Both the IRS and the Better Business Bureau encourage you to do your homework before hiring anyone.

- Get a recommendation from friends or through an organization like the National Association of Tax Professionals. Call them at 800-558-3402 or go online to *www.natptax.com*.

- Make sure the person you are considering has a Preparer Tax Identification Number (PTIN).

- Ask about fees. The amount should not be based on a percentage of your refund.

- Make sure any refund you are due will be sent directly to you or deposited in your account.

- Get contact information that will be good even after tax season ends — in case questions come up or you get audited.

Stay involved. As appealing as it may sound, you can't just drop off your paperwork with the preparer and flee.

- Review the entire return and make sure you understand everything. You, as the taxpayer, are legally responsible for what is filed.

- Never sign a blank return or one that has been filled out in pencil.

- Get a copy of your return.

- Ask that your return be electronically filed. It is safe and fast.

- Get all your personal records back.

Finally, do you know how to file a complaint against a shady tax preparer? Complete Form 14157, Complaint: Tax Return Preparer.

Mail it to: Internal Revenue Service
            Attn: Return Preparer Office
            401 W. Peachtree Street NW
            Mail Stop 421-D
            Atlanta, GA 30308

Connect with the IRS on the go

Are you expecting a big refund and want to know the second your return is processed? Or maybe you're just a tax tip junkie. Then you'll be happy to learn the IRS has moved into the mobile age with their smartphone app, IRS2GO. Whether you have an iPhone or Android device, you can download it for free.

---

3 easy ways to avoid an audit

Tax season is stressful all by itself. Add in the threat of an audit, and you've put new meaning to the word "taxing."

While many audits are random, the IRS computers also automatically flag thousands of returns because of certain triggers. These returns draw special attention and are more likely to be audited. Here are some things you can do to lessen your chances of raising a red flag and, if you are audited, help you escape without penalty.

E-file. The IRS believes submitting a tax return the old-fashioned way — with paper forms and a pen — increases the odds of making an entry error. In fact, they report the error rate for a paper return is 20 percent, while the rate for returns filed electronically is 1 percent.

Double-check every entry. Any math error, mismatched Social Security number, blank signature block, or other type of inconsistent information is automatically flagged for attention by the IRS computers.

Keep accurate, detailed records. Take every deduction you are entitled to, but be prepared to back them up. You'll be especially scrutinized if you:

- are self-employed and file Schedule C — Form 1040. Because you are a business owner, you can take advantage of oodles of deductions. Based on experience, the IRS knows it's tempting to underreport income and exaggerate deductions.

- claim a home office deduction. The restrictions on this deduction are tough. Before you take it in error, review the specifics to see if you qualify.

Reap a tax reward for supporting aging parents

One out of every four adult children provides personal care or financial help to a parent. If you're one of them, you may be able to claim your parent as a dependent and reduce your taxes — even if your parent doesn't live with you.

Your parent, grandparent, great-grandparent, step-parent, or in-law may also qualify as a dependent if all four of these are true.

Your relative's income is very low. For example, in 2013, the dependent relative's gross income must be less than $3,900. Gross income includes taxable income such as interest and dividends from investments and those parts of Social Security income that are taxable.

You provide more than half your relative's support. Support generally includes cost of food, housing, clothing, transportation, travel, recreation, and medical and dental expenses not reimbursed by insurance.

You cannot claim your relative as a dependent if more than 50 percent of these support costs are paid for with your relative's income, savings, loans, or Social Security, or with money from government programs like food stamps. But figure the total dollar amount of the person's support costs and calculate your contribution to it. If you've paid more than half the support costs, you may qualify to claim your relative as a dependent.

Of course, determining what counts as support costs can be tricky, so talk to your tax advisor or check IRS Publication 501: *Exemptions, Standard Deduction, and Filing Information.* This publication includes examples and details about what qualifies as support, and a worksheet to help figure out your total contribution to support. It may also help answer questions and avoid mistakes about income or other requirements for declaring a relative as a dependent. See *4 sources of free tax help* earlier in this chapter to learn how to order or download IRS publications.

You and your relative meet the filing rules. You can't claim your relative as a dependent unless:

- your relative does not file a joint return, or the joint return is filed solely to get a refund because he doesn't owe taxes.

- the person is not a qualifying child of any other taxpayer.

- you or your spouse cannot qualify as a dependent of another taxpayer.

Your relative has North American ties. Your relative must be a U.S. citizen or a resident of the U.S., Canada, or Mexico.

Tax laws change regularly, so check IRS Publication 501 to make sure you meet all the dependent relative requirements. If you can claim your relative as a dependent, make sure you include their Social Security number in your tax return.

If your parent is not a U.S. citizen, attach form W-7 to your return to obtain an Individual Taxpayer Identification Number. The IRS will assign a number and use it in place of a Social Security number.

What to do when siblings share support

The IRS says you can't claim your parent as a dependent because you and your siblings split the cost of her care. But don't give up yet. One of you can still claim your parent. This tax break may apply under the following circumstances.

- You and your siblings jointly provide more than half of your parent's support.

- You personally provide less than 50 percent of your parent's support, and each sibling contributes less than 50 percent.

- The person who claims the parent as a dependent provides at least 10 percent of the parent's support, and all other requirements for claiming the parent as a dependent are met.

- Each person who provides more than 10 percent of the parent's support fills out and signs Form 2120 *Multiple Support Declaration*, and everyone who isn't claiming the dependent provides a written statement waiving the right to claim the dependent that year.

6 tax tips for people with disabilities

Check out these tax breaks and helpful IRS resources especially for people living with a partial or full disability. They can make your life easier and save you money.

Take advantage of accessibility resources. Visit the IRS Accessible Forms and Pubs page at *www.irs.gov* to download tax publications and forms in Braille-ready file, large print, and other accessible formats. To order hard-copy Braille or large print versions of tax forms and publications, call 800-829-3676.

Enjoy a bigger standard deduction. Regardless of your age, you qualify for a higher standard deduction if you or your spouse is legally or partially blind on December 31. To claim the deduction for partial blindness, you need a letter from your optometrist or ophthalmologist certifying that your vision loss meets IRS requirements. For details see IRS Publication 501: *Exemptions, Standard Deduction, and Filing Information.*

Shrink your gross income. Many disability pensions count as wages, but those from the Department of Veterans Affairs and some government pensions are tax-free. To find out whether yours can be excluded from gross income, see IRS Publication 525: *Taxable and Nontaxable Income.*

Claim an extra tax credit. You may qualify for the Tax Credit for the Elderly or Disabled if you're age 65 or older and meet the income requirements. If you aren't yet 65, you may still qualify if all of these are true:

- You meet the income requirements.

- You've retired on permanent and total disability.

- You received taxable disability during the tax year.

- You had not reached mandatory retirement age by January 1 of the tax year.

To learn more about this tax credit and find out if you qualify, see IRS Publication 524: *Credit for the Elderly or the Disabled.*

Submit medical costs. If insurance, your employer, or a government program doesn't pay for disability-related supplies or reimburse you for their cost, you may claim them as a medical expense. For example, costs for the following may be deductible:

- a guide dog or other service animal to help the blind, deaf, or disabled

- a wheelchair

- hearing aids, eyeglasses, contact lenses, or artificial limbs

For more information, read *Beat the new minimum for medical deductions*, earlier in this chapter, and get vital details from IRS Publication 502: *Medical and Dental Expenses.*

Deduct impairment-related work expenses. If you have a disability that limits your ability to work, you may be able to claim the cost of special equipment or attendants that help you do your job. To learn more about what expenses qualify and how to deduct them, see IRS Publication 529: *Miscellaneous Deductions*.

5 steps to lower property taxes

Your mortgage may go away, but your property taxes never will. And while this levy could range from a low of $300 in Louisiana to a whopping $6,500 in New Jersey, the average American pays just under $2,000 a year in property taxes. Wouldn't you love to reduce that?

The amount you pay is based on a calculation involving your home's value, the percentage of the property value that is taxed, and the tax rate. And that's where the trouble begins.

Home values, especially in recent years, have changed faster than you can say "housing bubble." Tax assessments simply aren't keeping up with how quickly home prices have yo-yoed up and down. In fact, experts say about half of all taxable property is overassessed — and an inflated property value translates into a too-high property tax bill.

The best solution involves you, the homeowner, taking the initiative. After all, it is your money. Appeal your property's assessment. It's legal, free, and fairly easy. Yet not even 5 percent of taxpayers challenge their assessment.

The National Taxpayers Union, a nonprofit, nonpartisan citizen group, has put together steps to follow if you want to appeal your tax assessment.

- Note any deadlines or legal requirements for filing the appeal. Call your assessor's office or check their website for information.

- You are entitled to see your property tax card, usually available at the local assessor's office. Check the description of your property and any math. Note mistakes and discrepancies.

- Locate up to five comparable properties. Make sure they are recent and as similar to your property as possible. Including foreclosures will probably help your case.

- Talk to the assessor first. Obvious errors can be changed quickly and easily, without resorting to a lengthy appeals process. If he doesn't agree to make changes, file your appeal.

- Rules vary from state to state, but usually you're required to submit a written summary of your case with as much documented support as possible. You may have to attend a formal hearing before a board of taxpayers.

If you don't feel up to the task of appealing the assessment yourself, you can hire a tax lawyer or a property-tax consultant to do the work for you. They will generally charge a percentage of the tax reduction — as much as half. Make sure your savings will be worth the expense.

WARNING

Beware reassessment scam

The Better Business Bureau has received over 600 complaints involving property-tax consultants, according to a *Wall Street Journal* report. Swindlers eager to prey upon financially strapped homeowners are trying to cash in on high property tax bills.

The scam often begins with a letter that looks official, but actually comes from a private company offering to file a property assessment appeal on your behalf.

In addition to an upfront fee, they often ask for a certified copy of your property deed and your Social Security number. Your best bet — toss the letter in the trash and file an appeal yourself.

Work off your property taxes

A small investment of your time could reduce or eliminate your property taxes. And surprise — it's courtesy of your government.

Many towns, cities, and counties across the country offer a Property Tax Work-Off Program to older adults. Instead of paying property taxes, people just like you are lowering or erasing their property tax bill by working part time for their local government.

Restrictions and eligibility vary, but there are usually age, income, and residency requirements. Local programs often set their own rules using state guidelines. And you must have a skill that your city or town can use.

For example, the town of Whitinsville, Mass., will place volunteers in various town hall offices and schools, the library, and the senior center. Boulder, Colo., residents eased their tax bill by doing data entry, manning phones, teaching, and performing groundskeeping tasks.

What's more, some people need only work for a few weeks out of the year to shrivel their tax bill. To find out whether your local government offers a similar program, contact its Human Resources department, Senior Citizen or Elder department, or Taxpayer Assistance office.

3 ways 'tax free' bonds could cost you

Interest earned on municipal bonds — those issued by state and local governments — is often assumed to be tax-free. But check carefully before you buy, or you may end up owing Uncle Sam more than you thought.

State tax. Check the laws for the state where you file your tax return and the state where the bond is issued. Some states only tax out-of-state bondholders, while others tax all municipal bondholders.

Federal tax. Before you buy a municipal bond, get a copy of its prospectus and check its tax status. Some aren't exempt from federal taxes. Examples include Build America Bonds or bonds issued to fund a sports stadium.

Social Security benefits. Tax-free interest from municipal bonds raises your provisional income, a figure calculated by making certain adjustments to your gross income. When provisional income is too high, part of your Social Security benefits may be taxed. For details, see IRS Publication 915: *Social Security and Equivalent Railroad Retirement Benefits* or talk with your tax professional.

WARNING

'Senior freeze' loophole you can't ignore

Many states offer a Senior Property Tax Freeze exemption, which provides a special tax break if you meet age, income, and residency requirements. The exemption "freezes" your home's equalized assessed value (EAV) — the taxable value of your property — at the amount calculated the previous year. It's designed to protect you from property tax increases. And it works quite well, as long as property values increase.

When real estate values plunge, however, you can actually end up paying more in property tax. That's because your EAV stays high and is multiplied by an ever-increasing tax rate.

Don't automatically apply for the Senior Freeze exemption if it looks like you won't benefit. And don't forget to reapply once the market bottoms out. This will lock in a low value for the following year.

Estate Planning & Legal Matters

Protect your family's financial future

3 safe paths to a low-cost will

It's not too late to draw up a will if you haven't done it yet. This piece of paper is the most important part of your estate plan because it lets you have a say in where your assets will go. Otherwise the state will divvy it up, and those you love may not benefit the way you'd like them to.

Drawing up a will can be expensive, but you have some choices that can help bring down the cost.

Write the will yourself. If you don't have a large estate and your bequests are fairly straightforward, you can create your own will using an online service or software.

You can find will-writing services at websites like *www.nolo.com*, *www.legalzoom.com*, and *www.legacywriter.com*. Or search online for software, such as Quicken WillMaker Plus.

These programs will walk you through the process by asking you key questions about your last wishes. When you're finished, you can print the will, then follow directions for signatures and other steps to ensure it's legal.

Fees for do-it-yourself wills usually average $40 to $100. If your quote is much higher, your estate may be more complicated than you thought. In that case, it's best to play it safe and get help from an attorney.

Ask a lawyer to review your document. The hardest part of creating a will is thinking through your bequests and deciding where everything goes. If you can do it ahead of time, you'll save yourself the hefty fee a lawyer will charge to guide you through it.

Find the cheapest online service or software you can, go through the questionnaire, and create your will. Then print it out and take it to an estate planning attorney to review. You'll feel better knowing your document is legal and you haven't missed anything important.

Hire a paralegal service to help. If you don't feel up to doing the work yourself, but can't afford a lawyer, look for a paralegal typing service in your area. Their personnel will help you prepare your will at a substantially lower cost.

How to guarantee your last wishes are met

As your life changes, your will should too. But only 14 people out of 100 bothered to update their wills or make any changes in estate documents during the previous five years, according to a *Consumer Reports* survey.

Don't be one of those whose family suffers because you neglected to stay on top of your financial affairs. Update your will when any of these three things occur, and you'll guarantee your wishes will be met.

- You've had a change in status, such as divorce or remarriage. You'll want to ensure your estate plan reflects your new circumstances.

- You need to change a beneficiary. Perhaps you have a new child or grandchild you'd like to include in the will, or someone named in your will dies. If you don't change your bequests, your heirs may not get what you intended.

- You've acquired new assets or they've changed in value. Or you no longer have an asset, which means if you don't change your will, the person it was bequeathed to will get nothing.

While you're updating your will, make sure you include a residuary clause if you haven't already done so. This will describe what to do with assets left over after your bequests have been fulfilled. Otherwise, they will be distributed as if you had no will.

WARNING

Make the right beneficiary choices

The beneficiaries you select for your IRAs, insurance, retirement accounts, and annuities are separate from those named in your will. It's important to keep these updated as well.

Don't make the mistake of naming your estate as beneficiary of your insurance or retirement accounts. The proceeds will become part of the estate and subject to taxes, which could leave your heirs with little or nothing.

If the retirement plan goes into the estate, it must be paid out in full and taxed within five years. If you name an individual as beneficiary, he can take the distributions out over many years, which will be less of a tax burden. Plus he can keep earning tax-free interest on your retirement plan for his entire lifetime.

Stow critical docs safely

Everyone has important documents they need to keep track of. But which ones need the safety of a bank vault and which should stay at home?

The best place for never-toss, hard-to-replace personal documents is in a safe deposit box. Make sure these four types of items are secure.

- personal — birth, marriage, and death certificates; divorce decrees; citizenship papers; adoption papers; military records; passports; social security cards

- household — mortgage, deeds, titles, household inventory

- financial — stock certificates, bonds, income tax returns

- estate — wills, advance directives, living wills, power of attorneys, insurance policies. If you don't have a co-owner on the safe deposit box, you should keep the original estate documents at home and place copies in the box.

Documents that need easy access are better off at home. Keep them in a lockable box you can grab on your way out the door if you must evacuate your house for any reason. Here are 12 things you should include:

- list of contact information for employer, bank, insurance company, and utilities

- copies of both sides of each credit card

- copies of both sides of each family member's driver's license

- list of insurance companies with policy numbers

- list of banks and account numbers

- family medical, dental, and immunization records

- personal checks, check registers, latest bank statements

- pay stubs

- social security statements

- investment statements

- loan documents

- receipts for major purchases

7 ways to save money for your heirs

Taxes and probate will take the biggest bite out of your estate. Use these ideas to help cut the government out of your inheritance money.

Beef up your life insurance. You can leave your heirs a tidy sum, and they won't have to pay a dime in taxes. Just designate them as beneficiaries on your life insurance policy. They won't have to report the benefits as income, so it's a tax-free windfall.

Share your property. If you have real estate holdings in your name only, you can file a "quit claim deed" to set up "joint tenancy with right of survivorship" (JTWROS). After death, the property will pass to the joint tenant without going through probate.

This is easier than retitling your deed and can be done at your local county records office. Joint tenancy ownership can be used on almost all types of property, not just real estate. But be careful — if you set up a JTWROS with anyone but your spouse, the property may be considered a gift and incur taxes.

Consider a bypass trust. Thanks to a change in the tax laws in 2013, couples may no longer need to create complex trusts to save their estate from the tax man. The new portability law allows the unused portion of a person's estate tax exemption to roll over to their spouse when they die. That means a couple can leave up to $10.5 million to their heirs tax-free.

But a trust may still be a good idea, especially if your state has its own estate tax. Funding a bypass trust up to the state exemption amount could save you a hefty amount of state taxes. It's a simple legal loophole that's easy to create. Talk to your financial advisor about whether a bypass trust is right for you.

Surprise your heirs with an annual gift. You can reduce your taxable estate by giving away up to $14,000 per year to as many people as you want — twice that if you're a couple. This annual exclusion is tax-free.

Help your grandkids with college. If you want to give even more, you can set up a 529 college savings plan account for your grandchildren. You're allowed to fund the first year with five years worth of the annual exclusion — $70,000 for an individual or $140,000 for a couple.

Donate to your favorite charity. Charitable donations can easily lower your taxable income below estate tax level. Make sure you check IRS regulations so your contributions do what you want them to.

Seek out a tax-friendly state to retire. You may not have a large enough estate to warrant federal taxes, but it may be a different story when it comes to your state. In addition, your beneficiaries may be subject to an inheritance tax.

Wherever you plan to retire, make sure you know the laws regarding taxes. Your best bet is to find a state with low or no death taxes.

WARNING

Death-tax trap you need to avoid

Think twice about adding your son's or daughter's name to your bank accounts. If your child dies first, that decision could result in hefty inheritance taxes on your own money.

That's because the government considers that person as owning a portion of your savings, which you "inherit" upon their death. Seven states currently levy such a tax, and banks are not required to tell customers about it.

Don't get caught in this unfortunate trap. Ask your bank about your state's death-tax laws before adding anyone to your accounts. Or avoid the problem altogether by granting your heir a financial power of attorney.

10 deathbed secrets you shouldn't keep

Discussing your end-of-life affairs with your adult children is not something most people think about, but the sooner you do it, the better. Here are 10 things you must tell them about to ensure a smooth transition after you're gone.

Do yourself a favor and attach the first six lists to your will, or put them in a safe place and let your family know their whereabouts. That way, you'll ensure your heirs don't lose any valuable assets.

Financial information. Gather all your banking, credit card, and investment account information, and create a document listing the financial institutions' names and account numbers. Include the name and number of your financial advisor.

Insurance policies. List your policies and how much they're worth, their account numbers, and the institution they're from. Don't forget any policies from employers or organizations you belong to.

Property ownership. Make a list of any houses, land, vehicles, or other major property you own. Also include the names of your brokerage and mortgage accounts.

Recurring bills. Don't make your children rifle through files trying to determine what bills they need to pay. Write down all your account names and numbers, and include the monthly payment, if applicable. Be sure to include automatic withdrawals from your bank account.

Computer access. Your online accounts may be locked forever unless you give someone access to your user names and passwords. If you don't want to write them down, look into an Internet password managing service like Dashlane (*www.dashlane.com*) or LastPass (*www.lastpass.com*).

These free programs will store all your logins and passwords in an encrypted file under one secure login. You can then include that login with your other paperwork, or leave it with a trusted relative or friend.

You also might want to check into programs like Legacy Locker (*http://legacylocker.com*) and Secure Safe (*www.securesafe.com*), which help you create a plan to pass on all your digital data.

Location of safe deposit boxes. Follow the suggestions in *Stow critical docs safely* earlier in this chapter. Then make sure someone has access to your safe deposit box by naming a co-owner. Write down the name of the bank and box number, and don't forget to mention where you keep the key. Let your children know if you're storing any valuable items.

Partnership or corporate agreements. If you or your spouse are in business for yourselves, make sure your children know about any business arrangements with others you may have. In addition, note the whereabouts of your last three years of tax returns.

Health care plans. Let your loved ones know if you have a living will, health care power of attorney, do-not-resuscitate (DNR) order, or an organ donation card. Discuss your health care wishes should you become incapacitated.

Burial instructions. Cremation or burial? Mass or memorial service? Don't leave your loved ones guessing about your last wishes. Make note of them in a document separate from your will. If you've paid for cemetery plots, leave them the paperwork with the details.

Specific bequests. You've decided to leave your grandfather clock to your son and all your jewelry to your daughter. Take the time to explain your decisions ahead of time, or leave a separate note with your will. If you don't, you may spark a feud among your heirs. According to an AARP study, one in five people over age 50 have squabbled with their family over an inheritance.

Do you need a living trust?

Many people believe trusts are only for the rich. But revocable living trusts can be helpful to people with smaller estates as well. Consider one if you want to:

- avoid the time and expense of probate. Everything you place in the trust will pass directly to your beneficiaries upon your death without going through the courts.

- maintain privacy. The document is not made public unless your heirs challenge it.

- avoid or reduce estate taxes. As a married couple, you can include language in the trust that ensures you can claim your estate tax credits.

- protect out-of-state property. Placing all your properties in a living trust will keep your heirs from going through multiple probates.

- plan for disability. If you become incapacitated, your trustee can immediately start managing your assets without court approval.

Keep in mind that a living trust may be more trouble than it's worth if you have just a few assets. Your IRAs, life insurance, and bank and brokerage accounts don't need to be in a trust because they pass directly to your designated beneficiaries.

When you sell property, such as your home, you must do it through the trust or transfer it back to yourself. And placing your car in the trust can complicate car loans and insurance.

Talk to an estate attorney to see if a living trust is right for your situation.

Keep your savings out of probate

You and your spouse have separate savings and checking accounts. Guess where that money will end up when one of you dies? That's right, in probate.

Make things easy on your family by designating a beneficiary for your accounts like you do for insurance and retirement plans. It's called a payable-on-death (POD) account. Ask your bank for a POD form, and fill it out with the name of the person you want to inherit the money. You can change your beneficiary at any time.

No one can access your money while you're alive. After you're gone, they just need to show your death certificate and proof of their identity to collect the funds.

One caution — make sure you have other cash available in your estate for your executor to pay bills and taxes. Otherwise, your heirs may have to come up with the money themselves.

Save thousands on funeral costs

No one likes to think about their own funeral or that of a loved one, but if you want to save money, early preparation is key. The best way to keep the lid on funeral costs is by checking out the available options before you need them.

If you have Internet access, go online to *www.funerals.org* to get started. Or check the Yellow Pages for a local Funeral Consumers Alliance or memorial society, which you should find listed under "funeral services."

You may find a lot of information about prepaid funeral plans, but most experts advise against them. If you decide to go that route, make sure the money is placed with a reputable insurance company and not held by the funeral home you're working with.

Here are some good ways to shield your savings.

Select a funeral home carefully. Call or visit several in the area and ask for an itemized price list. By law, they have to give you that information.

The Federal Trade Commission has actually developed a "funeral rule" to protect consumers in transactions involving funeral arrangements. For information, go to *www.consumer.ftc.gov* and search on "funerals."

Shop your favorite warehouse store. Believe it or not, you can buy caskets at Costco or Walmart and save a bundle over those offered at your local funeral home. You can also look for headstones elsewhere.

Consider cremation. This service can be done for close to $1,000, so check around until you find a reasonable price. Make sure you ask whether it includes the crematory fee and "alternative" casket, as well as any other fees. You can also provide your own urn or other container.

Rely on the church minister. Ask your loved one's minister to perform the service. They will usually charge just a small fee. The minister may also be willing to go with you to the funeral home to help you deal with billing and other financial issues.

Plan a separate memorial service. Keep your costs low by holding a memorial service at home, in church, or in a hall. You may want to hold a private viewing following the death, then schedule the memorial for family and friends later.

Donate to medical research. If you're not squeamish about donating your body to science, you can save your family a substantial amount of money. Facilities will usually cremate the body for free and return the ashes in about a month. You can make arrangements in advance, so if it's something you're considering, let your family know.

Remember your veterans' benefits. If you or your loved one served in the military, you're eligible to be buried in a national or state cemetery for free. That goes for spouses, too. At the very least, you're entitled to a burial allowance.

"Both my mother-in-law and father are buried in national cemeteries, one in North Carolina, the other in Florida," says Renee Frost. "My mother-in-law predeceased her husband, who is the veteran, and there was no problem obtaining a burial site. He will be laid to rest on the other side of her when he passes.

"The national cemeteries are lovely, peaceful places and a fitting resting place for the men and women who have served our country. I'd advise anyone who is eligible to check them out."

For more information, contact the Veterans Administration at 800-827-1000, or go online to *www.cem.va.gov*.

Surprise help for funeral expenses

Funerals can be expensive, and every little bit helps when you're trying to cut costs. One thing to check into is life insurance. Don't forget to look for insurance policies the deceased may have forgotten about or perhaps didn't know about.

Check with your loved one's employer or past employer, worker unions, retirement fund, banks, credit cards, and investment accounts. Many of these have life insurance policies tied in, but you may have to track them down.

---

5 smart ways to save on legal fees

Some things in life require a lawyer's help, but no one wants to break the bank over legal fees. Remember that you will probably be charged for any interactions, including phone calls and emails, so it helps to find a way to cut costs. Here are a few ideas.

Ask what you can do yourself. Your attorney may let you do preliminary research or draft your own documents, which he can later review.

You can also organize your paperwork before consulting with him. If you show up with a box full of papers, you'll pay for the hours the lawyer spends sorting through them. Organize everything first, and also make extra copies of any important documents.

Combine your legal questions. You may be there to draw up a will, but if you bring up other estate questions, or even legal problems you're having with your tenants, you'll save yourself another consultation fee.

Choose one person to act as legal contact. If more than one person is involved — in an estate disposition, for example — you don't want everyone calling the lawyer for updates. Those phone calls can run up your costs. Pick someone to act as the family representative, and have that person keep the others in the loop.

Check on billing alternatives. Paying by the hour can run into thousands of dollars. But many lawyers will offer flat-rate billing, especially on routine matters such as traffic problems, divorces, and wills.

If it's a personal injury or other high-payout case, look into negotiating a contingency fee, which is a percentage of the amount awarded if you win your case.

Look for group membership rates. Your company or an organization you belong to may offer reduced rates for legal services from local attorneys. As an AARP member, for example, you can get an attorney referral and a 45-minute free consultation, as well as a small discount on billing rates.

Find free legal help through Eldercare

Legal problems can be overwhelming to anyone, but perhaps more so for older adults, who deal with issues like a fixed income, health care, housing, long-term care, and possibly even abuse, neglect, or age discrimination.

Fortunately, the federal government has provided legal protection for older adults through its Eldercare program, a public service of the U.S. Administration on Aging. Seniors can find free or low-cost legal assistance in their area by going online to *www.eldercare.gov* or by calling 800-677-1116.

In Georgia, for example, seniors can access a legal hotline staffed by attorneys. They serve older Georgians and their families, including grandparents raising their grandchildren. The attorneys manning the hotline can give legal advice but will refer you to other attorneys or services if needed. Services are free for adults 60 years of age or older.

Along with local help, Eldercare provides links to national websites with useful information on a variety of legal issues, including fraud, identity theft, consumer issues, and Elder Law.

The Eldercare Locator can connect you to dozens of other services for older adults and their families, such as financial assistance, home repair and modification, transportation, housing options, and in-home services.

Most people don't know about these helpful senior programs, so don't let these resources go to waste.

Be case-savvy to save time and money

You may have no desire to be a lawyer, but if you have a legal issue to take care of, you'd better start cracking the books. The more you know, the less your lawyer will have to fill you in on, and the less money you'll fork over for his time.

Look for materials published by trade associations and non-profit public interest groups that might be associated with your type of case. The Internet can be a huge help as many sites publish information on a wide range of legal topics.

Check out websites such as *www.nolo.com*, *www.findlaw.com*, and *www.justia.com*. You can also access the legal centers of major law schools like Cornell at *www.law.cornell.edu* and Harvard at *www.law.harvard.edu*.

Health Care

Win the war against rising costs

Health insurance and Medicare

Common Medicare mistakes you can easily avoid

Medicare enrollment starts three months before the month you turn 65 and lasts for three months after. You're expected to make some major decisions during that time, but don't slip up — missing a signup date can mean big penalties down the road.

You'll be automatically enrolled in Parts A and B if you are drawing Social Security or receiving Railroad Retirement Board (RRB) benefits when you turn 65 years old. If you delay drawing your benefits, you must sign yourself up for Medicare at age 65. Do that by calling the Social Security Administration at 800-772-1213.

Part A. You won't pay premiums for Part A if you paid Medicare taxes while working. If you didn't, you may have to buy it. In that case, you'll pay an extra 10 percent each month, or $44 on a typical $441 premium, if you miss the signup date.

Part B. Premiums for Part B cost around $105 per month and go up 10 percent for each full year you signed up late. Miss your enrollment by two years, and you could pay 20 percent more per month for the rest of your life.

Part D. Medicare's drug plan follows the same enrollment schedule as Part A. You must sign up for some kind of drug coverage when you get Part A — through Medicare, the VA, your job, or elsewhere. If you go more than 63 days without any, you'll pay penalties when you finally do sign up. How much depends on how long you go without coverage. Skip it for three and a half years, for instance, and you can expect to owe an extra $13 or more each month.

Medicare supplement (Medigap). Your Medigap Enrollment Period begins when you join Part B and lasts for six months after. There's no official penalty for failing to purchase a Medigap policy then, but put it off and you'll end up paying more or even be denied coverage. During that initial signup period, insurance companies must sell you a policy regardless of your health. After that window, they will take your medical history into account. The result could well be higher premiums or a refusal to cover you.

4 ways to save $500 or more a year

Prescription drugs aren't cheap, but they needn't break the bank. Are your medications taking a bite out of your fixed income? Learn how to keep more money in your pocket with these Medicare Part D smarts.

Get Extra Help. Have limited income? The government's Extra Help program could save you money on Medicare costs each month by paying for all or part of your prescriptions. Most people who qualified paid no more than $2.65 for generic and $6.60 for brand name prescription drugs in 2013.

More than 2 million seniors who qualify for the program don't take advantage of it. That's like throwing away free money. One study found that joining Extra Help could save the average senior $529 each year.

Some people think their income is too high to qualify. Many are wrong. Others feel overwhelmed by the application process. Don't let that stop you. Ask a family or friend for help applying. Call Social Security at 800-772-1213 to get started.

Call SHIP. Your state may help with your drug costs if you don't qualify for Extra Help. Call 800-MEDICARE to get the phone number for your local State Health Insurance Assistance Program (SHIP).

Shop each year. Premiums rise and your prescriptions change. In fact, some plans' premiums rose by double digits from 2012 to 2013. Make sure you shop around every year during the open enrollment period, October 15 through December 7. The comparison tools on Medicare's website make it easy to look for a better deal. Visit *www.medicare.gov/find-a-plan*, or call Medicare directly at 800-MEDICARE.

Check the benefits. Before you sign up for a particular plan, ask whether it:

- covers the medicines you currently take. If not, you may have to pay the full cost yourself.

- charges copays or coinsurance. With copays, you pay a flat dollar amount per prescription, no matter what the drug actually costs. With coinsurance, you pay a percentage of the drug's price, which adds up fast on expensive medicines.

- limits how many pills you can order at one time. Buying in bulk could save on drugs you take every day.

Challenge high Part B premiums

Medicare relies on your tax returns from two years ago to set your premiums. Seniors who earn more than $85,000 individually or $170,000 as a couple face higher Part B premiums than the average older adult.

Problem is, a lot can happen in two years. Divorce, job loss, retirement, the death of a spouse — each could send your income plummeting. Your Part B premiums may not drop accordingly, since Medicare uses old tax information.

If you have experienced a life-changing event and a big drop in income, ask Medicare to recalculate your premiums. Contact your local Social Security office for help filing the appropriate forms.

Spot medical scams that target seniors

Fraud drains millions of dollars from Medicare each year and can wreck your credit, even endanger your life. Spotting and reporting it could actually earn you money.

Medicare rewards people who help them catch crooks defrauding the system, and the pot is about to get sweeter. Under the old rules, Medicare awarded whistle-blowers a maximum of $1,000. New rules set the top reward at $9.9 million. Keep your eyes peeled for telltale signs of these scams.

Identity theft. Thieves can steal your identity, damage your credit score, and waste thousands of Medicare dollars by stealing your Medicare ID number. They can risk your health, too, if someone else's information ends up in your medical records.

- Be suspicious of anyone offering free goods or services like wheelchairs, groceries, or transportation in exchange for your Medicare number. The truth is, if it's free then they don't need your Medicare number.

- Hang up if someone claiming to be from Social Security or Medicare calls and demands payments or asks for your Medicare number.

- Watch for bills or collection notices for medical services and equipment you never received. Someone may have stolen your Medicare ID number.

Medicare fraud. A few doctors, pharmacists, and other health care providers try to steal money from Medicare by billing it for goods or services you never received. Here's how to foil their scheme.

- Save the receipts and statements you get from your providers, and write down the date of your doctor visits and other services.

- Compare these to your Medicare Summary Notice, if you're on Original Medicare, or your plan statements if you're on Medicare Advantage. These documents tell you what you have been billed for. Look for equipment, tests, drugs, or services you didn't receive.

- Call the provider first if you spot a mistake. If they don't resolve the problem, call 800-MEDICARE to report the suspicious charges.

Advantage scams. Don't buy Medicare Advantage, Medigap, or Part D drug coverage from someone who cold-calls you by phone or knocks on your door. It is illegal for insurers to call you first about buying their plans or to ask for your bank or credit card information over the phone.

Get better coverage for less

Medicare may not be enough to cover your health costs, with its high deductibles and unlimited copays, say experts like Robert Fitzgerald, who sits on the Medicare Advisory Board of the National Association of Health Underwriters.

Fitzgerald should know. As an insurance agent who specializes in Medicare, he helps people choose Medicare supplement (Medigap) and Advantage plans every day. Here's his advice for choosing coverage that bridges the gap.

Medigap. You'll pay more upfront for a supplement plan, (Medigap), says Fitzgerald. "That's the downside." But the benefits are better. "The upside is that you can get treatment anywhere in the country that accepts Medicare." Medicare Advantage plans, on the other hand, limit you to certain doctors and hospitals.

Medigap doesn't cover prescription medicines. You'll need to buy Medicare Part D for that. The two together will likely cost $135 to $200 a month, according to Fitzgerald. And Medigap premiums tend to rise over time. "Everybody loves you when you're 65," he says, but as you get older, the rates will go up.

"Some of the plans go up a lot faster" than others. Fitzgerald warns people not to be fooled by Medigap plans that start out with super-low premiums. They lure you in with low prices then jack up your rates. "Over time, they're the ones that get you."

Medicare Advantage. These plans generally cost less than Medigap. Many don't charge premiums. You may have copays for doctor visits and such, but the plans cap your annual out-of-pocket expenses. "Most of the plans I'm seeing cap costs between $3,900 and $6,700" a year, says Fitzgerald. When shopping for a plan, make sure:

- your doctors and your preferred hospital are in the carrier's network. You'll pay more for out-of-network care.

- the drugs you take are covered. "Prescription drugs could be the most expensive part of the plan," Fitzgerald says.

- you buy a PPO-type plan, rather than an HMO. HMOs may be cheaper, but they set much stricter limits on where you can get care. That can be catastrophic if you develop a disease and need an out-of-network specialist.

- you focus on plans that don't charge premiums. After all, Fitzgerald reasons, "if I'm going to pay a premium, why wouldn't I get a supplement," or Medigap plan, instead?

- to compare the extras in plans that are close in price and coverage. See if either offers extras like dental or vision care.

Medicare's website, *www.medicare.gov/find-a-plan*, lets you compare Advantage plans based on where you live and what medicines you take. The site asks you to select the two pharmacies you use most often, then recommends plans that fit your needs.

Fitzgerald recommends going through the process twice, however, and choosing different pharmacies each time. Some have special deals with insurance companies. If you pick CVS and Rite Aid, you may miss out on a plan that gives you free generics at Kroger.

WARNING

Choose the right plan the first time

Whether you lean toward a Medicare supplement (Medigap) or Medicare Advantage plan, do your best to choose wisely the first time. Switching between Medigap and Advantage can be expensive and even impossible.

A healthy senior may pick Medicare Advantage when he turns age 65 because it's cheaper than Medigap, says Medicare expert Robert Fitzgerald. "And then you get sick, and you want a Medicare supplement because that covers more."

Try to switch to Medigap during the next enrollment period, however, and you may not qualify. Insurers must sell you a Medigap policy when you turn 65 years old, regardless of your health history. That's not the case when applying for a Medigap plan after age 65. Insurance companies will scrutinize your medical history and may refuse to cover you, Fitzgerald explains. "If you've had cancer or another serious disease, forget it."

Shop and save in new exchanges

The new insurance exchanges could be a boon to people between the ages of 50 and 64. It could even help them retire early.

Most people who don't have health insurance through Medicare, Medicaid, their employer, or another source are now required to buy it themselves. They can get it through an insurance company, an insurance broker, or their state's insurance exchange, otherwise known as the Health Insurance Marketplace.

The law that established the Marketplace also prevents insurance companies from denying you coverage or charging you more based on your health problems. They can only charge more based on age and smoking status. Even then, they can't charge more than three times what a young, healthy person would pay for the same policy.

That's important, because many people nearing retirement have high blood pressure, diabetes, or other chronic conditions that have made it almost impossible to buy health insurance in the past.

Now you may not have to stay in a job you dislike until you turn 65 just for the health coverage. You may be able to buy affordable coverage on your own through your state's Marketplace. Start with the website *www.healthcare.gov.* Click on "Get Insurance," then choose the state you live in. The site will tell you where to shop for insurance based on that.

- If you live in a state that is letting the federal government run its insurance exchange, then you'll shop for your policy through *www.healthcare.gov.*

- If you live in a state that runs its own exchange, you will see a link directing you to that state's exchange.

No computer? No problem. You can get the same information by calling 800-318-2596.

Some people will qualify for subsidized insurance. Use the Kaiser Family Foundation's calculator at *www.kff.org/interactive/subsidy-calculator* to find out if you're one of them and how large a subsidy you're likely to get.

Don't fall for fake plans or skimpy coverage

Health insurance is confusing, and crooks prey on that. They're betting you won't realize that the policy they just sold you is fake, and the insurance company they claim to represent doesn't really exist.

Plenty of honest, legitimate insurance companies are out there. Here's how to separate them from the scams.

- Ask to read the policy, especially the fine print, before you sign up. Don't cave in to aggressive salespeople who insist it's a "limited time offer."

- Scam artists may use names that sound similar to a real insurer. Call your state's insurance commissioner to verify that the company is legitimate and licensed to sell in your state.

- Watch out for policies that require you to join an association or union. Those organizations may be fake, too.

- Check a company's reputation by calling your local Better Business Bureau or visiting the website *www.bbb.org*.

Some insurance policies are outright fake. Others are real but a bad deal. Say "no thanks" to these types of coverage.

Medical discount plans. They aren't the same as insurance. Health insurance pays for part of your care. Discount plans only give you a list of doctors and pharmacies that may — or may not — be willing to accept a discount for their services.

Most of the discounts are much smaller than the ones loudly advertised. Add enrollment fees and monthly premiums, and you may not save anything at all. Worse, if you end up in the hospital, you could be stuck paying from your own pocket.

Hospitalization insurance. Some policies pay as little as $100 a day while you're in the hospital. That won't come close to covering the cost of your care.

Disease-specific insurance. Critical illness policies pay a lump sum if you are diagnosed with a certain condition, such as cancer, heart attack, or stroke. Unfortunately, the fine print can render them useless. A cancer policy may not pay if you have a slow-growing cancer that isn't life-threatening. And the payout may shrink as you get older. These policies also don't cover serious chronic conditions, like diabetes, which are much more common.

You're better off getting a good disability policy and saving up for unexpected illnesses through a Health Savings Account or regular savings.

Get wise to the latest Medicare scam

Only people who have no insurance need to shop for it through the new insurance exchanges, also known as the Health Insurance Marketplace. If you're enrolled in Medicare or Medicare Advantage, you are already insured. So relax — your Medicare coverage won't be changing.

It's illegal for anyone to sell you a Marketplace policy if they know you have Medicare. Watch out for fraudsters who claim you need to sign up for a "national insurance card" or some other plan. There is no such thing. Never give your Medicare number, Social Security number, or bank information to someone who knocks on your door or calls you out of the blue.

Shop for Medicare coverage safely at *www.medicare.gov/ find-a-plan* or by calling 800-MEDICARE. People who need to get coverage through the Marketplace can learn about plans at *www.healthcare.gov*.

Cut costs with tax-free savings account

You've heard about the importance of fully funding your 401(k) during your working years, but what about your HSA? Health savings accounts (HSAs) are a tax-free way to tuck away cash for future health care.

They're only available to people who have a high-deductible insurance plan. If you're one of them, take advantage of it. Stuff your HSA with the maximum amount of cash allowed by law each year until you retire.

You won't be able to contribute to the account once you move to Medicare. But you will be able to use the savings to pay your out-of-pocket health costs during retirement, including Medicare premiums, copays, and deductibles.

That's like getting a health care discount, since you don't pay taxes on the money you put in or take out of your HSA. Miss that opportunity, and you could essentially pay more for medical care in retirement. Call the IRS and request publication number 969 to find out what expenses your HSA can cover.

Long-term care

Alternative to nursing home saves you thousands

What do you need to change about your home in order to live in it until you die? "Start thinking about it now. Be as prepared as you can," urges Dennis Lippy, owner of Home Free Home Modifications, a construction company that remodels homes for people with physical limitations.

As a Certified Aging-in-Place Specialist (CAPS), Lippy has helped many seniors modify their homes so they can age in place. Many people hire him because they don't want to enter a nursing home. "A lot of them can't afford it. You spend $30,000 or $40,000 a year on a nursing home, versus $5,000 on a stair lift and $10,000 on a bathroom." The potential savings are huge, not to mention the comfort of living in your own home.

"Our motivation is independence," says Lippy. "What can we do to gain somebody's independence?" His advice — figure out how you would get from the car to your bedroom or bath if you had to use a walker or wheelchair. Add a ramp outside to avoid steps, and a stair lift inside to reach the second floor.

And concentrate on your bathrooms. "Sixty to 80 percent of accidents happen in bathrooms." Add a grab bar in the shower or tub. Convert your bathtub to a roll-in shower in case you need a wheelchair down the road.

An experiment in Baltimore proves you don't need to spend thousands of dollars on home improvements. As little as $1,200 can make your home safer and more livable.

Experts at the Johns Hopkins University School of Nursing are spearheading a project to help seniors stay in their homes, lower their risk of falling, and avoid entering nursing homes. Called Community Aging in Place — Advancing Better Living for Elders (CAPABLE), it hires handymen to make $1,200 worth of repairs to the homes of Baltimore seniors.

Sarah Szanton, Associate Professor at the Johns Hopkins School of Nursing, heads the project. She says the most beneficial repairs are sometimes the simplest ones, for instance:

- repairing banisters and steps.

- adding railings to both sides of stairs.

- installing better lighting on stairways.

- taping down rugs and electrical cords.

- installing grab bars and hand-held shower heads in bathrooms.

Look for a contractor who is a Certified Aging-in-Place Specialist, like Lippy. CAPS contractors have special training in making homes more accessible for people as they age.

Free help with home remodeling

Making your home more accessible is the one thing you must do if you want to continue living in it as you age. Thankfully, there's free help to do it.

- Title III of the Older Americans Act sets aside money to fund home modifications and repairs. Call the Eldercare Locator at 800-677-1116 to find your local Area Agency on Aging. They can help you apply for these funds.

- Medicaid programs in many states also pay for home modifications. Contact your state to learn more.

- Volunteers with Rebuilding Together, Inc., help low-income seniors modify their homes. Call the national office at 800-473-4229 to find a local chapter near you.

- The U.S. Department of Agriculture offers low-income seniors in rural areas up to $7,500 in grants to repair their homes and make them handicap accessible. Call your local Rural Development office to apply.

- Some long-term care insurance policies let you access benefits to make your home more accessible and avoid entering an assisted living facility or a nursing home.

- Medicare may pay for an occupational therapist to visit your home and suggest changes to make, if your doctor orders the evaluation. Call 800-MEDICARE to learn more.

Medicare covers in-home health care

Medicare has done an about-face on covering home visits by nurses and physical therapists. Until recently, it would only pay for these visits if you had a condition that would improve with time. That left many homebound seniors with chronic health problems out in the cold.

No more. Medicare now covers care aimed at helping you maintain your current health and avoid getting worse. That could mean a physical therapist to help you cope with arthritis, or a nurse to help a loved one with dementia or diabetes.

This applies to medical care, not personal care or homemaker services. So while a skilled nurse or therapist may be covered, an aid who helps you shower or makes meals won't be. It also doesn't apply if you need a full-time nurse. In addition, your doctor must certify that you are homebound and need the services.

Little-known tips to qualify for Medicaid

Nursing homes cost more than $200 a day and rising, based on national averages. Don't just wonder how you can prevent a spouse's care from driving you to bankruptcy. Apply for Medicaid.

Medicaid isn't just for people with a low income. It can help middle-class seniors pay for nursing homes, assisted living, and even in-home care. You have to be almost impoverished to qualify for traditional Medicaid, but most states offer special programs with looser limits. Most people qualify for Medicaid by falling into one of two groups.

Special income level. Forty states cover people in this category. In 2013, you could earn as much as $2,130 a month in Social Security, pension payments, and other income and still qualify for Medicaid. That's three times higher than the income limit for traditional Medicaid.

You'll qualify for nursing home care if you fall into this group, but some states cover in-home and hospice care, too. Medicaid will expect you to pay part of the costs of these services.

Medically needy. Thirty-three states cover people who have sizable incomes but huge medical bills. If your medical bills dwarf your monthly income, you could qualify. Each month, you will be responsible for paying a certain amount of your own medical bills. Then Medicaid will kick in and pay the rest. Racking up enough medical bills to trigger Medicaid isn't hard, especially if you're in a nursing home.

Both of these programs limit your assets, not just your income. Generally, you can't have more than $2,000 in assets if you're single and $3,000 if you're married. But don't despair. Despite all of these limits, you're really never too rich to qualify for Medicaid. You just have to know the right way to go about it.

When you first apply, Medicaid will look over your finances for the last five years. Some people give their money away to family or friends so they can qualify for help. If the state thinks you tried this trick, it will penalize you with a waiting period. The more money you try to hide, the longer you'll have to wait until Medicaid covers your care.

Fortunately, you don't need offshore accounts or underhanded accounting tricks. There are plenty of ways to dispose of your money legitimately without triggering a penalty.

Spend it wisely. Medicaid counts checking and savings accounts, stocks, and Certificates of Deposit as assets, but it doesn't count your home, your primary car, and a few other items. Spend your money on those, and you won't get nailed.

- Medicaid doesn't count your main car, so splurge. Trade in your old clunker for a newer model.

- Remodel your home to make it easier for you or your spouse to live in as you age. Add grab bars, convert your bathtub to a roll-in shower, lower thresholds, widen doorways, or install a wheelchair ramp.

- Buy a small life insurance policy. You're allowed to have a policy with a face value up to $1,500.

- Set aside up to $1,500 for burial arrangements.

Stash your cash. Plan ahead, and qualifying for Medicaid will be much easier. You can place your assets in an irrevocable trust to protect them, but you must do this five years before applying for Medicaid. Otherwise, you'll face a waiting period.

Miller trusts are a good option in states without a Medically Needy program. You can place monthly income like Social Security and pension payments in a Miller trust without penalty. You can't, however, place cash from a savings or checking account in one. These will still count toward your asset limit.

Buy the right insurance. Spend down some of your assets by buying a Partnership-Qualified long-term care insurance policy if your state allows it. It will pay for your care until you hit its maximum payout limit. Then Medicaid will kick in and cover the rest.

Squirreling away your money in order to qualify for Medicaid can be confusing, and doing it wrong comes with tough penalties. Get advice from an Elder Law attorney before moving your money around. They specialize in helping seniors with long-term care and estate planning.

The website of the National Academy of Elder Law Attorneys can help. Visit its website at *www.naela.org*, click on "Find an Attorney," and type in your ZIP code to see a list of Elder Law attorneys near you.

WARNING

Protect your inheritance

Maybe you need long-term care but you're afraid Medicaid will take all of your money, leaving your heirs with nothing. Surprisingly, the opposite could happen. Your heirs could get more money if you apply for Medicaid than if you don't.

When you die, the program may claim part of your estate to cover the amount it spent on your care. The difference is, Medicaid negotiates lower rates with nursing homes and other providers than what private citizens like you pay.

So the amount of money Medicaid tries to get from your estate will likely be less than what you would have paid out of your own pocket.

Smart way to get the care you need

Many people think Medicare will help pay for nursing home care, but they're wrong. Medicare only covers long-term care under very limited circumstances. Even then, it may not foot the whole bill. Medicaid offers better coverage, but it's designed to kick in after you have spent nearly all of your own money on care.

That's where long-term care insurance (LTCi) comes in. You pay premiums on the policy, and when you need help with basic daily activities like bathing, dressing, or eating, the policy pays part or all of those costs.

Generally, policies pay a set amount for each day you need care. The amount it pays depends on the policy you buy. And some go beyond nursing homes. They may pay for in-home care, adult day care, assisted living, and respite care.

LTCi policies aren't right for everyone. Experts say you should shy away from this insurance if:

- paying the monthly premiums would pose a financial hardship now or in the future. Your premiums will almost certainly rise over the years, perhaps by 50 percent or more. If you let your policy lapse because you can no longer afford the premiums, you'll lose all the money you paid.

- the premiums make up more than 7 percent of your current income.

- your assets are worth less than $30,000, or your only source of income is Social Security or Supplemental Security Income (SSI). Medicaid will likely cover the cost of your long-term care, in which case you won't need LTCi.

- you have serious health problems, or you're in your 70s or 80s. Insurers may deny you based on poor health, and policies are harder to get the older you are.

Don't fall into any of those categories? Then long-term care insurance could be a good investment, particularly if you have sizable assets you want to leave to your heirs. Look for a policy that:

- does not exclude any pre-existing conditions you have.

- is sold by a financially stable insurance company. Strong companies may not need to raise premiums as much as financially shaky ones.

- has inflation protection, so your benefit increases each year to keep up with inflation.

Ask the insurer for the policy's outline of coverage before buying it. This document details the policy's important features, provisions, and benefits. Look it over carefully to make sure you're getting the coverage you want.

Cut LTC policy costs up to 90 percent

Long-term care isn't cheap, but neither is long-term care insurance (LTCi). A 60-year-old couple can expect to pay $3,381 a year for LTCi that pays $150 a day for three years, with 3-percent inflation protection.

You could do better. A few key discounts can slash as much as 90 percent off the cost of a policy.

Find the right agent. Shop for a policy with the help of an insurance broker who sells policies from several different companies. It pays to shop around. The American Association for Long-Term Care Insurance found you could pay 90 percent less at one company than another for virtually the same policy.

Don't buy direct. For that reason, don't try to buy a policy directly from the insurer. They aren't allowed to sell LTC policies directly to the public. Contact them, and they may put you in touch with an agent who will steer you away from their competitors' policies. As a result, you may not end up with the best deal.

Shop before your birthday. The longer you wait to buy a policy, the more expensive your premiums will be. You could pay 7 percent more simply for buying the policy after you reach age 61 instead of at age 60. That's a difference of $100 or more a year.

Get it before getting Medicare. The free "Welcome to Medicare" screening you receive at age 65 could save your life by uncovering hidden health problems. That's exactly why you should buy LTCi before having it done. It could reveal health conditions that will disqualify you from getting a policy or make your premiums unaffordable.

Dodge high health premiums. Do you already suffer from a chronic condition? Not all companies will charge you higher premiums because of it. What one insurer deems a risk another may shrug off. It's one more reason to shop around.

Be aware of gender bias. Insurers have begun charging 40- to 60-percent higher premiums for women than men. That's because women usually live longer and need more care. Not all LTC policies have jacked up their prices by gender, so keep shopping. You may find a policy that hasn't.

Double up. Spouses can shave 15 to 40 percent off premiums by buying both of their LTC policies from the same insurer.

Extend the wait. Pick a policy with a longer deductible, or elimination period, for major savings. A policy that makes you wait 90
days between the time you need long-term care and when it begins
paying out will cost 12 to 15 percent less than one with a 30-day
elimination period. Longer waits can cut the cost even more, up to
40 percent.

Opt out of inflation. Policies that increase their benefits annually
to keep up with inflation tend to cost more than those that don't.
Insurance that pays a higher daily benefit but has no inflation protection may be more affordable.

Lump your payments. Most people opt to pay their premiums
monthly, but paying a full year's worth all at once could trim the
price by 8 percent.

Cheaper alternatives to LTCi

Long-term care insurance (LTCi) isn't the only way to protect
your savings and assets. Consider these alternatives.

- Self-insure against catastrophic illness. Stash the
  same amount of money you would have spent on
  LTCi premiums each year into a high-yield savings
  account or other investment. Tap that money if you
  end up needing long-term care.

- Buy permanent, not term, life insurance if you're single.

- Look into longevity policies. These pay out once
  you reach a specific age, such as 85, ensuring that
  you don't outlive your savings. For more information, see *Get guaranteed income for life* in the
  Insurance chapter.

- Add an LTC rider to your life insurance policy. A combo policy like this is typically cheaper than traditional LTCi. Also, health conditions that would disqualify you or raise your rates on an LTCi policy may not affect a combination policy.

Doctors and Dentists

Take advantage of free tests and treatments

Changes to Medicare mean you now get free checkups, weight loss counseling, and screening for diseases like heart disease — no copay necessary. Don't miss out.

- Get a free "Wellness" visit every year. It includes a vision test, review of your medications, and screenings for high blood pressure, weight problems, and dementia, among other services.

- Sign up for a free annual heart check, especially if you're at risk of heart disease or already have it. Your doctor will check your blood pressure, discuss whether you should take daily aspirin, and tell you about foods that can protect your heart.

- Lose weight with free counseling. Medicare covers free weight loss counseling sessions for people who are very overweight, with a body mass index (BMI) of 30 or higher. Sessions meet once a week for a month, then every other week for five months. Lose 6.6 pounds or more in the first six months, and you'll receive free counseling for another six months.

These services are only free if you have them done in a primary care setting, like your family doctor's office or a health clinic. Nursing homes don't count.

Whittle the bill for office visits

Stop spending all of your money at the doctor's office. These three tricks can slash your bill up to 40 percent.

Check on assignment. Are you enrolled in Medicare? Shave 15 percent off your doctor bills by only using doctors and specialists who accept Medicare assignment. Doctors who don't accept assignment can charge you an extra 15 percent on top of your copay.

Say Medicare agrees to pay a doctor $150 for your office visit. If he accepts assignment, you pay a 20 percent copay, or $30, and Medicare covers the rest. If he doesn't accept assignment, you'll pay an additional 15 percent of that $150, for a total of $52.50.

Pay in cash. What if your specialist doesn't accept Medicare, or you don't qualify for it yet? Remember that money talks. Tell the doctor's office you are footing the bill yourself, and offer to pay in cash if they'll give you a discount.

It worked for Carol Rogers after a $600 outpatient procedure. "When I got to the front desk, the lady asked about my insurance." Carol told her she would be paying the whole bill out of pocket. Upon hearing that, "she offered me the cash price, which was $350," saving Carol $250, or 40 percent.

Be upfront. Tell your doctor if money is tight. Be honest if you are having trouble paying for a prescription, or if you can't afford the treatment he wants you to have. Chances are good he can change your treatment plan to make it more affordable.

Get healed at half the price

Seeing the doctor may feel like a rip off — a scant few minutes can cost $100. But office visits are no longer the only game in town. New options have cropped up for treating basic illnesses. Before you haul your sick self into the doctor's office, consider these cheaper alternatives.

Call for free help. You have your own nurse on-call 24 hours a day with certain insurance companies. Cigna, Humana, UnitedHealthcare, and Aetna are a few that offer 24-hour nurse hotlines. Wondering what's causing your cough? Not sure how to treat that back pain? Call the nurse. Check the back of your insurance card for the toll-free phone number.

Consider convenience. Nurse-staffed walk-in clinics, whether standalone or inside drugstores, can save you a bundle on minor illnesses and injuries. "When we get sick, we hardly ever go to our regular doctor," says Sharon Dement. "It's too expensive with our insurance." Instead, she and her family see a nurse practitioner at a nearby walk-in clinic for everyday illnesses. "It's $50 for your first visit and $40 for every visit after that." Compare that to the $100 or more she'd pay at a doctor's office.

"It's great for when we just have something like pink eye or strep throat," Sharon explains. But don't use these clinics as a substitute for your regular doctor when dealing with more serious conditions.

Dial a doc. Telemedicine services connect you by phone or computer with a full-fledged doctor. For a fee, you can get a one-on-one consultation, diagnosis — and, in some cases, a prescription — without leaving your home.

If you have a "smart" cellphone or a computer with a Web camera, look for a telemedicine service that allows you to video chat with your doctor. That way, they can actually examine you using the camera on your phone or computer.

You'll pay anywhere from $10 to $50 for a consultation, less than half the price of a typical office visit and a fraction of emergency room costs. Check out services such as American Well, at *www.americanwell.com* or 855-818-DOCS or Teladoc at *www.teladoc.com* or 800-TELADOC.

WARNING

Plan ahead to prevent disaster

Health care is a crucial part of your retirement budget, but many people don't consider those costs when they plan for retirement. That may be the single biggest mistake people make.

Medicare copays and premiums, drug costs, and out-of-pocket needs like hearing aids and eye and dental care are likely the largest retirement expenses you haven't thought of.

Retirees now spend more on health care than on food. Failure to plan now can lead to tough choices in the future between the care you need and the basic necessities of life. What can you do?

- Take care of yourself. The healthier you are, the less care you will need, and the lower your costs will be.

- Shop smart when it comes to drugs, tests, and medical treatments.

- Consider getting Medigap insurance to cover what Medicare doesn't, or a good Medicare Advantage policy.

- Set money aside in a Health Savings Account before retiring, if you have access to one.

5 ways to clamp down on high test costs

The expense of an illness starts adding up before treatment even begins, from a $100 bone density scan to an $800 MRI. It's easy to feel helpless when your doctor insists you need a particular test — but you're not. Get control over the cost of tests and screenings with these saving strategies.

Find freebies. Medicare and insurance companies now pay the full cost of some preventive tests at no charge to you, as long as they're done by an in-network provider. You may be entitled to free blood pressure and cholesterol checks, mammograms, and colonoscopies, to name a few. Call Medicare at 800-MEDICARE or your insurer to learn more.

Crack the code. Ask your doctor to assign a preventive code to routine tests in the paperwork she submits to Medicare or your insurer. Tests done for preventive reasons can cost much less than if they're done to diagnose a problem.

Shop around. When Carly Davison needed a thyroid ultrasound, she decided to do a little shopping. She called several imaging centers to compare the prices for her procedure. "I saved a lot of money."

Different providers may charge wildly different prices, even in the same city. Call your insurance company for a list of in-network testing facilities, or call and find one that accepts Medicare. Ask each one what they charge for the tests you need.

Question the need. Doctors like to play it safe, in part to avoid malpractice suits. That makes some tests expensive overkill. With so much money on the line, you're within your rights to ask your doctor whether or not you really need a particular test. Joe Hoffman has done just that. "I have saved a good bit of money over the years by asking the doctor or nurse how badly I need a test they're recommending." He suggests asking them three questions.

- "What's the worst that could happen" if you skip the test and take a wait-and-see approach?

- "If I put up with the problem as it is right now, will it get worse?"

- "What warning signs should I look for" that suggest the problem is getting worse?

Joe has a high-deductible insurance plan, so he generally pays out of pocket for tests and office visits. Explaining that to the doctor also helps. "Usually that results in the doctor admitting the test isn't really that necessary anyway."

Dodge duplicates. If you're like most people, you see a whole team of doctors and specialists. Make sure they don't each order the same test. Keep track of what you've had done, and carry copies of the results to doctor appointments just in case.

Take the bite out of dental bills

What hurts worse — getting a crown or paying for it? Caring for your teeth shouldn't leave you in the poor house. Try these strategies to ease the "ouch" in your wallet.

Pay cash. Everyone likes cash. Your dentist may like it so much she's willing to give you a discount for paying with cash instead of a credit card. Just ask. The savings could be huge on a pricey procedure.

Make it a family affair. Does everyone in your family use the same dentist? Ask for a family discount. Think of it as snagging a good deal for buying in bulk.

Go when it's slow. Ask the office staff when the slowest part of their week occurs. Then ask if they'll cut you a deal for scheduling your appointments during those days and times. It's a win-win.

The dentist fills a slot that might normally go vacant, and you get the work you need for less.

Call for quotes. There's nothing wrong with calling other dentists and asking what they charge for a crown or filling. Shopping around is a must if you need lots of expensive work.

- Ask your current dentist to print out your treatment plan, along with the dental codes, tooth numbers, and cost of each step.

- Call around to get estimates for the work. You may also want to get a second opinion about what you need done.

- Take your new quotes back to your current dentist and ask if she can match a competitor's lower prices.

Check the website *www.brighter.com* to get an idea of what procedures cost where you live. Simply type in your ZIP code and choose the service you need.

Try someone new. Find a better price elsewhere? Sweeten the pot by asking about "new patient" specials. You may score a free cleaning or discounted dental work.

Cut costs by 91 percent

Brighter, an online dental marketplace, partners with dentists in some cities to get you discounts up to 91 percent on cleanings, fillings, crowns, and more. If your city is one of them, you'll see a list of dentists and prices when you enter your ZIP code and select a service. You must schedule your appointment through *www.brighter.com* to score your deal.

Skip care without risking your teeth

Not everyone needs annual dental X-rays and two cleanings a year. Some people do just as well with less and save hundreds of dollars in the process.

Cleanings. People who don't have diabetes, don't smoke, and have never had gum disease may do fine with one cleaning every year, according to a new study. You need two cleanings a year, though, if you have even one of these risk factors, and three or more cleanings if you have two or more risk factors.

X-rays. Getting bitewing X-rays once a year may raise your risk of meningioma, a type of brain tumor linked to ionizing radiation from dental X-rays. X-rays today use lower doses of radiation than ever before, but there's no harm in asking your dentist if you really need a new set of bitewings. He may suggest they can wait.

Don't skimp on your teeth to cut costs. Gum disease affects more than your mouth. It may contribute to pneumonia, heart attack, stroke, and arthritis — all of which cost more to treat than having a simple cleaning or X-ray.

Hospital costs

Guard your estate from sky-high medical bills

How do you make sure your wishes are followed after you die or are incapacitated, and hospital care at the end of your life doesn't bankrupt your estate? It's called an "advance directive," and it's a combination of:

- a living will, which tells your family and doctors how much care you want in different medical situations.

- a durable power of attorney for health care, which designates someone to make medical decisions on your behalf if you can't.

Together, these legal documents form an advance directive. They're generally free and easy to fill out, and experts say they could save you and your loved ones a bundle of money.

A quarter of all the money you ever spend on health care will likely be spent in the last few months of your life — perhaps to keep you alive even when doctors know you won't recover.

The statistics are startling. Roughly six out of 10 people die in hospitals, sometimes after long stays in intensive care at a cost of up to $10,000 a day. That can drain any inheritance you had hoped to leave your spouse or children.

Part of the problem is that most people never create an advance directive. Only one in five Americans has one. Worse, their doctors usually don't know they have one and may order expensive, unwanted medical care. Don't be one of those people. Give some thought to your wishes before the unthinkable happens. Follow these five tips to write a living will that will give you peace of mind.

Do it now. Set up your advance directive documents before you get sick. Do it while you're physically, mentally, and emotionally healthy to ensure you make well-informed decisions.

Lynn Buckley wishes her father had done it before he developed dementia. "I remember trying to explain to dad what we were doing as we were filling it out, and asking questions about prolonging life," she recalls. "That's a difficult discussion to have with somebody who's mentally alert, much less someone with dementia."

Talk with your doctor. Fill out your advance directive with your doctor's help. She may point out potential medical situations you hadn't thought of and can explain any medical terms you don't understand. Buckley's parents used an elder care attorney who gave them a detailed questionnaire to help them think through different scenarios. "The questionnaire was helpful, because it asked about really specific situations that you don't think about."

Tell your family. Make your wishes clear to your family and to any doctors or specialists you see. Don't rely on a piece of paper to do it for you. Medical circumstances could crop up that aren't covered in the document. If your family knows how you do and don't want to live your last days, they'll have an easier time making tough decisions on your behalf.

Get it on record. Give a copy of your advance directive to each of your doctors and make sure they put it in your medical file. The same goes when you enter an assisted living or a nursing home. Also give copies to family members, close friends, and the person you chose to make medical decisions for you.

Buckley took it a step further. Her parents had living wills, do-not-resuscitate (DNR) orders, and durable power of attorneys for health and finance. "I made multiple copies of all these documents and kept them in a gigantic notebook. No matter where I went with my parents, I took this notebook," she explains. "It saved me over and over and over again."

"No matter where we went, be it the hospital, emergency room, or urgent care," no one ever had her parents' documents on hand. "Their own doctors never had the paperwork, even though I knew I had given it to them."

Each time, the extra copies she kept in her notebook proved handy, especially near the end. "We had to file their documents with the medical records department at the hospital, and we were in the emergency room numerous times after that." The emergency room staff never seemed to have those forms. "If I couldn't show them the document, they were not going to believe it," Buckley says.

"If you don't have the document with you," chances are "they're not going to pay any attention to it."

Cover your travel. Some states have their own advance directive form. If you split your time living between two different states, fill out forms for each. Give a copy to your doctors and local hospitals in both states.

Fill out a living will for free

Advance directive forms are often available for free or low cost. Find them through these organizations.

- AARP offers advance directives online by state at *www.aarp.org/relationships/caregiving/info-03-2012/ free-printable-advance-directives.html.*

- Aging with Dignity provides a thorough, easy-to-understand directive called Five Wishes, available online at *www.agingwithdignity.org* or by phone at 888-5-WISHES. The form costs $5 but shipping is free.

- Caring Connections allows you to print one free copy of each state's advance directive form, including District of Columbia, at *www.caringinfo.org.*

- Compassion & Choices offers advice and a variety of end-of-life forms. Visit *www.compassionand choices.org/what-we-do/advance-planning/ advance-directive* or call 800-247-7421.

The U.S. Living Will Registry will store your advance directive documents online for a small fee and make them available to all of your health care providers. Visit *www.uslivingwill registry.com.*

Top 5 forms you need to have

You know you need a will, but that's not the only thing. Make sure you have these five important documents in case something happens to you.

- A living will, so you have a say in how much care you receive if you are too ill or injured to answer for yourself.

- Durable Power of Attorney for Health Care, where you name someone you trust as your Health Care Proxy to make medical decisions if you can't answer for yourself.

- A prehospital medical care directive, sometimes called a do-not-resuscitate (DNR) order, to alert ambulance or emergency room staff that you don't want CPR.

- An authorization to release health care information, which allows doctors to discuss your condition with your Health Care Proxy if something happens to you.

- A regular Durable Power of Attorney, assigning another trusted person to make decisions about your finances if you are unable to.

Someone who is terminally ill or knows they are nearing the end of life may also want to fill out a Physician Orders for Life-Sustaining Treatment, which is more specific than a living will. It addresses issues like whether you want a feeding tube or antibiotics if doctors know there's no chance you will recover.

3 ways to keep hospital costs at bay

Getting care doesn't have to cost a fortune. Check out these alternatives and learn ways to save while you're there.

Plan ahead. Before you get that procedure done at a hospital, call the office of the doctor who will be doing it. Ask if she works at any other facilities. You may pay less if she can do the same procedure at an outpatient center. Shop around for tests, too. An X-ray or MRI almost always costs less at an outpatient facility than a hospital lab.

Save ERs for real emergencies. It's the day after Thanksgiving, you broke your finger, and the doctor's office is closed. Seems like you'll be heading to the emergency room. Not so fast. An urgent care clinic can handle many of the same problems for a fraction of the cost. Sprains, mild cuts, even broken fingers and toes can be patched up there for less.

Even cheaper are the nurse practitioner-equipped clinics popping up in drugstores like CVS and Walgreens. They can treat basic illnesses, including strep throat and ear infections for around 80 percent less than an emergency room.

Keep costs low once you're in. You can't always avoid checking into the hospital, but you can take steps to cap the cost.

- Check your patient status every day that you're there. Being classified as "outpatient" or "under observation" rather than "inpatient" affects your insurance and Medicare coverage.

- Are you covered by insurance? Ask the hospital whether each doctor, specialist, and anesthesiologist you see is in-network. Also ask the hospital to send your tests to an in-network lab.

- Keep track of what medicines you do and don't take while in the hospital, and which tests are completed or canceled. The hospital may bill you automatically for drugs and tests you did not receive.

Haggle with hospitals for major savings

You can bargain with car salesmen and dicker at flea markets. In fact, it's expected. Why should hospitals be any different? Experts say you can slash the cost of care, if you're paying out of pocket, simply by negotiating the price of a procedure before you have it done.

Hospital sticker prices leave plenty of room for negotiation. The U.S. Department of Health and Human Services found that a hospital in Ada, Okla., charged an average of $5,300 for a joint replacement, while a hospital in Monterey Park, Calif., charged a whopping $223,000 for the same procedure.

Start by asking the hospital or doctor's office for the exact billing codes for the procedure you need. Next, find out what hospitals in your area typically charge for it. If it's a surgery, be sure to ask for prices on all aspects, including anesthesia and facility fees.

You can call each hospital and ask or do some sleuthing on the Internet. Several high-quality websites have sprung up to help you compare costs and score the best deal.

- *www.healthcarebluebook.com*
- *www.nerdwallet.com/health/hospitals*
- *www.fairhealthconsumer.org*

Use this knowledge as leverage to land a better deal at your preferred hospital. Haggle in person, if possible. It's harder to turn down someone face-to-face than over the phone.

Ask to speak to someone who can discuss pricing with you. Tell them you'll be paying out of pocket, if you don't have insurance, and ask for a self-pay discount. You could knock 25 percent off the bill this way, especially if you agree to pay up front in cash.

"Our local hospital offers a 25 percent discount on the bill if you pay within two weeks of billing. It's written in mice type at the bottom of the bill," says Carl Douglas. "We always take advantage of it." If you can't afford even that amount, ask if you qualify for charity care or financial assistance.

Whatever price the hospital agrees to, get it in writing and have someone with authority sign it. The person who ends up billing you may not know about your special deal. Having a written agreement could save you headaches down the road.

Smartest way to save on health care

Too many people make the choice to skip their medicines or skimp on dosages in order to save money. Research shows you'll actually spend more by trying these tactics — thanks to hospital visits — than if you had taken your meds in the first place.

People with congestive heart failure who took their medications as prescribed spent $8,881 less each year than those who didn't stick to their prescription regimen. Those with high blood pressure spent $3,908 less, with diabetes spent $3,756 less, and with high cholesterol spent $1,258 less.

Help your health and your wallet — fill your prescriptions and take your medicines as directed. Tell your doctor if you have trouble affording them. He may be able to prescribe cheaper alternatives or point you toward financial assistance programs that can help.

How to snag free care and big discounts

The hospital wants their money now, but what if you don't have the cash on hand? Don't panic. You have a good shot at landing financial assistance. Here's how.

Apply for Hill-Burton help. Some hospitals are required by law to help people who need care but can't afford it. They agree to do a certain amount of procedures for free or reduced-cost.

- Call the Hill-Burton hotline at 800-638-0742 to find a participating hospital.

- Speak to someone in the admissions or business office, ask if they have any Hill-Burton funds remaining, and ask for a copy of the Hill-Burton Individual Notice. This tells you where in the hospital you should go to apply.

- Head there and tell them you want to apply for Hill-Burton assistance. Fill out the form they give you and gather any documents they ask for.

- When you turn everything in, ask for a Determination of Eligibility. The Individual Notice will tell you how long the hospital has to accept or deny your application.

Surprisingly, you can apply for help before or after a hospital stay, and even if your bill has gone to collections. Each facility decides which services they will perform, and they only have to do a certain amount of them. Once they reach their quota, they can turn down people who apply for the program. Hill-Burton can be used to cover Medicaid, but not Medicare, copayments.

Check into charity status. Find out if the hospital that treated you is not-for-profit. If so, call and ask to speak to a financial counselor about charity care. Depending on your income, you could get 50, 75, or even 100 percent of your bill erased. But you have to ask — hospitals may not tell you about these programs. Is the hospital for-profit? Don't worry. You may still qualify for financial assistance, so be sure to ask.

You may have to haggle with any doctors or specialists who billed you separately. The hospital's assistance may not cover their services.

Catch costly hospital billing errors

Hospital errors don't just happen in the operating room. They happen on bills, with serious consequences. As many as eight out of 10 hospital bills are wrong. Catching those mistakes could save you hundreds — even thousands — of dollars.

Ask the hospital for an itemized bill, not the general one it automatically sends out. In most cases, hospitals are required by law to give you a detailed statement if you ask for it. This should list the prices of all the supplies, tests, services, and procedures you received. Once you have that bill in hand, go through it with a fine-tooth comb looking for mistakes like these.

Double billing. Check to see if the same description or code appears twice on your bill, or once on the doctor's bill and again on the hospital's. This is more likely if you spent time as both an inpatient and outpatient during the same stay.

Phantom charges. Hospitals automatically run certain tests when you check in with particular problems. You can refuse one or more of them, but make sure you don't get billed for them. The same goes for any supplies you don't use from the kit you receive when admitted.

Upcoding. Were you given generic drugs in the hospital? Be sure you weren't charged for the name-brand versions.

Charges on discharge day. Most hospitals don't bill you for the day you were discharged, so check. Also look for tests, procedures, or prescriptions that were charged after you had already left.

Unbundling. Hospitals may try to charge separately for items that are usually grouped together under a lower flat fee. Things like toothbrushes and hospital gowns, for instance, should be covered by room fees. Look for charges for multiple lab tests on the same day. Call your insurer and ask if those tests should have been bundled together for less.

Extra meds. Don't pay for an entire bottle of aspirin if you only took two pills. And if you brought your own medications from home, check that the hospital didn't charge you for those very same drugs.

Inaccurate operating time. Ask the hospital for your anesthesia records and take note of exactly what time your surgery started and ended. Then compare those times to the number of minutes of operating room use you were billed for.

Wrong room type. Did you share a room with another patient? Then make sure you were charged for a semiprivate, not a private, room. If you had to stay in a private room because no semiprivate rooms were available, the hospital should still charge you the semiprivate rate.

The mysterious codes that hospitals use on bills can make mistakes hard to spot. Call the hospital or doctor's billing department and ask them to explain specific codes and charges, or look them up on the Internet by typing "cpt" followed by the code number into a search engine like Google.

If you find an error, talk to the hospital's patient representative first. Call Medicare or your insurance company if the hospital has already filed a claim with them. You can also get professional assistance.

The nonprofit Patient Advocate Foundation will help people with debilitating, chronic, or life-threatening diseases resolve billing errors for free. Call them at 800-532-5274 or find them online at *www.patientadvocate.org*.

Big bills can slash your taxes

Turn hefty hospital bills into a boon come tax time. Simply keep the receipts for big-ticket medical expenses and use them as tax deductions next year.

You can deduct out-of-pocket medical costs once they reach 10 percent of your adjusted gross income, as long as you itemize your deductions. If you recently endured an expensive stay in the hospital, for example, it's worth it. See IRS Publication 502 to learn exactly which expenses are deductible.

Prescriptions and Supplements

Drop the cost of brand-name drugs

Some expensive drugs simply aren't available as generics, but that doesn't mean you're stuck paying the sticker price.

Ask about equivalents. Ask your doctor or pharmacist if your medicine has a therapeutic equivalent, another drug that has the same effect in your body. Then ask if the therapeutic equivalent has a generic version. If so, the cost of your prescription could drop dramatically.

Snatch up samples. Don't waste money filling a full prescription for a brand-name drug that you've never tried. Ask your doctor for samples, first. You'll get to test-drive the new drug and find out if it works before you spend a fortune on it.

Seek out coupons. Drug companies sometimes give away coupons for popular brand-name drugs. Ask your pharmacist if he knows whether any coupons are available, or look for special deals on the drug maker's website. Coupons may only lower the cost of your medicine for a few months, but if it's a drug you need then every little bit helps.

WARNING

Save money — and your liver

One in six people with liver damage got it from taking supplements. Most ended up in the hospital. Some suffered organ failure. A few even died or needed liver transplants. Supplements and herbal remedies for weight loss, immune system health, cough and cold treatments, and depression led the pack in liver damage, but ordinary multivitamins were fingered in a few cases, too.

More and more studies are finding that many supplements don't improve your health and may actually harm it. You may be better off spending your money elsewhere.

Fill your prescriptions for free

There's no reason to pay full price for your medications when deals like these abound. Some stores offer a long list of drugs at absolutely no charge. Others charge only a few dollars for a three-month supply. Don't despair if your prescriptions don't fall into those categories. Hundreds of programs provide free and discounted medications to people in need.

Freebies. Publix, Meijer, United Supermarkets, Price Chopper, and Schnucks pharmacies are just a few that give away life-saving drugs. Some limit the freebies to antibiotics, but Publix and Meijer also provide free metformin, a drug used to treat diabetes, and lisinopril, an ACE inhibitor. Many more chains participate in programs like these, so be sure to ask.

Cheapies. Pharmacies in nearly every major chain of grocery, drug, and big-box stores have a list of $4 drugs. Wal-Mart, Wegmans, and Kroger pharmacies sell hundreds of generic medications at $4 for a 30-day supply, or $10 for a 90-day supply. Ask your regular pharmacy about their low-cost generics. If they don't participate, look for one that does.

Discount deals. Don't let lack of money keep you from getting the medicines you need. Plenty of financial assistance programs are out there for people who can't afford their prescriptions. You may be able to get yours filled for free or at a deep discount.

- The Partnership for Prescription Assistance will help match you with one of 475 public and private programs that provide free and discounted drugs to people in need. Call 888-477-2669 or visit the website *www.pparx.org*.

- Apply for free and low-cost medicines through the website *www.rxhope.com*. Choose your medications, review the eligibility requirements, and print out the application forms. Have your doctor's office finish filling them out and apply on your behalf.

- The nonprofit, mail-order pharmacy Rx Outreach provides more than 500 drugs for chronic conditions to people with low incomes. You could pay as little as $18 for a six-month supply of medicine, $13 for 100 insulin syringes, absolutely nothing for a blood glucose monitor. Apply online through *www.rxoutreach.org*.

Free help with food, medicine, and more

It's out there — extra help paying for your prescriptions, in-home care, utilities, food, housing, and all the necessities of life. More than 2,000 federal, state, and private programs exist. Finding them was hard, until now.

BenefitsCheckUp can connect you with the right organizations for your situation. It's a free service of the nonprofit National Council on Aging.

Hop online and head to *www.benefitscheckup.org*, then answer a series of questions about your circumstances. The website will create a report that describes each program you may qualify for. You can apply for them online or print out paper applications.

---

5 surefire ways to cap prescription costs

Even with insurance coverage, prescriptions can take an enormous bite out of your budget. Start trimming those costs. The way you shop for medicine has changed, in some ways for the better. Pharmacies are everywhere now — on the Internet, in big-box stores, and through the mail. And they're fighting for your business. Put the increased competition to work for your wallet with these tips.

Let technology do the legwork. Type your ZIP code and the names of your medications into the website *www.goodrx.com*. The site will compare drug prices at your local and mail-order pharmacies and tell you which one offers the best deal.

Make pharmacies fight for your business. Check the prices at your local pharmacies, then call the one you like best and ask if they'll match a lower-priced competitor. This can work well with independent pharmacies, which don't always offer deals as good as the national chains. When comparing costs, be sure to ask pharmacies for their lowest possible price. They may offer customers in their loyalty programs a special discount.

Remember to check prices at warehouse club pharmacies, like Costco and Sam's Club. Unlike their groceries and other goods, you don't need a membership to take advantage of their low prices on prescription drugs.

Buy in bulk. Call your insurance company and ask if they have a prescription mail-order service. You could save a bundle on drugs you take often by having them mailed to you in bulk.

Find preferred pharmacies. No mail-order program? Ask your insurer if they have any deals with preferred pharmacies. Insurance companies sometimes negotiate additional discounts with a particular chain.

Shop safely online. Internet pharmacies may promise incredible deals on your medications, but be careful they aren't selling you a bunch of hooey. The Food and Drug Administration has shut down thousands of online pharmacies for selling fake or dangerous drugs.

Astoundingly, LegitScript.com says that more than 37,000 Internet pharmacies — a whopping 95 percent — are not legitimate. Follow these tips to buy with confidence.

- Make certain the pharmacy is located inside the United States and is licensed by the state where it's based. Call that state's board of pharmacy to check, or look up the pharmacy at a verification website like *www.legitscript.com*.

- Never buy prescription drugs from a pharmacy willing to sell them without a prescription.

- Only shop through websites that have a licensed pharmacist on hand to answer your questions.

Glasses and Hearing aids

Spot great deals on eyewear

Your eye doctor's office is the worst place to buy glasses, contacts, and accessories. You'll pay hundreds of dollars more than the eyewear is worth. Try these options and save.

Reuse your frames. Order new lenses for your old frames when your prescription changes. Both Costco and Wal-Mart will put lenses in your existing frames for as little as $10.

Shop wholesale. Head to Costco or BJ's for eye exams, glasses, and contact lenses at prices that are hard to beat. Some of these stores boast optical departments with optometrists on staff for eye exams. At Costco, expect to pay around $49 for an exam, $35 for basic frames, and $20 and up for single-vision lenses.

Buy online. You can find almost anything on the Internet, including incredible deals on eyeglasses and contacts. For instance, a pair of designer Ray-Ban frames that cost $210 at LensCrafters are $136 at the online store *www.framesdirect.com*. The same goes for contact lenses. FramesDirect.com charges $184 for the same contacts that cost $272 at LensCrafters.

The idea of spending that much money on a pair of glasses sight unseen can be a little scary. Fortunately, a few online stores like Warby Parker let you try on frames at home before you buy them. Go to *www.warbyparker.com* and choose five pairs. The company will ship them to you, free of charge, for a five-day trial period. You decide which pair you like best, order the frames and lenses, and mail back the testers.

Shave thousands off the cost of hearing

Hear that? It's the sound of all the money you could save on your next set of hearing aids. Forget about paying full price. There's no need when you have options like these.

Fix it, first. Before you spend thousands on a new hearing aid, try fixing your old one. A good cleaning and a few small repairs could have it working like new for one-tenth of the cost.

- The Department of Veterans Affairs (VA) repairs VA-authorized hearing aids. Call the VA Audiology and Speech Pathology Service that issued them to you. You will need to mail them in for repair but should get them back within three weeks.

- Not a veteran? Check the Yellow Pages for a local hearing aid professional, or contact a business that repairs hearing aids by mail, such as Kansas Hearing Aid Repair at 800-976-0601. Expect to pay around $100 for the fix.

Use your military benefits. Veterans can receive free and discounted hearing aids through the VA and Department of Defense.

- Military retirees may be eligible for free hearing aids and batteries through the VA. Enroll at a VA Medical Center or Clinic and ask your VA Primary Care Provider to refer you to the Audiology and Speech Pathology Clinic for an evaluation.

- The Retiree-At-Cost Hearing Aid Program sells aids to military retirees at discounts up to 85 percent. A top-of-the-line pair that retails for $5,000 could cost as little as $755. Call the VA Health Care Benefits line at 877-222-8387 to find a participating audiology center or visit the website *www.militaryaudiology.org*.

- Army retirees enrolled with the Lyster Army Health Clinic at Ft. Rucker, Ala. are eligible for great deals on hearing aids. This program serves veterans and their spouses throughout the United States. Call 334-255-7056 to enroll.

Ask an insurer. United Healthcare sells their own line of hearing aids called "hi HealthInovations" directly to the public, no insurance necessary. Prices range from $749 to $949 apiece, 30 to 50 percent less than you'd pay in a store. Members snag an even better deal. You'll pay as little as $479 each if you have an insurance policy, including a Medicare Part D Plan, through United Healthcare. Call United Healthcare at 855-523-9355 for more information.

Head to a wholesaler. Costco sells name-brand hearing aids at below-retail prices, with basic models starting at $500 each. Costco hearing aid centers also offer free hearing tests, free hearing aid batteries, and free cleanings.

Locate a Lion. The Lions Club gives hearing aids to people who can't afford to buy them through its Affordable Hearing Aid

Project (AHAP). Call Lions AHAP at 630-203-3837 to find your local Lions Club and apply for the program.

Pay less for important supplies

Medicare changes could mean huge savings on diabetic testing supplies, walkers, oxygen tanks, and more. Now, companies that sell or rent medical devices must bid against each other to win a Medicare contract. The items are cheaper as a result — and so is your copay. Thanks to the new system, you have three ways to get medical supplies through Medicare:

- directly from the doctor's office or hospital before being discharged, but only if the device is "medically necessary," like a walker.

- by taking your prescription for the item to a pharmacy or medical supply store that accepts "Medicare assignment."

- by getting the prescription filled through a mail-order supplier that has a contract with Medicare.

Call 800-MEDICARE (800-633-4227) to find mail-order suppliers, or type your ZIP code into the Medicare website at *www.medicare.gov/ supplier directory.*

What if you don't qualify for Medicare yet or can't afford the copay? Not to worry. You'll find the supplies you need for free or cheap from these sources.

Seek out nonprofits. Nonprofit organizations around the country provide free and low-cost medical equipment to people in need. Friends of Disabled Adults and Children in Georgia, Clinics Can Help in Florida, and GoodHealthwill in Colorado and Wyoming are just a few. Check your telephone book for nonprofit suppliers of durable medical equipment. The website *www.rmmor.org/nonprofits.htm* has a partial list of groups around the country.

Hop online. The websites of brick-and-mortar retailers like Walgreens, Wal-Mart, and CVS offer a much wider selection of medical equipment than you'll find in-store. Amazon.com carries nearly every item under the sun, including wheelchairs and walkers, at competitive prices. Remember to factor in shipping charges when comparing online deals.

New rules don't apply to everyone

Medicare changes regarding medical supplies only apply to people enrolled in Original Medicare. If you have a Medicare Advantage Plan, your insurer will tell you when, or if, your supplier changes.

Groceries & Dining Out

How to eat on the cheap

3 ways to actually save with bulk buying

Buying in bulk can save up to $100 a month on your grocery bill if you play it smart. Find out how.

Know what to avoid. Skip oils, nuts, spices, and foods with high oil content because the bulk versions will probably go bad before you finish them. This also applies to bread and fresh produce unless you freeze them. For all other items, use this rule — if you are not dead sure you can finish the entire product by the expiration date, do not buy it in bulk.

Find the best candidates for bulk buying. Not everything is worth buying in bulk. But with dozens of uses and pennies per use, you will go through these two in no time. Vinegar and baking soda are not only good for cooking, but for cleaning and deodorizing, too.

Bulk buying saves you 58 cents per gallon of vinegar and 96 cents for every 16 ounces of baking soda you use.

But those savings are only for two products. Other good candidates for bulk buying include:

- dry beans
- pasta
- white rice
- canned goods
- frozen fruits and vegetables
- personal care items
- cleaners
- paper goods
- staples, like salt, pepper, and tomato sauce
- foods or ingredients you use up quickly

Watch for red flags. Before buying a warehouse club membership or a supermarket's bulk buy special, decide where to store each of your bulk purchases, and make sure you have enough freezer, refrigerator, or pantry space available.

Don't buy a product in bulk if you cannot store it properly because part of it will probably go to waste before you can use it. And be careful with all bulk products because even nonperishables and frozen foods can go bad if given enough time.

For each item you plan to buy in bulk, compare unit prices first to make sure the bulk price really is cheaper than the prices you can find elsewhere.

Bulk buying for singles

Try these tactics to help make buying in bulk more worth-while for a one-person household:

- Buy multipacks of canned goods or family packs of loose frozen items, so you can only remove and use the amount you need for a single serving.

- Find another single person or small household to split your bulk buy purchases and costs with.

- If a warehouse club membership is too expensive, keep an eye out for bulk sales or case lot specials on nonperishables at your supermarket.

Stop paying full price

When are groceries the cheapest? Learning the industry sales cycles will save you money. In fact, if you play your cards right, you may rarely need to pay full price on many of your groceries.

Put time on your side. If you've ever bought a grocery item on sale only to discover a deeper discount two weeks later, blame sales cycles. Most grocery products have one.

At the beginning of the cycle, the price of an item rises for several weeks until it reaches its peak price. Then the price falls for several weeks until it hits the rock bottom price and restarts the cycle. That rock bottom price may be more than 50 percent lower than the peak price.

If you know when the next rock bottom price is due, you can stock up and save. And if you know when all future rock bottoms will happen, you can always stock up enough to avoid buying until the

next rock bottom. In fact, after learning how to predict sales cycles, one person reported saving $30 on her grocery bill every week.

Predict sales cycles. Although an individual item, such as a particular brand of frozen chicken breasts, may have a sales cycle that is always the same length, the length of the cycle may be different for other items in the same store.

What's more, the sales cycle for an individual item may vary depending on where you live. In general, sales cycles are between six and 12 weeks long, but you must track them to find out the length. Here's how.

Pick the seven supermarket items you buy most frequently or pay the most for. Write down their prices every week, even if you don't buy the item on every shopping trip. Within a few months, you'll know how many weeks to wait between rock bottom prices and can plan your stockpiling and purchases accordingly.

Once you know the sales cycles for the first seven items, start tracking a new set of seven so you can save even more. Just remember that different stores may have different cycles for the same item.

Line your pockets with soft drink savings

Buy a 12-pack of canned Coca-Cola every week, and you may be spending $217.36 a year or more. Save money on soft drinks without giving up the sweetness of the treat. Switch to buying two 2-liters instead. Although you will drink roughly the same amount, you will save $115.44 by this time next year.

For even bigger savings, switch to sweet tea. Make six pitchers of sweet tea a month instead of drinking cola, and the savings add up to $192.60 a year or $16.05 a month. Drink water or unsweetened tea instead, and you will save even more.

Put an end to impulse buying

Roughly 62 percent of supermarket sales come from impulse purchases, and that's no accident. Grocery store marketers tweak everything from the location of milk to the music playing in the store to nudge you toward making an impulse purchase.

Learning how to defend against these marketing tactics could save the average shopper $25 a week or more. Here's how to start.

Plan your menu. Before you shop, plan all snacks and meals, including entrées, sides, desserts, and drinks, for the next week. To save extra money and help resist impulse purchases, plan around the sale items listed in the newspaper, store circular, or on the Web. Adding unplanned items to your cart is tougher when you know exactly what you need for the next week.

Make a list. Using your menu plan, make a grocery list. Mark off each item on your list when it goes in the cart.

Beware of specials. Items displayed prominently at the ends of aisles may not be on sale. Be sure you know the regular price of an item before you buy it on sale. Even some genuine sales may not be bargains. For example, a 10 for $10 sale may seem like a deal, but only if you can eat the entire product before it spoils or expires.

Limit shopping time. After 30 minutes in the supermarket, shoppers spend an extra 50 cents for each additional minute in the store. What's more, marketing experts know you're more likely to buy what you look at longest. They try to slow your pace, encourage browsing, and keep you in the store longer.

For example, grocery marketers place milk and bread far apart so you must walk by more products. That's also why they locate the most popular items in the middle section of an aisle. So don't shop when the store is crowded because you'll be forced to linger in the aisles longer. Instead, aim to finish shopping within 30 minutes.

Never shop while hungry. Marketers make sure delicious smells waft in from the bakery and deli to tempt you to buy more. That's why the bakery is often near the front of the store.

Leave the kids and spouse at home. They will want items beyond what is on your list. In fact, grocers place the most tempting cereals and treats at the right eye level for children. One woman even found that taking her kids to the supermarket raised the bill by 20 percent.

Compare your list to your receipt. Roughly 76 percent of shoppers buy up to five products that aren't on their lists. If you have tried other impulse-resisting tactics, but still find items on your sales slip that weren't on your list, leave your credit and debit cards at home. Shop only with enough cash for the groceries you need.

Smart way to resist checkout lane goodies

Sales of impulse buys like magazines and gum are down at least 5 percent, and retailers believe they know why.

Consumers no longer browse the magazines or gum in the checkout lane display because they are too busy with their smartphones. The problem has become so serious that Kroger and other retailers are experimenting with new locations for checkout lane products.

So if you worry about making impulse purchases while waiting in line, take your smartphone, cellphone, or some other distraction with you to the checkout. Sales figures suggest this little trick really works.

Top-quality products at incredibly low prices

Your regular supermarket may not be the best place for grocery shopping. As Janet Shaw discovered, considering other options can make a real difference in your food bill.

Meet the hard discounter. "I switched to shopping at Aldi's when my work hours were reduced, and it was important to find ways to save on expenses," Janet says. "I cut my grocery bill by about a third."

"Their prices are lower than at a regular store, and the quality of their products is very high," she explains. "In addition to canned and boxed items, they also sell great fresh produce that is much less expensive than at a traditional grocery store."

Aldi's, Save-a-Lot, and several others are a special type of grocery store called a hard discounter. These stores emphasize high-quality products at startlingly low prices. How can they afford this? Aldi's does it through trade-offs like these:

- "Aldi's stores are not fancy," says Janet. "Products are displayed in the boxes they are shipped in, so stocking the shelves is faster and easier."

- Aldi's only accepts cash or debit cards, so leave your checkbook and credit cards at home.

- Aldi's does not provide free bags. "They do sell paper and plastic bags for a few cents apiece," Janet says, "Or you can usually find empty boxes to carry your goods to your car. But taking my own reusable bags is more convenient."

- Aldi's charges a temporary 25-cent fee for using a shopping cart, but you get your quarter back when you return the cart.

You may also see more store brands, less selection, and fewer brand names than you are used to.

"I can't do all my shopping at Aldi's so I do need to go to another store for the other things I need," Janet admits. "But it's worth the savings to shop at two stores."

Explore other money-saving options. If you don't have a hard discounter nearby, investigate one of these instead:

- Farmer's market. Organic produce may be much cheaper there than at traditional supermarkets.

- Dollar store. Some dollar store products may be significantly cheaper than the same items at your regular grocery store, so compare unit prices to find out. But also check expiration dates, and read labels carefully if you have any concerns.

- Ethnic markets. Compare prices at your local Asian, Italian, or other ethnic market to see which items you can stock up on for less.

Save more on what you already buy

Americans throw out around 25 percent of the food and drink they buy. In fact, the average family of four spends up to $2,000 every year on food that never gets eaten. Try these tips to use more of the food you already buy, and see how much you can save.

Rotate your stock like a supermarket. Grocery stores "front and face" their shelves nightly, moving older items to the front and tucking newer items behind them. Do the same in your pantry and refrigerator when you restock your inventory with new groceries. You will be more likely to use older items first, before they can spoil or expire.

Start dating again. Use permanent marker to put a date on frozen foods and bulk items when you bring them home.

Take inventory. Put together an inventory list of the pantry items you keep in stock for regular use. Check how much you have left of each one before you go grocery shopping, so you won't buy extras you don't need.

Learn storage limits and stretch them. Visit *stilltasty.com* or your local library to find out the shelf life, freezer life, or refrigerator life of a food, and learn how you can keep it fresher longer.

For example, you might discover you can make that bunch of bananas last a few more days if you wrap the crown — the brown part connecting all the bananas — in plastic wrap. You may also find that produce lasts longer, and is easier to find in a crowded refrigerator, if you keep it in closed mason jars.

You could even test how much longer cereal, chips, flour, sugar, and other bagged items can last if you seal them tightly with clothespins or chip clips, or put them in resealable bags.

Stall for time. Freeze and date foods if you know you won't be able to use them before they go bad. You can freeze most foods, but don't freeze these:

- fried foods, except french fries and onion rings

- salad vegetables like cabbage, celery, cress, cucumbers, lettuce, parsley, and radishes

- baked or boiled potatoes

- cooked spaghetti, macaroni, or rice without sauce

- desserts with meringue, cream, or custard fillings, or icing made with egg whites

- milk sauces for casseroles or gravy

- crumb or cheese toppings for casseroles

- sour cream

- gelatin

- fruit jelly, mayonnaise, or salad dressing

Keep a diary. Record which foods you throw out and why they had to be discarded. If you notice any repeat offenders or discard things for the same reason every time, plan how to prevent the problem.

For instance, if you buy a healthy food like broccoli but throw it out because it's boring, dip or drizzle it in pasta sauce, Worcestershire sauce, teriyaki sauce, vinaigrette salad dressing, or — if you are really brave — hot sauce.

High-tech way to shop and save

Carol has eaten her favorite brand of hot cereal every morning for years. To avoid its high price tag, she either bought the cereal on sale or shopped at discount stores, but her cereal luck could not last.

"They eventually stopped carrying it, and it literally never goes on sale at Kroger anymore. So I was stuck paying almost $4 for a box," Carol says. That encouraged her to change her strategy.

Score savings over and over. Carol discovered that her cereal was available by the case at *www.amazon.com*.

"When I do Subscribe & Save, it comes to $3.30 a box, and it's shipped free automatically so I never run out," she explains.

By choosing to use Amazon's Subscribe & Save program, she can save up to $30 a year on just one item.

Comparison shop online. You may already comparison shop locally by checking your supermarket, warehouse store, and other outlets. In addition, start regularly checking the online prices of all your nonperishable grocery items at *www.amazon.com* and the websites of your local stores. Note whether you must pay shipping or other extra charges and whether the item is a bulk buy.

If the price is cheap enough for significant savings, and if shipping or other costs don't wipe out those savings, consider ordering the item instead of buying it locally. If the item is a bulk buy, make certain you have room to store it properly so it will last until you use it up.

Check Amazon's Subscribe & Save option. Amazon offers a 5 percent discount on any one item from its Subscribe & Save program, but boosts the savings to a 15 to 20 percent discount if you subscribe to five different items. If an item is not cheaper with the 5 percent discount, calculate the 15 percent discount to see if that is cheaper than your local prices. If you find five items that are cheaper with either the 5 or 15 percent discount, your discount will be 15 percent on all five items if they always arrive during the same month.

Of course, unlike your regular Amazon purchases, Subscribe & Save is not a one-time order, but a subscription that arrives at regular intervals. You select how often the order is delivered, ranging from every month to every six months.

Shipping is free and no fees apply, but you still pay sales tax. Shipping starts the month following your Subscribe & Save order, so you have time to use up old stuff.

And don't worry about receiving purchases you don't want. You receive e-mail reminders shortly before Amazon begins processing your order so you have a chance to make changes to your subscription. You can also cancel your subscription at any time.

WARNING

Check before you choose Subscribe & Save

Amazon's Subscribe & Save program is not always your best bet, so remember these tips.

- Check local sales. Some shoppers have reported that sales at local stores sometimes beat the Amazon Subscribe & Save price. Others point out that the Amazon price may change at any time. Watch sales and the Amazon price to see if you should continue your subscription.

- Plan carefully. If you run out of something before your next shipment, you may have to pay full price locally to buy the product.

- Schedule cautiously. You may not get the 15 percent discount during any month when four items or less arrive.

Become a food preservation ninja

Don't let a big batch of produce go to waste. Learn how to do home canning, drying, freezing, and even pickling with online publications from the National Center for Home Food Preservation. You can find them at *nchfp.uga.edu*. Preserving your own food can also be much cheaper than buying it at the store.

Transform leftovers into gourmet meals

Don't spend money on new foods to replace languishing leftovers or soft fruits and vegetables. Reinvent those foods instead with these tips.

Give produce a second chance. Mary Ross discovered that a high-powered blender is the secret to using up fruits and vegetables before they go bad. She makes a delicious smoothie every morning with a mixture of whatever she has on hand.

"The brand I use recommends filling half the blender with greens and half with fruit and nutritional extras like nuts or flaxseed," Mary explains. "It really helps when the strawberries or grapes get soft, and we don't have time to eat them all. Plus you can't taste the veggies, so it's a great way to sneak them into your kids' diets."

Divide and conquer leftovers. Chop or dice leftover meats and vegetables or puree the vegetables. Then decide which kind of cuisine they should go into.

- Mexican or Southwestern. Add to burritos or chili.
- Italian. Sprinkle on pizzas or add to pasta sauce.
- Asian. Mix into stir-fries or fried rice.

- Summer. Toss them in a salad.

- Winter. Add them to soups or stews.

Create a C.O.R.N. buffet. Pull out several nights of leftovers and reheat them. Put them on the table or countertop, and let everyone serve themselves from the Clean Out the Refrigerator Night buffet.

Clean out the pantry week. Pick a week when your goal is to use up pantry items that you might be tempted to throw out if they stay there much longer.

To find recipes that will help you use up these items, use Google to search for "recipe" and the ingredients you want, or try recipe sites like *www.recipekey.com* or *www.supercook.com*. If you don't have Web access, ask friends and family for recipe ideas and visit the library.

Boost your budget with recipe substitutions

Recipe substitutions can help you avoid expensive ingredients and prevent costly food waste. For example, if a recipe calls for meat, always replace half the meat in the recipe with beans, and you can buy less meat to cut costs.

But that's not the only way substitutions save money. Say you find the perfect recipe to use up several pantry items nearing their expiration date, but one of the recipe's key ingredients is wine. Don't buy any vino. Just substitute cranberry or grape juice for red wine, or substitute white grape juice or apple juice for white wine.

Use the library or the Internet to make a list of substitutions for expensive ingredients and ingredients you may need for recipes that clean out your pantry or refrigerator. Also check for substitutions where the substitutes are ingredients you need to use up.

Save up to $600 by switching from bottled water

You can get your daily recommended 64 ounces of water three ways, but only two of them will save you money. See the numbers for yourself.

If you buy bottled water in bulk, you can get a discount. A 24-pack of 16.9-ounce bottled water costs $4.98. To drink 64 ounces a day, you need to finish roughly four bottles every day. To do that, you have to buy 61 of those heavy 24-packs every year at a cost of $303.78 — and that doesn't even include sales tax. To drink the same amount of tap water, experts estimate you would spend just 50 cents a year.

In other words, a one-person household could save up to $303.29 a year or roughly $25 every month just by switching from bottled water to tap water. A two-person household could save more than $600 a year or nearly $50 each month.

But if you would rather not drink tap water, you can still save money. Just buy a faucet water filter, filtered water dispenser, or filtered water pitcher.

For $50 or less, you can get one that improves the taste of your water and reduces mercury and copper. Even with the cost of replacement filters, a one-person household could save up to $200 the first year and $250 each year after. A two-person household could save as much as $150 the first year and $200 during each of the following years.

Find discounts on specialty diet products

Buying specialty foods because of allergies, diabetes, problems with gluten, or other health issues can put a big dent in your food budget. Saving money on these food items is tough, but not impossible. Here's how you can find the discounts that don't show up in the Sunday newspaper.

- Write or email the manufacturer of a product you use, explain why you appreciate the product, and ask if coupons are available.

- Check magazines or websites dedicated to the health condition that restricts your diet, and see if they contain coupons or recommend ways to get discounts.

- Join a local or online support group for your health condition. Trade information about coupons and discounts with other group members, and find bulk-buying buddies for bulk deals that are too big for one person.

- Check *www.amazon.com* to see if bulk versions of your favorite nonperishable products are available at a discount.

Coupon hater's guide to coupon savings

Use these tips to spend less time finding and clipping coupons, while scoring bigger bargains.

Compare store brands. Your grocery store's house brand or generic brand may be cheaper than using a coupon for a national brand. Experts suggest you can save as much as 25 percent off your grocery bill just by switching to store brands.

Oddly enough, the store brand may be made by the same manufacturer who produces the brand name product. Start trying the store brand versions of various products to find out if they are right for you. Keep buying the ones you like, and you may get such steep discounts that you rarely need coupons for those items.

Use coupon databases. If you have Internet access at home or can use computers at the library, you can skip clipping from your Sunday newspaper coupon inserts. Instead, just collect the inserts from your paper each Sunday, write the date on them, and file them.

When you are ready to shop, use online coupon databases to tell you which inserts contain the coupons you want. Start with the database at *www.couponmom.com* and the one in the Tools section of *www.savingadvice.com*.

Only use coupons on sale items. Don't bother breaking out the coupons for an item that isn't on sale. Instead, collect coupon inserts from family and friends, so you can have several of the same coupon ready for an item when it goes on sale.

But don't stop there. You can do more than just score a deeper discount from combining the sale and coupon. If you have saved multiple coupons for the same product and they all have "manufacturer" written across the top, you can stock up by applying one coupon per item.

For items with a long shelf life and items you can freeze, this may mean you don't need to buy the item again until the next time it goes on sale.

If you have Internet access, you can make this job even easier by finding bloggers who match up the coupons and sales for you. These are available for most major grocery chains. To find them, try searching with terms like blog, coupon, sale, and the name of your grocery store.

Stick with the old standbys. Only collect coupons for items you always buy anyway, and don't waste time clipping other coupons to "try something new." To help find coupons for products you already buy, check their packaging.

While shopping, check each product's packaging for peelable coupons you can use before leaving the store. Before throwing away a can or jar, check the back of the label. You may find a coupon for that product.

WARNING

Watch out for new coupon scam

You find one link to a discount that's at least three times better than any other site's best offer for the same product. The Better Business Bureau suggests that's a warning sign of a potential scam. Here's how it works.

The link takes you to an official-looking website that requests contact information in order to send coupons to you. But once you provide that information, you are either sent to a promotion site for a questionable product completely unrelated to the product you wanted — or you may receive counterfeit coupons that look real, but stores won't accept them. Meanwhile, the scammer has your contact information and can bombard you with spam.

To dodge scams, avoid:

- sites that make you pay for a coupon.
- coupons without expiration dates and legal language.
- online coupons that offer unbelievably higher discounts than other coupons for the same product.
- sites that require you to fill out a form with personal information before you can download coupons or coupon codes.

Enjoy eating out for less

You already have a particular restaurant in mind, but you don't want to pay full price to eat there. Think like a bargain hunter to lower your costs.

Munch on midweek discounts. On Tuesday or Wednesday night, call ahead, and ask about that night's specials. You may discover half-price entrees, drink specials, or free desserts or appetizers. You may also enjoy fewer crowds and better service.

Join a loyalty or VIP program. This is great for restaurants you frequent often. The program can include a loyalty card, punch card, points system, or coupons by mail or email. And it can pay off well, as Sam Gardener has discovered.

"I have a VIP card at Maguire's, which builds up credit as a percentage of my purchases and qualifies me for VIP specials," Sam explains. "I usually allow the credit to build all year. Then, when friends visit at the holidays, I can take them all out, without spending a dime. So if there's a local spot you like, and they've got a member program for locals, take advantage of it."

Just be sure to read the fine print on your card or on the restaurant's website to make sure you get the most from your loyalty card and avoid unpleasant surprises.

Go for lunch. Lunch may offer smaller portions, but you can probably enjoy the same dish you'd have ordered at dinner for 25 percent less.

Search for a discount. If you have Web access, perform a search using the name of the restaurant and the word "coupon." You might be rewarded for your effort.

Visit the restaurant's website or Facebook page. You may find coupons, freebies, or special discounts. If you don't, you may still be able to score a discount or special offer by filling out a survey.

Check the backs of restaurant receipts. You may be able to fill out a survey to get a freebie or discount.

Skip desserts and drinks. These high-priced items may be adding more to your bill than you realize. Just switching from a regular drink to water may reduce your bill by as much as 20 percent.

Follow the restaurant on Twitter. You can also "Like" them on Facebook. In response, the restaurant may tweet or send you deals you can't get anywhere else.

Take advantage of the 'prix fixe' bargain

A three-course dinner at a local restaurant may normally cost $65, but you could pay as little as $40 if you know about the restaurant's *prix fixe* or fixed price menu.

A fixed price menu offers a single price for several courses that are usually sold separately or "à la carte" at higher individual prices. Watch restaurant ads, and ask around to find out which restaurants have a fixed price menu that is cheaper than their regular menu.

Every year, more cities are celebrating annual Restaurant Week. During this week, many restaurants boast a fixed price menu for the occasion. Check local news sources to see if Restaurant Week is coming to your town soon, and you may discover an extra opportunity to eat out for less.

Unleash super savings at favorite restaurants

When you don't have a particular restaurant in mind, let the deals help you decide where to go. To dig up the most discounts, use these tips.

Peck around for early bird specials. Check restaurant ads, and ask friends, family, and restaurant staff about early bird specials. You may save 25 percent or more if you are willing to eat dinner early.

Take advantage of membership privileges. If you join Senior Discounts.com for 13 bucks, they promise access to hundreds of dollars a year in senior discounts — and many senior discounts are unadvertised. Visit *www.seniordiscounts.com* to learn about the available discounts and what you can get from their free and paid memberships. If you're over 50, this is the one money-saving resource you have to know about.

Groups like AARP, AAA, and others also offer restaurant discounts. If you're a member of an organization or association, visit their website, or review the paperwork they gave you to find out which restaurants offer discounts.

Supersize your coupon discounts. Visit online coupon sites like Groupon.com and LivingSocial.com to get 50 percent off or more.

"Usually, the best Groupon deals are for restaurants," says Audrey Grant. "The best one I ever bought was $20 for $50 worth of upscale cuisine and stunning views at The Sun Dial Restaurant." The Sun Dial is a revolving rooftop restaurant in Atlanta. "Dinner at The Sun Dial can run $60 or more per person, not including tax and tip," Audrey explains.

"My husband and I used the Groupon on a beautiful, crystal clear afternoon," she recalls. "We had a lunch special which included dessert for $20 apiece," Audrey says. "When all was said and done, we paid less than $42 for an experience that would have cost any-where from $75 to $150 or more."

Just remember you may have to pay in advance, and your tax and tip will be based on the meal's full price. What's more, the offer may expire quickly, so read the fine print very carefully to make sure the deal is practical for you.

Buy a discounted gift certificate. Pick up a $25 restaurant gift certificate for $10 or a $50 certificate for half price or less. Just visit Restaurant.com or call toll-free 888-745-6991 between 8 a.m. and 8 p.m. Central Time on weekdays or between 8 a.m. and 5 p.m. Central Time on weekends.

You can get a list of all restaurants offering these coupons in your ZIP code or city, and narrow your list to your favorite type of restaurant, such as Italian.

Be aware that a minimum purchase will be required at the restaurant. To find out what other restrictions and rules apply, read carefully as you purchase online, or ask your customer service representative. Read the gift certificate to check for limits, too.

The key to big savings from your garden

In his book *The $64 Tomato*, author William Alexander tells how aiming for the perfect garden led to an average cost of $64 per tomato. But experts claim you can save money by growing your own herbs, vegetables, and fruits.

The trick is to plan carefully so your garden doesn't cost more than the delicious food it produces. Start with these tips.

Choose produce that's expensive at the supermarket. Determine which vegetables, fruits, herbs, and spices give you the most sticker shock, and make a list.

Grow stuff you like to eat. If you never use it, you can't save money. Remove items you dislike from your list.

Pick items you can store a long time or preserve. Narrow the list further by emphasizing items that have a long storage life or can be preserved by canning, drying, or freezing. Preserving prevents waste when your plants produce more than you can eat, and allows you to use your extra produce out of season.

Consider options with a great track record. In many parts of the country, tomatoes, sweet peppers, cucumbers, green beans, or leaf lettuce can provide good savings, but herbs may be your top bet for saving money. For example, herbs like basil and parsley are economical and easy to grow, but the same herbs bought fresh at the supermarket are pricey.

Avoid garden dropouts. Investigate your garden candidates to make sure they can survive long enough to help supply your kitchen. Ask your gardening friends, family, and neighbors what kinds of produce and herbs grow well in your area — and which varieties are best.

To find more information and investigate specific plants, use these resources, too:

- Surf to *www.extension.org* to find and visit your state's Cooperative Extension website. Look for "Select an institution." When you find it, enter your state or ZIP code, and click the "Locate" button. Links to your state's Cooperative Extension websites appear above where you typed. Click the link you want. If that link doesn't take you to the website, and a second set of links appears in the same spot, click a link to go to its website.

- Check the phone book for your county cooperative extension office, and call with your questions.

- Visit your local library or the Internet.

Look for answers to questions like these:

- What soil, drainage, and other conditions does the plant require?

- How hard is the plant to grow, and what are your chances of success?

- Does your yard get enough sunlight for the produce you want to grow?

- Can you protect the plants from pets, wildlife, insects, and disease?

- How big will the plants get, and how many can you fit in your available space?

Start small. To keep costs down, limit yourself to just a few items the first year, especially if you are a beginning gardener.

Garden without a yard

You can grow your own food even if you live in an apartment with no yard.

If your balcony or windows receive enough sunlight, try container gardening. You can grow salad greens, beans, peppers, cucumbers, cherry tomatoes, squash, radishes, beets, and chard in pots or other containers successfully.

If your light is too poor or container gardens are not permitted, check whether a community garden is available. A community garden provides the land for growing flowers or food. In some community gardens, you take home part of the harvest in exchange for tending the garden and helping to buy seeds and supplies.

To find a community garden, visit *www.communitygarden.org* on the Web. If you don't have computer access, call the American Community Gardening Association toll-free at 877-275-2242 or write them at:

> American Community Gardening Association
> 1777 East Broad St.
> Columbus, OH 43203

Smart ways to increase your harvest

Reap more from your garden space, even if it's small. Here's how.

Start seeds indoors. Growing from seed is cheaper than buying seedlings or plants. Learn how to start seeds indoors with inexpensive supplies like toilet tissue rolls for seed pots and plastic trays with lids for miniature greenhouses. You will stretch your growing season and save money.

Try succession planting. Your corn is harvested, and the plants are spent, so you pull up those old plants, recondition the soil, and plant peas to fill out the growing season. This is called succession planting. It works well for one-time producers like potatoes, corn, carrots, and greens, which you can follow with peas, other vegetables, or herbs.

To make sure your second crop can produce before the growing season ends, start seeds in containers at least one month before you expect to transplant them to your garden.

Get more from tight spaces. Fit more plants in your space and get more from each plant by growing them on trellises, cages, stakes, or even a fence. Try this with peas, cucumbers, pole beans, tomatoes, squash, and melons. You can easily make a trellis by tying string between two end posts or repurposing old bed springs.

Also, choose plants that produce many fruits or vegetables, such as tomatoes, carrots, and green beans.

Make extra dollars from extra produce

You have too much zucchini or other garden produce to freeze, can, or dry for the off season, so consider selling some using these clever ideas.

- Spread the word through friends and family that you have produce for sale.

- Put up a notice on community bulletin boards at your church, library, and other public outlets.

- Sell produce as part of your yard sale.

- Write a classified ad, and place it for free at *www.craigslist.org*. Include what you are selling, the price, a description, your availability, as well as the where, when, why, and how of the sale. For safety's sake, only accept cash, and make the exchange in a public place.

And remember, you can also make money from selling your extra seeds, herbs, or seedlings.

Transportation

Drive down the cost of getting around

Say no to dealer add-ons and save thousands

You don't really win if you've haggled your new car price down by several thousand dollars only to spend that much — or more — on hidden add-ons. Check the fine print, question the salesperson, and make sure you're not paying for extras you don't want or need.

Navigation system. Staying on course and on time can be priceless, but that doesn't mean you should pay an extra $2,000 for a built-in Global Positioning System (GPS) in your new car. If you own a smartphone, you probably already have a satellite-based navigation system. Otherwise, you can pick up a portable GPS very cheaply. Good ones range from $100 to $400.

Vin etching. It's an excellent idea to permanently engrave your vehicle's identification number (VIN) on the car's windshield or windows. In fact, police and insurance agencies recommend you do so to make a stolen car harder to dispose of and easier to recover. Your insurance carrier may even give you a discount if your car has VIN etching.

Doing this yourself is easy and cheap — a kit averages about $25 and takes under 15 minutes. A car dealer, on the other hand, may demand anywhere from $150 to $300.

Environmental protection package. A fancy phrase for rust-proofing and paint sealant, the dealer would love to charge you an extra $200 up to a whopping $1,200 for this. But most experts say you can safeguard your chassis and paint job just as well with the protective coating that comes standard from the factory plus regular washing and waxing. Cost to you — zip.

Fabric upholstery protection. Splatters and spills are part of a busy commute, but you can protect your car's upholstery with an inexpensive can of stain repellent spray. The dealer may ask $200 for this add-on, while a can of spray is less than $15.

Window tinting. This is not just a cool feature, it's a feature that will keep you cool by protecting your car's interior from the hot sun. It can also give you privacy and an added element of security. The dealer may charge around $400 for this, but if you take your car to a specialty shop, you could get it done for half that price.

An estimated total for all these features from the dealer is $3,525. Take care of these "upgrades" yourself, and you might spend around $400.

So how do you negotiate your way out of these extra charges? First, ask the dealer to show you a car without these add-ons or request they be removed from the vehicle you are interested in. Decide if you're willing to walk away from a deal if the add-ons become non-negotiable. Also, be sure you are prepared to spend the time and effort on do-it-yourself alternatives, if these are features you'd like to have.

One final thought — don't take anything for granted when negotiating a sale. You might not consider a spare tire and jack to be an "add-on," but some dealers might.

Turn car loan into $13,000 savings

You've finally paid off your car and that little voice in your head is busy listing all the things you can buy with the extra monthly cash. Stop for a second and think what would happen if you kept making that car payment — to yourself. It may sound crazy, but this could be one of the smartest things you'll ever do.

Let's say your car payment was $350 a month. Keep putting that amount into its own savings account, and in three years you'll have close to $13,000. Factor in some trade-in value on your existing car, and you could purchase a newer used car outright.

But don't stop there. Keep up this monthly saving habit and you may never have a car loan again.

Don't get fleeced by tricky leasing fees

Leasing a car is a lot like learning to tango. When everyone is in step, it can be a beautiful thing to behold, but a novice better be prepared to get their toes stepped on — a lot.

And, unfortunately, all that toe-stomping can translate into big dollar amounts. Here are just some of the expenses you may not anticipate when leasing your next car.

Watch out for sales tax. Most states charge sales tax only on the monthly lease payments. Others, like Texas and Illinois, charge sales tax on the full purchase price of the car — due upfront.

Factor in insurance costs. You may think of a lease as your chance to finally drive that ritzy car you've always wanted. Take a moment and contact your insurance company for a quote before you sign.

Calculate mileage penalties. Drive more than the number of miles set down in your lease, and you'll pay a penalty per mile. Negotiate extra miles into the lease if you think this may become an issue.

Don't forget gap insurance. Guaranteed auto protection, or gap insurance, protects you in a number of circumstances where you'd otherwise have to pay the leasing company — if the car is totaled or stolen, for instance.

Keep an eye on your money factor. This number is used to calculate how much you will end up owing the leasing company. It is not your interest rate, but you can calculate your interest rate from it. Do your homework so you understand the difference between these two numbers.

Beware early termination charges. If you end your lease early, you may have to pay a hefty fee to the leasing company.

Pass on protection products. Don't automatically buy plans that cover key replacement, dent repair, windshield protection, or other maintenance issues. Experts say they are rarely cost effective.

Pay attention to various fees. Besides the down payment, monthly payments, and any charges listed earlier, you might also have to pay:

- a refundable security deposit.
- license, registration, and title fees.
- an acquisition or processing fee.
- freight or destination charges.
- safety or emissions inspections.
- maintenance costs.
- a disposition fee when you turn in the lease.

Despite how complicated leasing seems and the multitude of unexpected fees, *Forbes* magazine reports leasing is growing in popularity.

Still, *Consumer Reports* emphatically states, "Buying is a better long-term financial choice."

Group membership means new car savings

Join an organization and save on your next new car purchase. Several offer car-buying discounts that more than make up for any membership fees you might have to pay. Check out groups like these:

- USAA (*www.usaa.com*)
- credit unions
- specific car manufacturers like Mercedes-Benz (*www.mbca.org*), BMW (*www.bmwcca.org*), or Audi (*www.audiclubna.org*)
- AAA (*www.aaa.com*)
- warehouse clubs like BJ's and Sam's Club

Avoid this trade-in nightmare

You still owe money on your car but you want to buy a new one from a dealer. Is it a good idea to negotiate using your trade-in?

If you've done your homework and you keep a sharp eye on the details in your contract, you might come out all right. But many consumer experts advise against it. Here's why.

- If the dealer offers you less than you owe on your trade-in, the difference will have to be paid off somehow. If you can't come up with the cash, you might have to roll this amount into your new car loan. That means you're essentially paying off two cars while only owning one. Bad idea.

- An unscrupulous dealer could neglect to pay off your trade-in loan in a timely manner. You are still responsible for the payments in the meantime — but may not know it. That could mean late payments, financial penalties, a mark against your credit, and a lot of stress. The only sure way to prevent this is to get the promise of your loan payoff in writing.

The most financially astute thing to do is pay off one car before buying another, especially if you owe a significant amount. Remember, your loan balance won't just go away. If you must sell before the title is free and clear, arrange to do so with a private buyer — you'll probably get more for your car by selling it this way.

Don't get dinged — top ways to save on body work

Scratches, dents, and scuffs may seem like tiny flaws, but they can have a big effect on your car's value and your wallet. According to the AAIA, Automotive Aftermarket Industry Association, collision repair shop sales were close to $38 billion in 2011. Keep your share in your pocket with these ideas for taking the sting out of that ding.

Soothe a scratch. You can buff out a minor scuff or light scratch yourself, using a commercial product that works pretty much like a mildly abrasive car polish. You might spend about $20, a half-hour, and some elbow grease.

If you can see metal in the chip or scrape, don't ignore the problem. This could lead to rust and more expensive damage. You can get miniature bottles of touch-up paint from an auto parts store or car dealer. They probably won't blend perfectly, but if the scratch is small, you should be happy with the cost — about $15 — and the results.

For anything bigger than a breadbox, you'll want to step the repair process up a notch. Look for your car's color code. It's often found on the driver side door jamb. Then go to the Internet, where you'll find companies selling spray paint kits that could match your color exactly. Check out Automotive Touchup at *www.automotivetouchup.com* where you can get a 12-ounce spray can for about $20 or a pint can for $45.

Experts say you'll get the best results if you:

- match the color carefully.

- let each coat dry thoroughly before applying another.

- blend the paint rather than taping off a section.

- apply a clear protective coat last.

Pay less for specialty repairs

Go to shops specializing in certain types of auto repairs — brakes, mufflers, or tires, for example — and you'll probably get a better rate than at a dealer or through a general mechanic. In addition, they usually offer quick service, promotions, coupons, and lifetime warranties.

Pop out a dent. Don't be afraid of a small dent or bend in your car's sheet metal, especially if the paint hasn't been broken. Try pushing on it firmly with your hand from the backside or pull with a suction cup on the front.

If this doesn't work, take it to a paintless dent repair shop, an inexpensive alternative to a traditional body shop. They will use special tools to force the dent out. And you'll only pay about $50 to $300 per dent. What's more, your insurance company might give you a discount or waive your deductible if you go this route.

Contact a tech school. Is there a vocational school or community college nearby? Call and ask if their auto body students need a little hands-on experience. Sometimes they will work for free — you pay just for parts.

Get competing estimates. When all else fails, you may have to call a pro. But don't just pick a name out of the phone book. Use a service like DentBetty at *www.dentbetty.com* that rates body shops based on performance reviews from thousands of customers. As soon as you provide photos of your car's damage, they will give you up to seven estimates from quality shops in your area.

5 surprising ways to save at the pump

Does it feel like you're always filling up your gas tank even though you combine your driving trips, empty the trunk out, and keep your car well maintained?

Here are five useful tips you may not have heard of that will help you squeeze every last mile out of your gas dollars.

Twist it till it clicks. You could lose up to 30 gallons of gasoline a year to evaporation if your gas cap is loose or missing, says the Car Care Council. At today's gas prices, that's like watching over $100 of your hard-earned money floating off into the clouds.

What's more, the escaping gas fumes combine with sunlight and heat to form ground-level ozone, a hazardous type of air pollution. So turn your cap until you hear it click to make sure it's tightened securely. And buy a replacement gas cap if you've lost yours.

Stick to the recommended oil. Use a different grade of motor oil than the one recommended by your car's manufacturer and you could lower your gas mileage by 1 to 2 percent. That's a price hike of 4 to 7 cents a gallon.

Park in the shade. Keep your car cool and you'll save gas two ways. First, you may have to run your air conditioning less if you don't start out in a car hotter than a pizza oven. Remember, every time you flip that AC on, you bump your fuel costs up anywhere from 13 to 21 percent. And even though the loss might be minimal, you can lose some gasoline to evaporation in a super-hot car.

Don't be a slowpoke. Your car is most fuel-efficient at 35 to 45 miles per hour. Driving slower doesn't save you gas. In fact, the slower you go, the more gas you use and the more wear on your engine.

Roll on with efficient tires. Experts will tell you to pick a tire for its handling and braking performance, then narrow the field by selecting one with low rolling resistance. You'll get better gas mileage with low rolling resistance models because they, basically, roll farther on less energy. And don't forget to keep them properly inflated.

Get around town without a car

Americans love their cars — more than 133 million of them are registered in the U.S. But they cost a lot of money to run. According to AAA, if you own a medium sedan, like a Honda Accord or Toyota Camry, and drive about 15,000 miles annually, you spend $8,000 or more every year on gas, maintenance, insurance, and fees. If you own a larger car or a gas-guzzler, and drive more miles, that number is significantly higher.

So — could you live without your car?

Walk a mile in your shoes. Take a closer look at your neighborhood and town. Is it pedestrian-friendly? If not, could you move somewhere that would allow you to ditch your wheels? One of the joys of retirement could be choosing a home where you could live virtually car-free — where shopping, churches, libraries, and entertainment centers are within walking distance.

Map out a one-mile radius from either where you live now or where you might live. About 28 percent of all car trips made in the U.S. are to places a single mile away. Almost half are within two miles. That's not as far as it may sound. Just think, by walking you could save money, keep fit, and help the environment.

Hop onto public transportation. The American Public Transportation Association says families that use public transportation — buses, trolleys, subways, trains, streetcars, ferries, water taxis, and trams — save more than $9,700 every year.

The HopStop website at *www.hopstop.com* offers transit maps, schedules, directions, and stations for dozens of major U.S. cities. They also have a free smartphone app for help on the go.

Catch a free ride. There may come a time when you simply can't drive anymore. Thankfully, organizations abound geared to helping older nondrivers find rides.

- Independent Transportation Network is a national nonprofit with locations in 21 states. Visit them online at *itnamerica.org* or call 207-857-9001 for more information.

- The National Association of Area Agencies on Aging provides services for older adults without private transportation or those unable to use public transportation. Their website is located at *n4a.org* or call 202-872-0888.

- The Beverly Foundation Legacy at *beverlyfoundationlegacy.org* will connect you with senior transportation options throughout the country.

Before you take advantage of a ride program:

- ask about any fees.

- find out exactly where you'll be picked up and dropped off.

- make sure you feel safe before, during, and after the transportation.

- jot down the schedule so there's no chance you'll get stranded.

If you just can't bring yourself to completely give up your car, you can still make choices that will save you money. If you own multiple cars, sell all but one. Trade a high-end car for one that's more fuel-efficient and cheaper to maintain. Then walk, bike, carpool, rideshare, and bus it whenever possible. It's a lifestyle known as living "car-light."

Home Utilities

Slash skyrocketing energy bills

4 easy ways to lower your electric bill

People over age 50 spend more money on electricity than any other utility, according to a study based on survey numbers from the Bureau of Labor Statistics. And as you get older, you'll spend even more of your monthly budget on utilities, in general, than younger folks.

That means you need to squeeze every penny you can from your utility budget.

Ask for a discount. Call your electric company to see if they will waive fees; discount your bill based on age, health situation, or income; or offer a reduced payment plan.

According to the U.S. Energy Information Administration, the average monthly electrical bill for a homeowner in 2011 was $110.14. Since a senior discount is usually about 10 percent — for those over age 60 and often under a certain income level — you could save about $132 a year.

Pay the average. Surprises are the worst thing that can happen to a budget. Unexpected expenses or a shockingly higher-than-normal bill will wreak havoc on your financial plan. That's what makes levelized billing such a smart idea. Your electric company will charge you the 13-month average of your bills, so you end up paying almost the same amount every month, regardless of seasonal highs and lows.

Check for billing errors. Everyone makes mistakes — even cable companies, phone providers, hospitals, and your electric company. If you receive a bill that looks higher than normal, call and ask for a reassessment.

The problem could stem from a meter malfunction, a meter reading error, a miscalculation on fees or taxes, or simply a mistake in your rate.

Find the cheapest provider. If you live in a deregulated state — meaning you can choose which company supplies your electrical power — take advantage of services provided by WhiteFence at *www.WhiteFence.com* to compare electricity plans from local providers.

Become even more informed by visiting *www.electricchoice.com* online. Here you can see which states are deregulated and look up the average kilowatt-hour price by state.

Most of these dollar-saving tips work just as well for other utilities, so put them into practice and pay less for water, natural gas, Internet, cable, and phone.

Lighting choices save you money

Reduce your electric bill — and help the environment — by making some "bright" lighting choices.

LEDs. The world of lighting is all abuzz over light–emitting diodes or LEDs. Originally used in cars, planes, traffic signals, video displays, remote controls, and hundreds of consumer electronics, you can now find LED lighting in general purpose bulbs and fixtures. Here's why this is good news.

- LED lighting is extremely efficient, using only 5 percent of the electricity of an incandescent bulb. You can save anywhere from $100 to $400 for each LED bulb over its lifetime.

- An LED bulb will rarely burn out. Instead, it just gradually dims. That said, according to a *Consumer Reports* review, LEDs claim to last 20,000 to 50,000 hours or around 20 to 40 years. This makes them perfect for those hard-to-reach fixtures.

- Although right now they are more expensive than most other bulbs, LED bulbs are very cost-effective because of their long life span. As technology improves, they will cost less to make and consumer prices will drop.

- Unlike CFLs, LED bulbs do not release any hazardous materials if they break. Although you are not required to recycle LEDs, some home improvement stores and recycling centers offer recycling.

- LED bulbs don't give off heat the way most other bulbs do, can be used with dimmer switches, and light quickly with no delay.

You may already be using LED bulbs for your holiday lighting. They are ideal for this because they are cool to the touch, use very little electricity, and last a long time.

Three-way bulbs. Light fixtures that take a three-way bulb are smart choices for multipurpose areas because you control how much energy is used. Turn on the lowest wattage for general room lighting and entertaining, then bump it up to a higher setting for task lighting or reading.

Motion sensors. Most people only think to use motion sensors outside, but you can easily and cheaply install motion-sensing switches in any room. This is a great idea for when you enter a room with your hands full, when children are visiting and forget to turn off lights, or if you have mobility issues and find it difficult to get to a regular light switch. You'll recover the cost of the switch — about $25 — quickly by only burning lights when necessary.

You can save money by making the most of the light fixtures you have in a room. A hanging, floor, or table lamp located in a corner, rather than against a single wall, will reflect its light off two walls and produce more usable light.

Top 5 energy-saving tips

Here are the five most important things you should do if you are on a fixed income and want to bring down your energy expenses.

- Ask all your utility companies if you qualify for a senior discount.

- Turn down the temperature on your water heater to 120 degrees.

- Install a low-flow showerhead.

- Lower your thermostat by 1 to 5 degrees in winter, and raise it by 1 to 5 degrees in summer.

- Unplug all chargers and appliances you can when they are not in use.

Be an energy detective to cut power bill

Sir Francis Bacon wrote, "Knowledge is power," back in 1597. Today, you could say that knowledge of your power is power.

The more you know about your energy consumption, the better equipped you are to rein it in. You need to learn which appliances run during peak rate times, which outlets draw the most power, when a particular electronic is drawing phantom power, and what difference the weather makes on your energy use. All this is easy with a home energy monitor.

There are three general levels of monitoring. Each gives you progressively more information — and carries a progressively higher price tag.

Outlet monitors. For less than $30, you can purchase a single outlet monitor. Plug it into the wall, then plug one electronic device or appliance into it and learn how much it costs per day, week, month, or year to power that device.

Use this information to decide what you can afford to keep plugged in all the time and what is running up your power bill. The Kill A Watt Electricity Monitor and the Belkin Conserve Insight Energy-Use Monitor are two popular examples.

Perhaps the best news is that some public libraries across the country allow you to check out these electricity monitors for a two-week loan.

Whole-house power monitors. As you might guess, this type of monitor tracks all the electrical usage in your home in real time. Depending on the model, you might physically hook this to your outdoor meter or electrical panel, or let it communicate wirelessly with your meter. You can see at a glance if your electricity usage is about normal for your household and also view the immediate impact switching appliances on and off has.

According to an interview conducted by *The New York Times*, an expert in the field of home energy analysis says simply having the details of your energy use front-and-center influences your behavior. And changing behavior usually translates into saving money.

The Black & Decker Energy Saver Series Power Monitor sells for about $100 and claims to save an average household up to 20 percent a month on their electric bill. Other models sell for between $200 and $400.

Home energy management systems. A more complete — but also more complex — approach is to use a system that interfaces with your home computer to monitor and analyze your energy use. Many allow you to control appliances, lighting, heating, and cooling remotely — often through a smartphone or tablet. Prices will vary, but expect to pay the most for this type of monitoring.

Charge your cellphone with solar power

Cellphones seem to constantly need charging and their chargers are constantly drawing electricity, even when they are not in use. That's a lot of utility dollars for one device. But if you live in a sunny climate, you can have a charged cellphone and a lower electric bill by using a solar charger.

For under $30, you can get either of these:

- a standalone gadget you plug into your phone that acts as a conduit for solar power

- a case that converts solar energy directly to your phone. This can be an add-on feature or integrated into the phone's design

Although different solar charger models will give you varying results, most need to be in direct sunlight for about 30 minutes to provide your phone with a minimum charge and around eight to 10 hours of sun for a full charge.

Save $298 with 3 small changes

Use the next 45 minutes to do these three easy things and you could save $298 a year.

Dial down the heat. Your water heater probably came with its temperature set by default to 140 degrees Fahrenheit. Lowering this to 120 degrees will not only reduce your risk of accidental burns, but save you money on your energy bill. It's estimated that making this small change to a 50-gallon electric water heater could save you about $72 a year.

For the best information, consult your owner's manual, but here are some general reminders.

- If your thermostat dial is not exposed and you must use a screwdriver to open an access panel, for safety's sake, first turn off the power to the water heater by flipping its breaker switch.

- If there is an upper and lower thermostat on your heater, change both.

- If your model does not have actual numbers on its thermostat, generally you can just dial it down from "Very Hot" to "Hot."

Lessen the flow. A low-flow showerhead reduces the amount of water that comes out of your fixture, which cuts not only the number of gallons you use per minute, but the amount of electricity or gas you use to heat the water.

According to the Environmental Protection Agency (EPA), the average family could save 2,900 gallons of water and about $46 in electric heating costs annually by installing low-flow showerheads.

Chill out. During winter, lower your thermostat 8 degrees for at least eight hours during the day and for 10 hours at night, and the EPA estimates you'll save $180 a year in energy costs.

Don't fret that you'll shiver at night, use an electric blanket or mattress pad and you'll sleep toasty warm. These are very energy-efficient and safe, plus models with dual controls are perfect for sleepers who may not always agree on one temperature.

Pull the plug on power drain with smart strips

Have you noticed the glowing LED displays, clocks, and illumi-nated power buttons on your electronics — even when they are turned off? That's one sign your chargers, gadgets, and appliances are constantly draining power simply because they are plugged in. The phantom energy they are using adds up to about 10 percent of your total electric bill.

You could race around plugging and unplugging items or you could invest about $40 in a small device called a smart strip.

It looks much like an ordinary power strip, but it cuts down on the amount of power your electronics use when they're either turned off or in standby mode, easily saving the average family $20 a month.

Most smart strips have three different kinds of outlets.

- There is one control outlet you'll use for the electronic that manages the switched outlets. When it is turned off, all the switched outlets turn off.

- Switched or auto-off outlets are for devices linked to the control outlet. So if you have your computer plugged into the control outlet, you might plug your monitor, printer, and scanner into the switched outlets.

- Constant outlets are always on. Use these to plug in items like your modem or router that you don't ever want to shut off.

Vacation checklist helps save utility dollars

You've stopped the mail, taken the trash out, and left a key with your neighbors. But did you go through your energy-saving checklist before leaving on vacation? The last thing you want is to come home to an out-of-control water, electric, or gas bill.

Unplug all chargers. It may not make sense, but cellphone, tablet, and power tool chargers all draw electricity even when nothing is plugged into them. So if you're not taking your charger with you, don't leave it connected to an outlet.

Along those same lines, wander through your house before you go, unplugging power blocks and appliances — they all use energy and are potential fire hazards.

Cut your washer's water supply. "When we moved our washer and dryer to a new laundry room upstairs, I became nervous about possible flooding," says Carrie Ann, a Missouri homeowner. "We set the washer into a floor pan and had our contractor connect the drain to a hose that led outside. But we soon realized the pan could only handle 2 to 3 inches of water." If a hose cracked or pulled loose, there would be gallons of water gushing over the floor, clearly more than the floor pan could contain. That's when the simplest solution became apparent.

"Now, whenever I leave home for any length of time, I just turn the water off behind the washer. The controls are easy to reach, and I know there won't be any disaster waiting for me when I get back. At least not in the laundry room," she adds.

Switch off the water heater. It takes a lot of energy to keep the water in your tank hot, and why would you want to spend that money if no one is home for a week or more?

- Switch a gas water heater to the "pilot" setting.

- Turn off an electric water heater by flipping its breaker switch or dialing down the temperature setting to as low as possible.

Set lights on timers. For less than $10 each, you can buy simple manual timers for lamps throughout your house. This is so much smarter than leaving lights to burn continuously — your home will have a more lived-in look plus you'll spend less on electricity.

While you're at it, pick up some dusk-to-dawn light sensors at a local hardware store for your outdoor lights. Nothing burns more energy and says, "Nobody's home," like porch lights on 24 hours a day. Screw on these sensors between your fixture and the light bulb, and they will automatically turn the lights on at dusk and off at dawn.

Surprisingly, most experts will warn you not to turn your air conditioning or heat completely off while you're away, especially if there could be extreme fluctuations in temperature. Wood floors and doors can expand and buckle in summer, and pipes can freeze and burst during winter.

A guide to greener electronics

Every November, Greenpeace, the independent campaigning organization for worldwide environmental issues, publishes its *Guide to Greener Electronics*. Without endorsing any product or company, they attempt to evaluate major electronics corporations based on how they and their products impact the environment.

If this sounds like something that could help you make a purchasing decision, visit them online at *www.greenpeace.org* and search for the latest edition of this guide by name.

Tweak your TV to reduce power pull

Bigger, brighter, jazzier television sets often mean bigger electricity bills. According to experts, the TVs in your home could be using as much electricity as your refrigerator.

If you're purchasing a new set, keep in mind an LCD TV typically uses less electricity than a plasma TV. But perhaps the most helpful thing you can do is look for the Energy Star label. You'll save energy and money, as well as help protect the environment. A suite of Energy Star entertainment products — including a TV, Blu-Ray player, audio system, and home theater system — could save you more than $200 in energy.

But even if you're not in the market for new electronics, there are simple things you can do to make the TV you have use less energy.

Unplug it. Seventy percent of your TV's energy is consumed while it is turned off — even newer models go into standby mode instead of complete shutdown, which means they are still drawing power. Every chance you get, switch off power strips your electronics are plugged into or pull the plug completely.

Tone down brightness. Most high-definition televisions (HDTVs) are shipped with settings best suited for the store showroom. That means brightness and contrast levels may be unusually high. These settings — sometimes called "vivid" or "dynamic" — use more energy and are not necessarily appropriate for home viewing. Change these in the setup menu.

LCD TVs have a similar "retail" setting, which really amps up the brightness level. Choose, instead, the "home" setting and your eyes, as well as your pocketbook, will thank you.

Reposition it. Your television — like all electronics — gives off heat. If it is located close to your air conditioning system's thermostat, the ambient heat from the TV could cause the thermostat to read hotter than the true room temperature. And that could cause your AC to run longer than it should. Find another place for the television, and while you're at it, make sure no lamps or other heat-producing devices are too near the thermostat.

Start it slowly. A "quick start" option on your TV means the picture will appear without delay when you press the power button. But it also means your set must stay in a constant state of readiness while in standby mode. That uses 94 percent more power than normal standby mode without the quick start option.

Switch modes. Many TVs come with a power-saver mode, although how much you'll actually save will vary with each model. You may notice a difference in brightness when this mode is switched on and many think this improves image quality.

7 kitchen habits that will save utility dollars

You may be surprised to learn that the average coffee maker uses almost as much electricity as a space heater. That's a good reason to flip your coffee maker off right after brewing and microwave cups individually as needed throughout the day.

You can make hundreds of small decisions like this in the kitchen that will add up to big energy savings. Here are just a few.

- Use a slow cooker to prepare single-dish meals whenever possible — it's one of the most energy-efficient appliances in your home.

- Keep the reflector pans on your stovetop bright and clean. Shiny pans help focus heat properly on the bottom of your cooking pots.

- Wait to start the self-cleaning cycle on your oven until you've just finished baking something and the oven is still hot.

- Use pots and pans with absolutely flat bottoms. A curved bottom leaves a gap that allows heat to escape.

- When using your oven, cook multiple dishes at the same time — even if they call for different cooking temperatures. You can fudge the heat setting up or down by 25 degrees without a problem.

- Copper-bottom stainless pans and enameled cast-iron pans will heat quickly and hold their heat longer than other types of pans. That usually translates into shorter cooking times.

- An electric-induction smooth cooktop is your most energy-efficient choice, according to the Department of Energy. If you opt for a gas stove, choose a model with an electric ignition rather than a pilot light.

3 surprising ways to insulate your home

Heating and cooling make up about half your home's energy bill — with the average family spending more than $1,000 a year. But with proper insulation, you could spend 30 to 50 percent less. Here are a few unusual ideas to help keep the elements where they belong, outside your home, and your dollars where they belong, in your pocket.

Paint on protection. Insulating paint is a great way to add a layer of protection to your home without the hassle of cutting drywall and laying fiberglass insulation.

One product called Insuladd, originally designed for NASA, claims to reduce your heating and cooling costs by 20 percent or more. Stir a pouch of their patented ceramic additive into your own paint, apply it to your walls, and it will keep heat from passing through in the summer, and reflect heat back into your living areas during the winter. Nansulate and Hy-Tech are similar products that work on the same principle.

These are not substitutes for traditional insulation, but an easy way to bump up your defenses. Use insulating paint inside or out, on your roof, attic, or basement, and watch your energy bill go down.

Hang a fabric barrier. Why not add your own personal decorating touch to a room while amping up its R-value. Hang quilts and pretty rugs on your walls for a cozy feel that will allow you to turn your thermostat down a few degrees in winter.

Block the sun's heat. An average home loses 30 percent of its heating and cooling through its windows and doors. If you don't happen to have newer, energy-efficient windows, you can still improve the performance of your old sashes by adding window film, designed to restrict the sun's infrared rays.

Old-fashioned films seemed to block more light than heat, but thanks to vast improvements in technology, modern window films reflect solar radiation while still letting in light. Look for products with a low Solar Heat Gain Coefficient (SHGC).

Be sure you keep all receipts for any insulating products you use in your home. Many utility companies offer rebates for these types of improvements, which will make them more affordable.

The secret to warmer winters

Wintertime means cold, dry air. And the drier the air, the higher you need to set your thermostat to feel warm.

That's why a good humidifier is a smart choice for your home during the cold months. Moisten the air, you'll feel warmer, and you can set your thermostat lower. It's a very cost-effective solution, too. You might spend less than $50 for a good single-room humidifier and just pennies a month to run it.

Another option is to refrain from using exhaust fans when it's cold outside. This allows any moisture from cooking and bathing to remain in the house longer.

When your home is comfortably warm during winter, studies show you might just feel better, too — both emotionally and physically.

Quick tricks for tiptop heating and cooling

Keep your heating and air system running efficiently with two simple tasks.

Change your filter every one to two months. Unless you have allergies or breathing problems, many experts believe you don't necessarily need top-of-the-line furnace filters. Purchase a cheaper filter and save a minimum of $7 per filter. Although buying filters by the case may not give you a price break, a box of six could last about a year. That gives you protection against price increases.

Vacuum your registers and returns. Some HVAC construction designs have the home's furnace filter right inside the cold air return — what some call the airbox. According to Ron, a longtime employee at a local hardware store, that makes it easy to complete two tasks at once. "Every time I change my furnace filter," he says, "I vacuum out the air box."

He's quick to add that everyone should routinely screw off the grating over their cold air return and check inside. "When I moved into my home, I opened mine up and found a piece of drywall stuck in there. And this was new construction."

He doesn't like to imagine what would have happened if he had never gone investigating. "Not only would dust have been trapped," he says, "but I never would have had any airflow."

At the very least, pull out your vacuum's brush attachment and run it over your home's heating and air vents every month.

Take the heat out of your natural gas bill

Furnaces have come a long way since the days of coal. Today's natural gas models deliver warm, soothing air with the push of a button or the turn of a dial. Although natural gas is clean, efficient, and abundant, Americans heating with gas furnaces spent an average of $657 during a recent winter. Here's how you can shrink that number.

Update it. Older is better for wine and cheese — not major appliances. Replacing an old gas furnace with a new, more energy-efficient model could save you over $100 a year. Furnaces typically last an average of 15 to 18 years, but if yours is over 10 years old, consider its efficiency.

According to experts affiliated with *This Old House*, if you replace an older furnace operating at 80 percent efficiency with a 97 percent efficient system, you'd cut your heating bills around 20 percent.

Besides saving money, you'll enjoy more consistent heating and will pollute the environment less.

Take into account these important considerations when buying.

- Purchase the correct size for your living space. Too small a unit will have you constantly bumping the thermostat up in an effort to stay warm. A unit that's too large means you've simply paid for more heat than you'll need or use.

- Look for a high annual fuel-utilization efficiency (AFUE) rating — an indication the unit can efficiently convert gas into heating energy.

- Check if you will be eligible for a tax credit during the year you purchase. Most recently it was as much as $150. If tax credits are offered, save your receipts.

Disconnect it. Sheryl Grable of north Florida has two reminders on her calendar every year — call the gas company to disconnect their service in April and call to reconnect in October. This saves her not only the minimal monthly fees during the summer, but in other ways, too. "The providers are so competitive in the fall," she says, "we can usually negotiate a nice low rate as well as waive any reconnection fees."

Others who have tried this say their gas providers are also required to conduct a free inspection of their gas lines, fireplace, and furnace before reconnecting — one more perk.

Regulations and policies will vary by provider and possibly by state, so call and get all the details before you try this yourself. And remember, if natural gas powers other appliances in your home — your water heater, for example — don't disconnect this service.

Turn it off. Older furnaces have a pilot light, which is a small flame kept constantly burning as a means to quickly ignite your furnace's burners.

According to the International Association of Certified Home Inspectors, pilot lights waste a large amount of fuel — anywhere from $7 to $18 a month with a single natural gas pilot light. If your furnace is located in your living space, this pilot light is also adding heat to your home — year-round.

Consult your furnace's owner's manual, a professional, or your gas company if you are considering turning your pilot light off for the summer. You may need to contact the gas company to have it relit in the fall.

Get reimbursed. Loyal customers, who pay on time, may be eligible for a refund of their initial deposit. It's at least worth a phone call to find out.

Simple way to save lots of water

Run — don't walk — to the nearest dollar store or Internet shopping site and pick up an inexpensive shower timer. For less than $5, you can get an hourglass, classic dial, electronic, novelty, or waterproof design. Some even come with a suction cup for easy wall mounting. Now you have no excuse for taking long, water-wasting showers.

Solve the great dishwashing debate

Put down that dishrag and walk away from the sink. You may be surprised to learn that washing your dishes in a dishwasher instead of by hand is smarter and cheaper.

Save dollars. According to experts at the EPA's Energy Star program, using an energy-efficient dishwasher for one year can save you nearly 5,000 gallons of water and cut your utility bills by more than $40.

Save time. It is estimated that using a dishwasher can save you over 230 hours throughout the year. That's almost 10 days you won't have your hands pruning up in soapy water.

In addition, your dishwasher can use hotter water, adding a level of sterilization you just can't get when you wash by hand.

But don't take all that efficiency for granted. You need to do your part to ease the utility burden on your dishwasher by following these tips.

- Scrape food off your dishes instead of pre-rinsing, and save up to 20 gallons of water per load.

- Run only full loads.

- Use the air-dry setting rather than heated dry.

Social Security & Extra Income

Surprising ways to boost your cash flow

Social Security

Reap benefits from Social Security changes

In spite of all the news reports about proposed changes to Social Security, change is not new to Social Security. Here is what you need to know about how Social Security has been changing and will continue to change — straight from an expert.

Uncover your true retirement age. "Full retirement age for many years was 65," says Social Security spokesperson B.J. Jarrett. "For individuals born 1937 or earlier, it was always 65."

"But that's changed," Jarrett says. "For the bulk of the folks who are retiring now, full retirement age is 66."

This applies to you if you were born from 1943 to 1954. You can still file for reduced benefits as early as age 62, but you cannot collect your full amount of Social Security retirement benefits unless you wait until age 66 to file for Social Security. Yet, the changes don't end there.

"For people born in 1955, that age is increasing to 66 and two months," says Jarrett. "For every year, it'll increase by two months until we get to those born 1960 or later."

If you were born after 1959, your full retirement age is 67.

Find services at your fingertips. Social Security's online services are available to you even if you don't have a home computer.

"There are ways that seniors, who may not have Internet access at home, can access our online services — whether it's at a public location, like a library, senior center, community center, or whether it's a family member who's helping them navigate the website, *www.socialsecurity.gov*," says Jarrett.

This doesn't mean you can't get offline help with Social Security, but those who log on have easy access to lots of information.

"You probably remember when you would receive a Social Security earnings statement each year in the mail shortly before your birthday each year," Jarrett says. "We no longer send paper statements, but we have a service online that allows you to sign up for your own personal Social Security account. You'll create a user name and password just like you would with your banking online or other online accounts, and then you can access your Social Security statement online."

To create the statements, the Social Security Administration keeps the same records it kept when statements were mailed regularly, but now everything is done electronically. Creating an account can also help you get copies of documents, like a benefit verification letter, without visiting a Social Security office. But that's not all the website offers.

"Individuals can actually go online to file a retirement application. Now it only takes about 15 minutes," says Jarrett. "There's no paperwork to do. You can do it at home in your pajamas in as little as 15 minutes." You can even sign up for direct deposit when you apply.

Many more services are available from the Social Security website, including tools that may help with retirement planning and a way to find your local Social Security office. Jarrett says he can't stress enough how important the online services are and will continue to be. But if you cannot get to a computer, don't know how to use one, or can't get help from a family member, you still have two ways to deal with Social Security questions or problems.

"We have an automated toll-free number. It's 800-772-1213," says Jarrett. "You can talk to a dedicated agent there to ask a number of questions on any type of Social Security subject you would like." Or you can ask for the location and phone number of your local Social Security office.

Best way to stay up to date on changes

"We often get questions about proposed changes to Social Security," says Social Security spokesperson B.J. Jarrett. But now Social Security can help with that, too.

"You can sign up for Social Security updates," says Jarrett. "You give us your email address, and then we'll alert you."

"You can customize what you want to know about," he adds. For example, if you want to know about legislative changes that involve Social Security — including new programs, changes to policy, or existing programs — you can receive emails when those changes happen. You can also find out about new online services, new press releases, and other topics.

"We'll let you know whenever something changes involving that particular subject," says Jarrett. "It's something I subscribe to myself."

Prevent costly Social Security blunder

You've planned well for your retirement. Don't blow it by making this common mistake.

Don't just follow the crowd. About half of all Americans claim Social Security at age 62, but this might not be your best option. Your monthly payment will be as much as 32 percent higher if you wait until your full retirement age to claim Social Security.

Delay until age 70, and your monthly payment will be a whopping 76 percent higher than if you claimed at age 62. What's more, you can probably expect to receive that higher payment for a long time because average life expectancy for people at age 65 today is at least 83 years.

But that's not all. Because full retirement age is changing, retiring early costs even more than before. According to Social Security spokesperson B.J. Jarrett, claiming Social Security at age 62 only reduced the monthly check by 20 percent for people whose full retirement age was 65. But he adds, "The further you are away from your full retirement age, the more of a reduction it's going to be."

"For folks whose full retirement age is 66, if they decide to take their reduced retirement benefit at 62, they would suffer about a 25 percent reduction in their full retirement benefit," Jarrett explains. That would permanently reduce a $1,000 monthly payment to $750. For people whose retirement age is 67, claiming at age 62 would shrink the monthly check by 30 percent — a loss of hundreds of dollars, or more, every year.

Those losses add up. In his book, *Social Security: The Inside Story*, author Andy Landis looks at Social Security's total lifetime payout. His calculations suggest an unmarried, healthy person who claims Social Security at full retirement age will receive a higher total lifetime payout by age 83 than if he had retired at age 62.

Retiring at age 70 instead of full retirement age gives you a higher lifetime payout by age 83, plus you get a significantly higher payment during your later years, when you may need it most. Even better, claiming later could put you ahead by thousands of dollars. According to Landis, delaying Social Security by even one year may result in making more money than some common investments do.

Of course, the best age for you to claim Social Security may vary depending on your health, life expectancy, and whether you are married, but you still need to know more about your options.

Calculate your monthly payment. To find out your full retirement age, visit *www.ssa.gov/retire2*, or call the Social Security Administration's toll-free help number between 7 a.m. and 7 p.m. on weekdays at 800-772-1213.

- If you have Web access, also visit the "Retirement Estimator" page *(www.socialsecurity.gov/estimator)* for estimates of what your monthly payments will be if you claim Social Security at age 62, at full retirement age, or at age 70. Just be aware that this calculator won't work if you already receive Social Security retirement payments. You can also experiment with possible scenarios about when you should claim using the free T. Rowe Price Social Security Benefits Evaluator at *troweprice.com* or the AARP Social Security Calculator at *www.aarp.org*.

- If you don't have Web access, part of your estimated benefit information may be available on your Social Security Benefits statement. If that statement is not available, call the Social Security Administration's toll-free help number mentioned previously for the information you need.

If you are married or divorced, claiming Social Security later may not always be your best bet, so see a financial planner to find out which of the many available options will net you the most money during retirement.

WARNING

Disarm the IRA 'tax torpedo'

Take withdrawals from your IRA while taking payments from Social Security, and your taxable income may rise enough for your Social Security payments to be taxed. You might even end up paying a higher tax rate.

But you can prevent this tax torpedo from putting a dent in your retirement budget. Delay Social Security, and take withdrawals from your IRA first. Waiting longer to take Social Security will mean a higher Social Security payment, perhaps high enough to lower the withdrawals you need from your IRA.

Wait long enough and you might be able to reduce withdrawals enough to cut or eliminate taxes on your Social Security payments.

4 ways to maximize Social Security payouts

Don't get short-changed on your Social Security. Check out the little-known rules that could entitle you to more.

Take advantage of your spousal benefit. If your husband qualifies for Social Security, you've been married more than one year, and you're age 62 or older, you may be eligible for a spousal benefit — even if you've never worked and cannot qualify for Social Security by yourself.

But you can't claim your spousal benefit until your husband files for his Social Security benefit. This doesn't necessarily mean he should file at age 62, particularly if he has usually earned more than you. The closer higher-earning spouses are to age 70 when they claim Social Security, the larger their benefit, plus their spouses receive a larger survivor benefit if widowed.

This could mean an extra $5,000 or more in Social Security payments over a lifetime. And remember, your spousal benefit is smaller if you claim before full retirement age (FRA), yet it does not grow if you claim after FRA.

Resolve timing problems with "file and suspend." If your husband files for his benefit at FRA, he can then request the payments be suspended. This file-and-suspend strategy means the monthly payment amount for his benefit can grow until he reaches age 70 or resumes receiving payments before age 70.

When he resumes collecting his benefit, the payment will be higher than when he suspended it. Yet, you can collect your spousal benefit while his payments are suspended.

But be careful when you file. If you're eligible for both your retirement benefit and a spousal benefit, and you file for either one before FRA, you're counted as claiming both benefits, and the payment amount is permanently reduced.

File-and-suspend works best when you've earned substantially less than your husband, and you're less than five years apart in age.

Grow your benefit with restricted application. If you haven't filed for Social Security even though you're eligible for it and have reached FRA, you can file a restricted application to receive only your spousal benefit. Meanwhile, your potential monthly payment grows until you claim it or reach age 70, whichever comes first.

Uncover benefits after divorce. If you're divorced, you may be eligible for a divorced spouse benefit. It doesn't matter whether your ex-husband has remarried or not, and you need not contact him.

To qualify, you must meet these criteria:

- Your marriage must have lasted at least 10 years before the divorce became final.

- You both must be age 62 or older.

- You must be unmarried or have remarried after age 60.

- Your benefit, based on your earnings alone, must be smaller than the portion of his benefit you may qualify for.

Keep in mind these strategies won't be right for everyone. In addition, the rules can be complicated and do change. For more details, call the Social Security Administration toll-free at 800-772-1213 between 7 a.m. and 7 p.m. Eastern time on weekdays.

WARNING

Outsmart Social Security scammers

Today's scammers go beyond stealing Social Security checks. Now that most Social Security benefits are paid by direct deposit, scammers steal your Social Security number and use it to redirect your payments to their bank accounts. To start fighting back, remember these tips.

- Never provide personal information, such as Social Security numbers, to an unsolicited caller or contact, even if that person claims to be from the Social Security Administration. Instead, call your local Social Security office to determine whether the caller is legitimate.

- Don't agree to send money to a stranger or to accept credit or debit cards in another person's name.

- Open a "My Social Security" account so no one else can use your Social Security number to open an account. To do this, visit *www.socialsecurity.gov/myaccount* — or visit your local Social Security office if you don't have Web access.

Rescue your retirement from new 'do-over' rules

You may be in trouble if you've been counting on Social Security's "do-over" option to boost your retirement income or help you get through hard times. The do-over rules have changed. Find out what's available to you now.

Originally, the do-over option was a loophole people used to get an interest-free loan from the government. From age 62 until age 70, you could withdraw your Social Security application, pay back benefits you'd received, and it would be as if you'd never filed for Social Security. You could later claim Social Security again, and receive the higher monthly check earned by waiting longer to file.

Even if you claimed Social Security before full retirement age, and retired early with reduced Social Security payments, you could use this option to avoid reduced benefits for life.

But now this law has changed, and some people are finding out the hard way. For example, say Stan lost his job in 2009 and couldn't find a new one. Lean finances might finally force him to claim Social Security before full retirement age. As a result, he'd receive a reduced monthly check for the rest of his life.

If an unexpected inheritance or other windfall had led Stan to file for the do-over option in 2012, he would have discovered he was not eligible because too many years had passed since he claimed Social Security. The new law only allows a do-over during the first 12 months after filing for Social Security.

If you're no longer eligible for the do-over, you can still suspend your Social Security payments, starting at full retirement age, but you don't pay back any money. Instead, you receive no Social Security checks during the suspension, but you accumulate valuable delayed retirement credits until you end the suspension or reach age 70, whichever comes first.

Each year of delayed retirement credits is worth 8 percent of the monthly payment you'd have gotten if you filed for Social Security at full retirement age. So if your full retirement age payment would have been $1,200 each month, suspending payments for just one year could mean nearly $100 extra every month afterward. Suspending payments for extra years could mean up to $400 more each month.

Simple way to make $720+ more each year

Waiting until age 66 to collect Social Security may seem too long. But retiring at age 62 means you'll collect only $900 per month if you're due $1,200 at full retirement. If you can hang in a little longer, you'll reap a big — and permanent — boost in benefits.

- At age 63 you'll receive $60 more each month or $720 more per year than you'd have gotten at 62.

- At age 64 you'll receive almost $140 more every month for a total of $1,679 more each year.

- Retiring at age 65 is worth almost $220 more each month or $2,639 more every year.

Extra income

Simple steps to your dream job

You've always wanted to work as a tour guide, floral designer, handyman, or another fantastic job, but it wasn't practical then. Finally, do what you've always wanted to do, and make some money at it, after you retire. Start with these four steps.

Do the math. Working during retirement can help make up for lost retirement savings or raise retirement income, but it may also affect taxes or Social Security benefits. If you will receive Social

Security payments while working, a work paycheck may boost your income enough to:

- temporarily reduce Social Security payments from age 62 to full retirement age.

- trigger taxes on Social Security payments starting at full retirement age.

- put you in a higher tax bracket.

Yet working may also raise the amount of Social Security benefits you're paid.

To learn more, visit the websites or call the toll-free helplines for Social Security (*www.ssa.gov* or 800-772-1213) and the IRS (*www.irs.gov* or 800-829-3676). If full-time work may reduce or tax your Social Security payments too much, consider contracting, consulting, or work that is part-time, temporary, or seasonal.

Plan your transition. The transition to a new retirement career averages 18 months, so start before you retire. To find ways to earn money doing what you love:

- Read magazines, newsletters, websites, blogs, and social media dedicated to the hobby, topic, industry, or work you like. Consider joining trade groups or associations.

- Use the library, your network of friends and colleagues, or social media to find someone already in a career you're considering. Interview that person to learn about the job.

- Consider talking to a career counselor — especially if your current employer offers one to retirees — or ask about access to a career center at your alma mater or a nearby university.

Job titles that combine what you love with skills you already have may be your best bet.

Train for your new career. After you choose a job, find out what additional training you need — and get it, but limit your training budget. You can save money with the tips described later in this chapter. Also, volunteer, moonlight, or serve as an intern to gain experience and determine whether the job suits you.

Prepare for the job hunt. Look for free and inexpensive classes nearby or online to teach you technologies often needed for job hunting. These include basic computing skills, Web-surfing, social media, and email. Not only can you use these skills to contact employers, but you may also fend off age discrimination.

Expand your network of colleagues by joining professional groups online and off, joining local networking groups, and using social media.

Make a list of your skills, experience, strengths, and expertise, including those that made you successful in your pre-retirement career. Use this information to rewrite your resume and create a social media profile. Emphasize your experience and the qualities that make you a good match for the job and company, rather than your long employment history.

Handy websites put you on the road to employment

Seniors, need a job or extra income? There is extra help to be found, even in these troubled times. Here is a sampling of the best senior-specific employment resources.

- RetirementJobs (*www.retirementjobs.com*)
- SeniorJobBank (*www.seniorjobbank.com*)
- Seniors4Hire (*www.seniors4hire.org*)
- WorkForce50.com (*www.workforce50.com*)

- JobSource (*ncoajobsource.org*)
- RetiredBrains.com (*retiredbrains.com*)

For something even more specific try:

- YourEncore (*www.yourencore.com*) for retired engineers and scientists.
- Employment Network for Retired Government Experts (*www.myfederalretirement.com*) for government workers seeking new jobs.
- JobsOver50 (*jobsover50.com*) for part-time work and internships.

For help with the transition to your next career, also visit sites like Encore (*encore.org*), Life Reimagined (*lifereimagined.aarp.org*), and AARP WorkSearch (*www.aarpworksearch.org*).

7 ways to cut training and education costs

Your encore career may require big training commitments like college courses or small changes like learning how to use social media for your job hunt. But that doesn't mean you're always required to spend big bucks. Instead, cut costs with these ideas.

- Check the local newspaper, senior center, continuing education center, or library for free or inexpensive local classes on basic computer and Web-surfing skills.
- Take free online courses if you already know how to surf the Web. For example, you can learn more about social media, popular software programs, email, and more at *www.gcflearnfree.org*.

- Visit *www.youtube.com/education* to watch free university lectures and other education videos, or take free online college courses at *www.coursera.com*.

- Find out if you can skip some college courses by passing a placement test for each course.

- Check whether your state or university offers tuition waivers or discounts to seniors or veterans.

- Investigate scholarships for your specific field or career, and check whether scholarships are available from professional associations you've joined.

- See if your employer offers tuition reimbursement if you're still in a pre-retirement job and the training or education you want would also benefit that job.

Add 30 percent to your nest egg after you retire

Today's retirees may not want the daily grind, but they also don't want to sit at home all day. "Whether mature workers are motivated by financial concerns or simply enjoy going to work every day, we're seeing more people move away from the traditional definition of retirement and seek 'rehirement,'"says Rosemary Haefner, vice president of Human Resources at CareerBuilder.

Join this trend by working part-time, and you could get a big payoff.

Find your buried treasure. Analysis from a leading financial company suggests you can increase your nest egg up to 30 percent if you earn 40 percent of your pre-retirement salary for the first five years of retirement. You may only need to work part time to earn that lower salary, but it packs a big financial punch because it can help you withdraw less money from your nest egg.

Withdrawing less means your nest egg will last longer, and tax-free investments inside that nest egg have more time to grow. So a simple, part-time job can make your nest egg last longer and grow even larger.

Discover your part-time options. Consider these 15 ways to make extra cash every month.

- Bank teller. You may be pleasantly surprised at how well this pays, but check the qualifications you need before applying.

- Retail associate. Work at your favorite retail store, and you may get an employee discount.

- Tour guide. These jobs may be available at museums, factories, historical sites, or even caverns. Some jobs may be seasonal.

- Research assistant. If you have an area of expertise, businesses or universities may pay you to track down information on that subject.

- Patient advocate, medical office worker, or other health care jobs. Determine which positions in health care you may qualify for and whether part-time work is available in those jobs.

- Newspaper deliverer. Finish working before lunch.

- Registration clerk. This is just one example of the variety of part-time jobs that may be available with your local, county, state, or federal government. If you have Web access, visit *www.usajobs.gov* and your state and local government's websites to see job postings.

- Crossing guard. Enjoy this outdoor work near schools or local government offices. School crossing guards don't work during summer and other school vacations.

- Bookkeeping. If you have an accounting background, small businesses may want to hire you as a part-time bookkeeper.

- Personal assistant. Help a businessman or homemaker with extra tasks for a few hours a day.

- Nonprofit organization jobs. You can find paid, part-time work at both national and local charity organizations.

- Delivery driver, bus driver, or chauffeur. You need a clean driving record, insurance, and an up-to-date license for these jobs.

- Home health care aide. Help a patient do routine household tasks, take medicine, and move around the house.

- Movie theater staffer. This job may come with free or discounted movie privileges.

- Your pre-retirement job. Ask about going part-time with a current or previous employer.

7 great ways to earn extra cash

Increase your cash flow, even if you're on a fixed income. Here's how to make more by working from home or being self-employed.

Give sewing or alterations a go. If you can sew well and have all the equipment you need, you can offer an alterations service or make products to sell. Spread the word through friends, family, flyers, and any other free advertising you can think of.

Try call center customer service. To do this job from home, you need a landline, a computer that meets the call center's standards, an Internet connection, and earphones. Calls are routed through a regular call center and rerouted to your phone. Alpine Access is a reputable call center company, but investigate any other call centers to avoid scammers.

Take up tutoring. Former teachers and current math whizzes can be ideal tutors for high school or college students, and the hourly rate may be higher than you expect. If you have a good Internet connection and computer, visit *tutor.com* to learn more about how you can become an online tutor.

Open a day care service. Babysit kids for working parents during the day, or offer "day care" during the very early mornings, weekends, or evenings when other day care services are closed.

Serve as a virtual assistant. Virtual assistants do small services for a business or individual via the Internet. For example, you may turn past secretarial experience into retirement income by providing services like data entry, answering emails, and scheduling from your home computer. To start, try working for people you know. After gaining experience and a good reputation, visit *www.elance.com* or *www.odesk.com*, and search for "virtual assistant."

Become a dog walker or pet sitter. Both these jobs may require local travel to the pet's home, as well as feeding, walking, and other pet care. Pet sitters may be asked to stay with pets overnight or to keep animals in their homes. To learn more about becoming a pet sitter, visit Pet Sitters International at *www.petsit.com* or write to 201 E. King St., King, NC 27021.

If you prefer dog walking, look for dog-walking businesses currently advertising for walkers, or sign a noncompete agreement, and apprentice with a pet sitter who does not live nearby. Smaller individuals may need to limit their dog-walking or pet-sitting services to smaller animals.

Start a housecleaning business. Make your cleaning skills a source of income. Spread the word that you're available to clean, and describe the services you offer.

Before you start a self-employment career, be sure to check the following things.

- Find out what permits, certifications, or licenses you need and what regulations and laws you must comply with.

- Make sure you won't violate any zoning laws.

- Determine whether your taxes will be affected, or if you must prepare separate taxes for your business.

WARNING

Beware of work-from-home scams

Most work-at-home offers are scams, experts warn. Be extremely suspicious of fees or costs you're asked to pay, guarantees of quick wealth, and anything that sounds too good to be true.

Always investigate potential employers, and be sure to ask many questions. To start your investigation, type the name of the employer or job promoter in a search engine along with words like "scam" or "complaint." Visit *www.bbb.org*, or contact the Better Business Bureau for information about the promoter or company. Also, use the search functions at *www.ftc.gov* and *www.scam.com* to search those sites for the company or promoter's name.

Ask the potential employer plenty of questions like these:

- What will my duties be?

- Will I be paid a salary or work on commission?

- How much will my first paycheck be and when will I receive it?

- What equipment am I expected to provide?

Earn real money doing what you love

Your fun hobby can make you money. Find out how other crafters, artists, collectors, and hobbyists are selling their products, and how you can join them.

Set up shop the easy way. If you can surf the Web, you can set up your own store at *www.etsy.com*. Etsy is a buying and selling community with 30 million members. The site does most of the heavy lifting for you, making it very easy to set up a store, payment system, shipping options, and product listings.

But that doesn't mean Etsy is expensive to use. You won't pay for membership at all. Instead, you pay just 20 cents to list each product for four months, 3.5 percent commission to Etsy on each item you sell, and you may pay a small commission to your payment processor. But your total cost may well come to 10 percent or less of your selling price.

Keep your costs down. Don't take up an expensive hobby to make products for Etsy. Instead, keep your old hobby, or try one of these 10 inexpensive hobbies you can turn into a retirement windfall.

- crocheting
- soap making
- candle making
- quilting from scraps
- woodworking
- needlework or embroidery
- tatting

- quilling

- beading

- polymer clay art

These hobbies can become expensive over time, so search the Web to discover ways to hold down costs.

Recognize the five common pitfalls to avoid. Before you open your store, discover the problems that can keep your products from selling — and how to solve them.

- You sell the same thing as everyone else. To see shoppers' alternatives to your product, hunt around on Etsy to find other items similar to yours. Think about ways to make your products unique, such as including a certificate of authenticity or creating products around a theme like dogs or wedding items.

- No one visits your store. Constantly promote your store by handing out business cards, spreading the word online, and so on. And, of course, don't forget to lace your product descriptions with keywords that attract online searches to your items.

- People visit, but can't see the product well enough to buy. Be sure your photos show enough detail, are well lit, make your items look fabulous, and are a pleasure to look at. Offer extra photos to emphasize impressive details. If your photography is poor, get help from an expert or friend who is good at photography.

- People visit, but don't find what they want. Your selection may be too limited, or products may not meet the customer's minimum standard of quality. Make sure your items are of high quality, and list enough of them to give buyers plenty of choices.

- The price is not right. Before you set prices, see what others on Etsy charge for similar goods. Price your items in that range.

This may sound hard, but plenty of help is available. Visit Etsy's Web pages for links to their "Seller Handbook," and read blogs like *www.handmadeology.com* and *www.everythingetsy.com.*

Choose a smarter start for your small business

Starting a small business can fulfill your retirement dreams or turn them into a nightmare. Consider these points first to lower your financial risks and raise your odds of a satisfying retirement.

- Retirement means you finally have enough time to turn your favorite hobby into a business, but be careful. Former hobbyists may discover they must spend less time on the hobby and more on business functions like marketing and finance.

- Starting a new business often requires long hours. Is this how you want to spend your retirement, or would you prefer to work fewer hours? And, if the job requires more than 40 hours a week, are you able to keep those hours?

- Ask your spouse how he feels about you starting the business, and talk to other family members who may be affected by your plans. Consider ways you can adjust your plans if your family isn't comfortable with the long hours and dedication it takes to start a full-time business. On the other hand, if your spouse and family are enthusiastic about the business, they may boost your odds of success.

- Starting a small business requires plenty of money, but a part-time side business costs less, gives you a chance to learn the business side of your hobby, and lets you test drive the business to see if it suits you, your family, and your retirement plans.

Hidden hazards of selling collectibles

You have a lovely set of commemorative plates Aunt Martha left you, and you're thinking of adding to the collection so you can make big bucks later. But, before you invest in antiques or collectibles to make money, discover the perils no one talks about.

- You must pay a 28 percent federal tax rate on profits, instead of the cheaper 15 percent capital gains rate you pay on stock and bond investments.

- A high number of fakes, flawed goods, or knock-offs may slash the price of your legitimate goods.

- You must pay the high costs of insurance and storage.

- You may face unexpected drops in the price your collectibles can fetch.

- High offers for products may vanish after the buyer's expert examines the goods.

- You may get stuck with hard-to-sell items.

- High dealer markups may push up your purchase price so much that you don't make enough profit to keep up with inflation. Profits that don't keep up with inflation are like a tiny pay cut every year, and those pay cuts add up. So watch or listen to the news to learn what the current rate of inflation is. If your collectibles aren't making at least that much, you may be losing ground.

In addition, you may be forced to buy at retail prices and sell at wholesale prices, making you more likely to lose money unless the price of your collectible rises like a rocket.

The truth about investing in collectibles is that avoiding losses may not be as easy as some people claim. So remember the one rule experts say you must follow if you want to be guaranteed not to lose money on collectibles. Don't buy collectibles to make money.

Instead, treat this poor investment only as a hobby, collect things you like, and find another way to boost your income.

Watch your yard sale profits soar

Try these five simple tricks that could double your garage sale income.

Price for maximum profit. If you have Web access, consider this tactic for items you price at $5 or more. Check *www.amazon.com* to find the price the item sells for new, print that Web page, and post it next to the price tag on the item. Upon seeing this, people may reduce the discount they expect, and pay an amount closer to your asking price.

If you don't have Web access, try a different approach. Instead of posting a price on every item, write "make an offer" on the price tags of some of your less expensive items. Some customers may offer more than you expect for these products.

Just be sure to find out what these items — and your more expensive "treasures" — are worth beforehand, so you won't accept any lowball offers. To find used-good prices for items, check *www.eBay.com*, local yard sales, *www.craigslist.com*, thrift markets, and online price guides from *www.satruck.org* and *www.goodwill.org*.

Set up for easy customer shopping. Show off clothing on racks, and organize other items on tables or bookshelves so they're clearly visible and easy to reach. Borrow shelves, tables, baskets, and racks if you don't have them. To make products more tempting, dust, polish, or clean them. Also, keep extension cords and batteries ready to test electronics.

Sell every last unwanted item. Thoroughly scour your house for possible merchandise to sell to be sure you offer enough items to tempt people to come to your sale. For example, sell broken items if they're safe. Label them as broken because some people buy products for their parts. Also, examine pockets and interiors of your merchandise for personal items hiding inside. You can even sell houseplants, seedlings, lemonade, baked goods, crafts, and leftover fabric.

Advertise heavily. Post at least 15 sturdy, easy-to-read signs with arrows to guide people to the sale. Start posting at major routes nearby, and work toward your sale location. Use waterproof ink, or cover with clear packing tape. To test the first sign, post it at a major route, and try to read it as you drive by.

Advertise in local newspapers, tell family and friends, and hang flyers on public bulletin boards. If you have Web access, advertise online at *www.craigslist.com*, Facebook, eBay classifieds at *www.ebay.com*, *www.garagesalehunter.com*, Twitter, or *www.tagsellit.com*. Include categories of items you'll be selling in every ad.

Handle money like a pro. Don't lose a sale because you can't make change. Arrange to have $50 in $1 and $5 bills, $5 in quarters, and another $50 in other coins and bills. To keep it secure, store both your change and your proceeds in a fanny pack you wear, not a money box.

If you have a smartphone, visit *https://squareup.com* to get a free credit card reader so you can accept credit cards at your sale. This could add a lot to your profits.

Last-minute strategy to make more money

Items left over from a garage sale make no money, so plan ahead to salvage profits from those leftovers. Before the sale, make signs that say, "Everything 50 percent off," but don't post them until the last few hours of the sale. This can help sell items customers have ignored.

If this strategy seems too drastic, plan how to quickly discount individual items. For example, make signs that say,

"Everything on this table 50 percent off," and move individual items to that table, as needed. Write discounts such as "25 percent off" or "50 percent off" on brightly colored adhesive labels, but keep them hidden until the late hours of the sale. Slap the labels on individual items for an instant markdown.

For higher-priced merchandise that you prefer not to mark down, try advertising them locally for free on *www.craigslist.org*.

Turn clutter into dollars

Sell a whole houseful of stuff on eBay, without lifting a finger — and all your listings are free.

Let professionals sell for you. You've probably taken old clothes to a clothing consignment shop where they sell the clothes for you, deduct their commission, and pay you the remaining profits. eBay consignment stores work nearly the same way.

For example, visit an iSold It store with your item in hand, and they'll determine its resale value. If the item meets their requirement for minimum resale value, they may agree to sell it for you on eBay or another online marketplace.

According to iSold It websites, they interview you to find the best information for the listing, take professional pictures of your item, write up the listing, and list your item on eBay. They also give you a link to the eBay auction, so you can see how your item is doing. Some stores even promise to charge you nothing for the listing unless your item sells.

When the item sells, the store collects payment and ships the product to the buyer. After delivery is complete, the store deducts fees and commissions from the buyer's payment and sends the rest to you. One iSold It website reports that commissions and fees can vary from 20 percent to 45 percent.

Find a consignment store. Visit *www.i-soldit.com* to check for a store near you, but don't fret if you don't find one close by. Other eBay consignment sellers may be available in your area. But, before using any eBay consignment seller, be sure to ask plenty of questions about:

- the services the consignment seller provides.

- fees and commissions the seller charges, when they're charged, and how much they cost.

- whether you pay if your item does not sell.

Enjoy extra income from a hobby

Consider whether activities you enjoy can make extra cash for you. That's what Bob and Jeanne Mott did. Bob began beekeeping as a hobby. It started with backyard hives, but grew until he also tended hives at a nearby farm.

The Motts soon realized Bob's hobby was producing something they could sell — local honey, and the farm was the perfect place to sell it. "They sell a lot of the honey there, and split the profit with us," Jeanne explains. But the Motts also spread the word to friends, family, and co-workers when their backyard honey is available for sale.

Although their profit isn't large, Jeanne says, "It sure has been handy." She adds, "There was a major car repair that came up, and we were wondering, 'Now what are we going to do.'" Their answer came from honey sales. "It was a godsend," says Jeanne.

Insurance

Get the best protection for the least expense

Car insurance

'Pay-as-you-drive' delivers premium discounts

Would you mind Big Brother tracking how you drive if it saved you money on your auto insurance? That's the theory behind usage-based insurance (UBI) — also known as pay-as-you-drive insurance. It takes advantage of telematics, the technology that sends and receives information from your car via wireless telecommunication.

This is the same technology used for satellite navigation and vehicle tracking. With it, your insurance company records how many miles you drive, whether or not you take turns and corners slowly, if you drive late at night, if you routinely travel faster than 80 miles per hour, and if you make sudden stops or hard accelerations.

They use the collected data to calculate how much to charge you. You are rewarded with lower premiums if you drive fewer miles and more safely. In short, UBI gives you some control over your insurance costs.

Iron out the details. Here are just a few important points that may put your mind at ease regarding UBI.

- Insurance companies cannot collect data without your consent.
- It's usually free to enroll in a UBI program and free to use the devices.
- The monitoring device is for one vehicle only.
- The data collected should not cause your premium to go up.
- One incident won't affect your rate.
- Insurers say they will not monitor whether or not you are speeding.

Get connected. If you decide to participate in a UBI program, here are the two most common ways your car sends driving data wirelessly back to your insurance company.

- You plug a small device from your insurer into a port under your dashboard — the same port mechanics use to run engine diagnostics.
- Your insurance company takes advantage of your car's existing built-in communications system like OnStar, In-Drive, or SYNC.

Many insurers allow you to monitor your driving performance online or with a smartphone app. You can get an overview of your driving habits, compare your driving to other family members on the program, and review specific days, times, or trips.

Start saving. Allstate, Progressive, and State Farm are just three companies that offer UBI programs. Savings will vary, but Allstate claims you'll reduce your premiums by 10 percent just for signing up for their Drivewise program, and you could save as much as 30 percent when it's time to renew — based on your driving score. Contact your insurance provider for details.

The National Association of Insurance Commissioners feels UBI is the wave of the future and predicts that 20 percent of all insurance in the U.S. will include some form of this technology by 2018.

7 quick ways to lower your insurance rates

You're a good driver with hardly a ticket or accident on your record — so why are your auto insurance premiums so high? Maybe you just haven't pursued all the discounts you are eligible for. Here are some of the easiest money-saving strategies.

- Boost your deductible to $1,000 and the Insurance Information Institute says you could cut your premium by 40 percent or more. Just make sure you have enough money handy to cover this higher amount in case of an accident.

- Bundle your home and auto coverage under the same carrier.

- Remove errors from your credit report.

- Take a defensive driving course.

- Drive fewer miles by taking public transportation or carpooling. The maximum mileage varies so check with your insurer for details.

- Look up the value of your older car. If it is worth less than 10 times the premium, drop collision and possibly comprehensive coverage.

- Simply ask for a discount. You may be surprised what you qualify for.

How to save money after a car accident

Odds are you will have three to four automobile accidents over the course of your driving lifetime. They will probably be distressing, regardless of how serious the injury or damage turns out to be. But they don't have to be expensive.

The following list is a must-do after any two-car accident.

- Call 911.

- Take care of the injured — including yourself.

- Trade information, including names and license numbers; year, make, and model of vehicles; license plate numbers; and insurance company names and phone numbers. Don't disclose your policy details.

After that, what you either do or don't do can make an accident even more costly than it has to be.

Stay calm at the scene. Emotions run high just after an accident. It's all too easy to say something you shouldn't when caught up in the moment.

- Don't apologize or blurt out the accident was your fault. At this point, you don't have all the facts and you could be making a costly assumption.

- Don't get into a verbal or physical altercation with other drivers. This will only make matters worse and possibly prompt legal action.

- Document the area and damage with a camera or smartphone. Some insurance companies, like USAA, offer phone and tablet apps to help you diagram your accident. With a tap, you can send it to your insurer and it automatically becomes part of your file. Taking advantage of technology in this way will speed up the process and could mean a fairer claim.

Know when to file a claim. Experts say it simply is not true that all claims will hike your insurance premiums. According to esurance.com, it depends on these factors:

- the severity of the accident

- your driving history

- who is at fault

- if the accident takes place in a no-fault state

- if your policy includes accident forgiveness for small claims

If the accident involves another vehicle, and there's even a chance you are at fault, filing a claim means you will be covered against any liability for harming others.

Realize, also, that repairs are frequently more expensive than they appear to the untrained eye and physical injuries often show up days later. If you don't file a claim right away, your insurance company may not cover these expenses.

The only situation where experts advise against filing a claim with your insurance company is if you are the only vehicle involved and the damage is so minor the repair cost is less than or close to your deductible.

Deal carefully with the adjuster. His job is to save his company money. That doesn't necessarily make him the bad guy, but he may not always have your best interests at heart. He must ask before recording you, so say no if you don't want him to. Don't be afraid to say, "I don't remember." And don't let him pressure you into any decision.

Don't be a victim of insurance fraud

Criminals often stage automobile accidents to swindle big money from insurance companies. They choreograph the collision, pay off witnesses, hire unethical attorneys, and even fake their own injuries.

The cost to you, the innocent victim, is high. As a result of this phony accident, you could be injured and your car damaged. In addition, your insurance company may raise your premium or even cancel your policy.

The National Insurance Crime Bureau says the following situations are highly targeted for staged accidents:

- urban areas because of high volume traffic
- wealthy communities where drivers are more likely to have better insurance coverage

- new or rental vehicles that are likely to be well-insured
- unaccompanied female drivers and seniors because they are less likely to be assertive at an accident scene

Drive defensively. In most cases, the fraudster tries to force you into some type of collision, often by slamming on his brakes, boxing you in, or cutting you off. Defensive driving is your best protection. Leave plenty of room between your car and other vehicles, and don't allow yourself to get distracted while driving.

Be wary of help. People who suddenly appear at the scene of an accident may be good Samaritans or part of the con. Avoid the tow truck that arrives before you called one. Bystanders that try to take you to a doctor or put you in touch with a lawyer should also signal danger.

Document the details. As soon as you are able, use a camera to record the physical damage and all parties involved. That way, there can be no dispute over the number of people in a car or who has visible injuries.

If you suspect you've been the victim of a staged accident, call 800-TEL-NICB (800-835-6422) or go online to *www.nicb.org*.

---

5 reasons to use an independent insurance agent

An independent agent is self-employed. He isn't tied to one insurance company, but rather represents many. There aren't a lot of them — about 37,500 in the U.S. — but in some circumstances, it could be worth your while to hunt one down.

- Independent agents work for you. Their livelihood depends on your repeat business so they want to keep you happy.
- You won't have to comparison shop — they do it for you, which should save you time and effort.

- An independent agent can offer you products from multiple lines. That means you'll get coverage best suited to your personal situation.

- If you've had a lapse in coverage, you probably face inflated prices on a new policy. An independent agent may be able to negotiate a better deal.

- When it's time to submit a claim, you call your agent, not an 800 number.

To find an independent agent, visit the Independent Insurance Agents and Brokers of America at *www.iiaba.net*.

Home and property insurance

4 things to consider when choosing an insurer

You buy insurance, then hope you never need it. But if you do, your insurer better come through for you. And it will — if you did your homework before purchasing a policy.

To help you choose the best insurance company, the Insurance Information Institute suggests reviewing these four things.

Licensing. Make sure the company is licensed where you live by contacting your state's insurance department. Go to the National Association of Insurance Commissioners (NAIC) website at *www.naic.org/state_web_map.htm* for help.

Price. Compare quotes on similar products from at least three different companies.

Service. Whether you are in contact with a customer service department or an agent, see if you're comfortable with them and try to gauge how efficiently they handle business.

In addition, the NAIC has a Consumer Information page on its website at *https://eapps.naic.org/cis*. Here you can check on complaints or fraud cases filed against an insurance company.

Rating. Several independent organizations classify the financial strength of insurance companies on a letter-grade system — A, B, C, and so on.

The point is to pay your premiums into a stable company that will be around when you need them. That means you need to choose a company that is consistently rated high — in at least the top two tiers — by more than one rating organization. They all have slightly different scales, including plusses and minuses, so get familiar with each agency's system.

You must create an account on some of these websites, but all the information is free.

Name	Web Address	Highest Rating
A.M. Best	*www3.ambest.com*	A++
Fitch Ratings	*www.fitchratings.com*	AAA
Moody's	*www.moodys.com*	Aaa
Standard & Poor's	*www.standardandpoors.com*	AAA
Weiss Ratings	*www.weissratings.com*	A+

Don't make these insurance mistakes

Most people pay $800 to $1,000 a year in premiums for homeowners insurance. You absolutely don't want to miss that payment, since keeping your home properly insured is one of the smartest things you can do. But paying too much or paying for the wrong coverage tops anybody's list of "dont's."

Don't ignore discounts. It's like throwing away free money if you are eligible for an insurance discount and don't ask for it. Alert your insurer to any features in your home that could qualify, including dead bolts, smoke alarms, security system, carbon monoxide detector, fire extinguishers, and heat sensors.

In addition, tell your insurer your age, if you are retired, if you live in a gated community, or if you've added any new features or updates to your home — like new wiring.

Don't forget to cancel PMI. You probably have Private Mortgage Insurance (PMI) if you put less than 20 percent down when you bought your home. Its purpose is to protect the mortgage company if you default on your loan. You'll pay anywhere from 0.5 percent to 1.5 percent of your loan amount per year. If your loan balance is $150,000, for example, you could pay about $1,500 in PMI annually.

Once your loan balance reaches 80 percent of the original value of your property, you can and should cancel PMI. If you forget, your lender is required by the Homeowners Protection Act of 1998 to automatically cancel PMI when the balance reaches 78 percent of the value. Unfortunately that doesn't always happen as it should. Since canceling PMI can be a lengthy and confusing process, go online to *www.privatemi.com/loanoptions/benefits/guide.cfm* for a step-by-step guide.

Once you've canceled, don't fritter away those extra dollars. This is a great opportunity to use them to pay down your loan principal. You'll love how quickly that helps you get out of mortgage debt.

Don't ignore flood coverage. Obviously, buying flood insurance when you don't need it is a huge waste of money. But before you pooh-pooh the idea completely, make sure of your facts.

- Flood insurance is never included in a standard policy, so don't assume you have even minimal coverage.

- FEMA (Federal Emergency Management Agency) reports nearly 25 percent of all flood insurance claims come from medium- or low-risk flood areas.

- Your emergency savings may not be enough to "bail you out" in case of a disaster. According to *Consumer Reports*, an inch of water in your home can cause $21,000 in damage and cleanup.

- Annual premiums for homes in medium- or low-risk zones can range from $60 to $2,000.

- Most private insurers don't offer flood coverage at all. Visit the National Flood Insurance Program online at *floodsmart.gov* for more information.

Are you covered?

It's a crazy, dangerous world out there. Thank heavens you have insurance. You are covered, aren't you?

- Your golf clubs are stolen out of your rental car in Scotland. They are covered unless you decided against "off-premises coverage."

- Halloween hooligans run riot through your bed of heirloom roses. You're covered for up to about $500 per item.

- Fido piddles on your neighbor's expensive Oriental rug. You're covered. Ironically, if Fido piddles on your rug, you're out of luck.

- Your neighbor's tree falls on your garage. You're covered, even if it toppled because of natural causes.

- All the food in your fridge spoils during a power outage. You may be covered under certain circumstances in some states. Check with your agent.

- Your aquarium develops a crack and leaks all over your expensive Oriental rug. You are covered for water damage from several types of plumbing accidents, but not aquariums.

How you can bounce back from disaster

Stand outside and look at your home. Look to the neighbor on your right. Now look to your left. Out of these three homes, two are underinsured. Are you one of them?

Experts say over 60 percent of Americans lack adequate homeowners insurance. That means if disaster strikes, millions won't have enough coverage to rebuild. In fact, the average underinsured homeowner will only receive 78 percent of the funds needed to replace their home.

Pick your coverage. The Rocky Mountain Insurance Information Association, a nonprofit insurance communications organization, explains three ways to insure your home.

- Replacement Cost will pay to rebuild your damaged property without factoring in depreciation. You will be limited to a maximum dollar amount.

- Extended Replacement Cost or Replacement Cost Endorsements protect against any gaps in your major policy — like the sudden increases in material and labor that often follow a natural disaster. These can add another 20 to 100 percent to your replacement value limit.

- Actual Cash/Cost Value (ACV) covers the cost to replace your home minus depreciation. This is generally less expensive because everything is valued on an "as-is" basis. For example, you'll be reimbursed for the value of your 12-year-old roof, not a new one. ACV is beneficial only when your home is a year or two old.

Calculate replacement cost. Just because home prices have plummeted in the last few years doesn't mean you should cut your coverage. In other words, the cost to replace your home cannot be calculated using market value, appraised value, or assessed tax value. Figuring out labor and materials to rebuild should be the basis for your coverage. Thanks to inflation and the state of the economy, this dollar amount rises every year. So if you've been in your home even a few years without reassessing your coverage, you're probably falling short.

Take a stab at figuring replacement cost yourself. This will at least give you some numbers to compare. Keep in mind, the National Association of Home Builders estimates the average cost of new construction in 2011 was $80 a square foot. Insurance experts report rebuilding costs, which must include demolition and debris removal, can start at $200 a square foot and go up.

There are several websites that walk you through this process for free or a small fee — most cost less than $10.

- AccuCoverage at *www.accucoverage.com*
- Building-Cost.net at *www.building-cost.net*
- HMFacts at *http://hmfacts.com*

In addition, your insurer will offer its own appraisal, or you can hire an appraiser for anywhere from $250 to $500.

Avoid expensive mistakes. Here are some issues you must consider when shopping for homeowners insurance.

- Your coverage will be woefully outdated if you fail to report home improvements and renovations to your insurer.
- If you were lucky enough to buy your home for a bargain, do not base your coverage on the amount of your mortgage.
- A low premium is not the holy grail of homeowners insurance, especially if it means lowballing your home's value. Your home is your biggest asset. Make sure it is covered.

Protect your possessions in 3 easy steps

Are your furnishings Chippendale or chip-n-dented? Doesn't matter — they are still your belongings and expensive to replace. In case of fire, storm, theft, or other disaster, you must be prepared.

Examine your coverage. The best time to revisit the type of personal coverage you have is before tragedy strikes.

- Replacement cost is just that — coverage that pays the amount needed to replace whatever possessions were lost or destroyed.

- Actual cash value coverage factors in depreciation. You'll be paid only what an item would be worth today.

Most policies default to actual cash value, so you'll have to specifically ask for — and pay about 10 to 20 percent more for — replacement cost.

Create a home inventory. Let's face it, a spiral notebook and a pencil could get the job done. But that won't be fast or efficient. Why not let technology turn this chore into something a little more productive — and fun.

- Use a digital camera to snap pictures throughout your house. If you're old school, print the pictures and write pertinent information on the back. Otherwise, upload them to your computer, save them to a disk, or store them on the Internet.

- Take your video camera room by room, describing contents as you go. Keep the video in a safe place away from your house.

- Take advantage of spreadsheets offered by many insurance companies and third parties. Download, print, and fill in. For examples, visit *statefarm.com* or *homeinsurance.com* and search for "home inventory checklist."

- Let free online tools do most of the work. Perhaps the most familiar of these is Know Your Stuff from the Insurance Information Institute at *www.knowyourstuff.org*. But, again, there are other options from insurance companies like American Family Insurance DreamVault and third parties like Belongings at *www.getbelongings.com*. They all walk you through creating an account; adding items, including pictures and values; generating reports; and saving your information to the Cloud — remote servers hosted on the Internet.

- Apps for your phone or tablet let you go mobile with all of the management tools found in Web-based software. Download an app from Google Play or iTunes and use your device to snap pictures and record other information. Many are free.

No matter how you document an item, at the very least note its serial or model number and purchase price. If possible, keep receipts, credit card purchase statements, and appraisals. And don't forget to update. Every year — say, on your birthday — take a quick run through your house, adding anything new to your inventory.

Process a claim effortlessly. Creating some kind of personal property record is important not only to make sure you have the correct amount and type of coverage, but so you and your agent know what you own. Then, when you suffer a loss, you use your home inventory, and not your memory, to submit a claim.

If you also hope to qualify for a tax break or disaster assistance, an inventory will help prove the value of anything you lost. Your claim should go more smoothly with this kind of proper documentation.

New flood maps affect rates

In 2012, the U.S. Congress passed the Biggert-Waters Flood Insurance Reform Act, which required the Federal Emergency Management Agency (FEMA) to, among other things, redraw flood zones. Many moderate-risk flood zones were changed to high-risk and vice versa.

This may impact your insurance options, since living in a high-risk zone often means you must have coverage. Go to *www.floodsmart.gov* or the FEMA Map Service Center at *http://msc.fema.gov* to search your address.

Life insurance

Do you need life insurance after 50?

That insurance check you write every month seems like an unnecessary drain on your finances — especially now that you're over age 50. After all, isn't this the time to let your policy expire? And those extra dollars sure could help out your budget. Experts agree you may not need life insurance anymore if:

- your mortgage is paid off.

- your children are self sufficient.

- Medicare benefits are about to kick in.

- you will soon start drawing Social Security.

- you have enough assets to cover known expenses and care for yourself.

- your estate is too small to owe estate taxes.

But there's a flip side to every issue — compelling and financially sound reasons to keep some type of coverage.

- Many seniors find themselves called upon to help support adult children, grandchildren, aging parents, and disabled family members. If you die before they do, an insurance policy would continue to provide for them.

- There is often a Social Security "blackout period" between the age you decide to retire and when you're eligible for benefits. Many surviving spouses have little or no income during this time.

- Older women, especially, can experience financial hardship after their husband's health problems drain their savings. To put this in perspective, about half of women over age 65 are widowed, but they can expect to live another 20 years. An insurance policy would provide a safety net.

- If your retirement income includes payouts from a traditional pension plan, a surviving spouse may not receive those benefits after your death.

So how should you plan for these situations? Find a financial planner with a good knowledge of insurance to help you make the best decision. Check out The National Association of Personal Financial Advisors at *www.napfa.org*, the Financial Planning Association at *www.fpanet.org*, or the Certified Financial Planner Board of Standards at *www.cfp.net*.

Unique financial opportunity for your children

A cash-value policy — also called permanent, whole, or universal life — builds up a reserve of tax-deferred cash in addition to giving you a death benefit. In times of need, you can withdraw as much as you've paid in premiums or take out a loan against the policy. If you own this type of policy, don't automatically cancel it or let it lapse just because you've reached a certain age. Talk to your adult children and see if they are interested in taking over the premiums. It may not be much of a financial burden for them, and they will benefit in the long run.

The single person's guide to life insurance

Suddenly, you are single. Whether widowed or divorced, finding yourself on your own means you, alone, are responsible for your financial decisions. It's time to make smart — not emotional — choices.

Collect any benefits. If you are eligible to receive any death benefits, file a life insurance claim with your spouse's policyholder. This would also be a good time to ask about an advance or loan against the benefit if you are facing immediate, overwhelming expenses.

In addition, make sure you claim all the benefits you are entitled to. This may include:

- individual policies

- a group policy through a bank, professional or social organization, credit card, or employer

If you're not certain of all the policies that could be in your spouse's name, call your insurance agent, contact your spouse's employer, look for certificates of insurance in your files or a safe deposit box, see if there are canceled checks to an insurance company, and contact any creditors or lenders.

Adjust your coverage. Now that you are single, you may not need as much life insurance as you did before. You can reduce or cancel your coverage and put those dollars into another type of savings or investment. There are situations, however, where you need to keep or even increase your insurance.

- Are there any children, grandchildren, or aging parents financially dependent on you that would need the death benefit from your life insurance policy?

- Do you need a policy to pay for any funeral expenses, or have you made other arrangements?

- Is it important to you to leave a final donation to a charity or special organization?

- Are you a "casual" saver, relying on a cash value policy as a type of forced savings plan?

If you answered "no" to these questions, you are free to revise your insurance and invest as you like.

Lastly, check the beneficiary on all your life insurance policies and change it from your spouse, if necessary.

Get guaranteed income for life

Are you feeling lucky? Are you willing to gamble a little on good genes and healthy living? If you think the odds are you'll live into your 80s — and beyond — longevity insurance could be a very smart move, indeed.

It works like this. Around age 65, you invest a good chunk of money into what is basically a deferred income annuity (DIA). In five, 10, 15, or even 20 years, you start receiving a set dollar amount — the longer you wait, the larger the payout. And you continue receiving payouts every year for the rest of your life. You can use this money for anything, including long-term care.

MetLife is just one of the financial institutions that has been selling this product for years. They offer this example. Say you invest $50,000 in a DIA when you are 65 years old. At age 85, you would begin receiving annual payouts of $35,205.

This means just when you might face outliving your savings, longevity insurance kicks in. It's one way to guarantee income for life. Of course, there are conditions.

- If you die before your payout period begins, in most cases you get nothing.

- Payouts are not usually adjusted for inflation.

- Part of your payout will be taxable.

This is an evolving investment product, so talk to your financial advisor to get the latest details.

Some experts believe this is an excellent option for seniors in good health, who have other investment income to live on for a decade or so, and can afford a substantial lump sum premium.

Real Estate

Smart strategies for buying, selling & renting

Smart ways to jump-start the selling process

To sell your home, you're going to need every advantage you can think of. Here are two things you must do before you put your house on the market.

Pay for a home pre-inspection. Imagine you're ready to close the deal on your house and the buyer's inspection turns up an expensive problem. Now you are forced to make a fast repair or risk losing the sale.

Dodge this particular bullet by having a home inspection done before you even list your home — maybe months before you're ready to sell.

When the inspector shows up, ask if you can follow him around your home as he works. He should point out and discuss significant issues as he finds them. Ask questions. Look over the inspection report carefully and make sure you understand it all.

Once you have the report, you can work to fix problems on your own timetable and within your budget. You decide when to repair or replace. You now have the time to solicit bids or do the work yourself, potentially saving hundreds of dollars.

You don't have to fix every defect found during the inspection. Just be aware you can't sweep problems under the rug, either. In some states, it's illegal to conceal a major issue on your property. A buyer will most likely pay for their own home inspection before closing and everything will come to light.

According to the American Society of Home Inspectors, the average cost of a home inspection is $318 and should take two to three hours. But this can vary, depending on your home's age and square footage. Isn't that a small price to pay for peace of mind?

Check out the competition. The more you know about your local housing market, the better equipped you are to make your home competitive. So before you stick a sign in your yard, get a handle on these issues.

- Pricing. A professional realtor can help set your asking price using comparables or "comps" — houses of similar age, square footage, and features. But before that happens, know generally what all houses are selling for in your neighborhood. Scan the local paper for ads. Drive by listings and pull their information sheets. Even attend open houses.

- Improvements. Are there new roofs on every home in your neighborhood — except yours? How do you think your old shingles will measure up? Certain improvements and remodeling projects may be important, even vital, to you making a sale, while others could turn out to be a big waste of money. Check out *Remodeling* magazine's *Cost vs Value Report* online at *www.remodeling.hw.net* to see what projects have the best resale value in your area.

- Decor. Go through model homes in new neighborhoods and make note of color and design trends. Flip through home decorating magazines in the grocery store or visit a few websites. You don't have to make big changes or spend a lot of money, but updating wall color or cabinet hardware can really make a difference.

Free insurance report gives your home an edge

Need an advantage in a competitive housing market? Order a Comprehensive Loss Underwriting Exchange (C.L.U.E.) Personal Property Report for free.

It lists every claim you've made on your homeowners insurance for the last seven years, including the type of loss, the date, amount, and the claim status.

Use a clean report to prove to a potential buyer there's no insurance loss history on the property that would keep them from getting homeowners insurance at a good price.

Order your C.L.U.E. report through LexisNexis toll free at 866-312-8076 or online at *https://personalreports.lexisnexis.com.*

How to sell your home fast for top dollar

It's a fact — the longer your house stays on the market, the less money you'll make. Increase your chances of a quick sale with these expert tips.

Price it right. What's the top reason a home doesn't sell? According to RE/MAX, a global network of top-producing realtors, it's because your asking price is set too high. Don't make the mistake of thinking it won't hurt to start high and drop your price later.

This strategy practically guarantees you will sit on the market for a long time and still have to drop your price eventually — which only makes you look desperate. Underprice by about 10 percent and you'll be more competitive, hopefully attracting multiple buyers.

Declutter. A clean, clutter-free home accomplishes two things. It gives the impression the property as a whole has been well-maintained, and it allows a potential buyer to not only see the space but imagine himself living in it. In fact, spend just $200 cleaning and decluttering your home, and you can expect to receive almost $2,000 more on your selling price.

Remove personal items, especially from walls and countertops, donate extra clothes to make closets look bigger, and purge, purge, purge.

Hold a garage sale to turn this into a moneymaking event and it won't seem like such a chore. If you can't bear to part with extra items, rent a storage space on a month-to-month basis and load it up.

Don't empty your house completely. Experts say vacant rooms actually appear smaller. If you'll be getting rid of major pieces of furniture before you move, wait until after your house sells, then hold an estate sale.

Stage it. Once all the excess is removed from your home, concentrate on making your rooms inviting. Arrange furniture into comfortable groupings. Make sure traffic can flow smoothly from one space to the next. Neutralize too-bold colors, but keep the rooms appealing with flowers or pillows.

This step doesn't have to cost you a dime if you use items and accessories you already have. Stumped for ideas? You can do this even if "simple" is not your style by copying arrangements or layouts from magazines.

A professional stager may be worth their price tag — anywhere from $150 to several thousand dollars — if you are really in a scramble. According to a survey by The International Association of Home Staging Professionals, a staged home is on the market for an average of 11 days, while an unstaged home averages 90 days.

Invite them in. Curb appeal is today's catch phrase in the world of real estate. It can mean the difference between a buyer walking in your front door and driving away forever. So if it's in your front yard, mulch it, trim it, edge it, wash it, or paint it.

Save $10,000 — go FSBO

Keep more money in your pocket by listing your home For Sale By Owner (FSBO).

The average price of a home in the U.S. in 2012 was around $177,000. While there is no set realtor commission across the country, a reasonable average is 6 percent. In this scenario, you would pay out over $10,000 to have someone help you sell your home.

While saving that much money may be reason enough to become your own agent, there are other benefits. You are in control of your price, listing, marketing, appointments, and negotiations. The downside — not only are you in control of these factors, you are responsible for them as well.

Only 9 percent of home sales in 2012 were FSBO. If you think you have the time and skills to be a part of that 9 percent, go to *www.fsbo.com* and choose this money-saving option.

Boost your marketing with online tools

"Nine in 10 home buyers today rely on the Internet as one of their primary research sources," says a joint study from the National

Association of Realtors and Google. "And 52 percent turn to the Web as their first step."

So if you're not marketing your house online, you're missing the boat. Even if you have a realtor, don't rely on them to create all the buzz.

- Use social media, like Facebook, to publicize your listing for free.

- Create a website with your home's address as the URL.

- Get a video of your home on YouTube. It's the top video research destination for home shoppers.

- Make sure your property is listed on the biggest real estate websites, like Realtor.com, Yahoo! Homes, Trulia, Zillow, HomeSeekers.com, RealEstate.com, and Craigslist. Be aware some sites only accept listings from real estate agents.

Avoid foreclosure with speedy alternative

Are you having a tough time affording your mortgage payments? Is a foreclosure looming? Avoid that messy and costly process with a deed in lieu of foreclosure, instead. You'll still walk away from your mortgage debt, but with less of a black mark on your credit score.

Basically, you hand over ownership of your property to your lender. In exchange, the lender cancels the loan and any foreclosure proceedings. Unlike with a short sale, you don't have to get involved with selling your house.

There are conditions, so call your lender's loss mitigation department to make sure you qualify, then talk to an accountant about how a deed in lieu of foreclosure can impact your taxes.

6 secrets for saving big at closing

Use these smart strategies to pay the lowest amount possible for your home.

Buy in the off-season. According to realtor.com, the official site of the National Association of Realtors, home sales are highest in the spring and summer, when families relocate around school holidays. Winter brings fewer sellers — and those often have a compelling reason to sell, such as a job relocation. That makes them highly motivated to make a deal. As a buyer, you're in a great bargaining position.

Clean up your credit report. The interest rate you'll pay on any money you borrow is largely determined by your credit score. You'll nab a better rate and lower closing costs the higher your score and the cleaner your credit history. Three to four months before you're ready to buy, check your report, challenge any errors, and pay off short-term debt — or at least get any credit card balance as far below your limit as possible.

Go with an alternative lender. Costco has teamed up with nine lenders, including First Choice Loan Services, Sterling Bank, and Bank of Internet USA, to provide mortgage services for less. The warehouse giant has capped lender fees at $600 for Executive members and $750 for all other members. You will still have to pay some third-party fees, so do the math and comparison shop before you commit.

Track price changes online. Trulia is a website that lets you get real estate updates in real time. Simply open a free account at *www.trulia.com* and this online marketplace will notify you when nearby houses are listed or sold, prices are cut, and open houses are scheduled. It's another tool that will help you time your offer to your advantage.

Get a home inspection. Home repairs can range from minor to the financially disastrous. You don't want to discover your dream home has black mold or a cracked foundation after the deal is done. A home inspection will give you peace of mind as well as leverage to negotiate repairs or a lower selling price. Have it done by a professional and make your offer contingent upon this inspection.

Pay cash. This isn't an option for everyone, of course, but if you can buy your home outright, you'll pay less in the long run — no mortgage interest — and the initial selling price may even be reduced. Because a cash transaction makes the process infinitely smoother for the seller, you will be in a great negotiating position.

3 ways a reverse mortgage can leave you homeless

A reverse mortgage can be a safe way to feel more financially secure as you age — if you're careful. But one misstep and you lose not only your source of income, but your home, as well.

This type of loan lets a homeowner over age 62 borrow part of the equity in their home as cash. There are no restrictions on how you use the money, and you don't have to pay anything back as long as you're living in the home. When you die, the property is sold and the proceeds pay back the loan.

It sounds simple, but as *The Wall Street Journal* reported in 2013, close to 10 percent of the current reverse mortgages are in default — that means almost 60,000 seniors are in danger of losing their homes.

Here are the top three ways this can happen.

Your name is not on the loan. Let's say you and your spouse apply for a reverse mortgage, but, based on your ages, the lender will give you a higher amount if the loan is processed only under your spouse's name. Then your spouse dies before you.

Since your name is not on the reverse mortgage, you must immediately pay back the loan, including fees and interest — even if that means selling your home to do so. In many cases, the property goes into foreclosure.

The fix is simple. Get both names on the reverse mortgage, even if you must add yours after the loan is initially processed.

You did not plan for a long retirement. If you take out a reverse mortgage too early in retirement, it's quite possible you'll live long enough to deplete this source of "income" and no longer have funds to pay property tax, insurance, or other homeowner bills. This constitutes a default on your reverse mortgage, and your home is subject to foreclosure.

Avoid this by tapping into as many other resources as you can before jumping into a reverse mortgage. And if you still decide to go this route, select a Home Equity Conversion Mortgage (HECM) insured through the Federal Housing Administration (FHA). Waive the lump sum option, and opt for fixed monthly payments for life.

You develop significant health problems. If you suffer a stroke, for instance, and must move into a rehabilitation center, your home is considered unoccupied after six months. Your reverse mortgage becomes due, and now you must not only pay for your health care, but also repay the loan or lose your home.

Protect yourself with an HECM that allows you to spend up to 12 months in a nursing home, assisted living facility, hospital, or other medical facility without penalty. Visit *portal.hud.gov* and search "HECM" for more details.

Reap financial rewards with rental property

People will always need a place to live, but not everyone is able or willing to own their own home. In fact, more than a third of U.S. households are renters. With rent at a national average of $884 a month, residential rental income is a $34 billion business. Would you like a piece of that investment property pie? If so, you need a little cash, good credit, a can-do attitude, and nerves of steel.

Owning investment property doesn't mean temporarily renting out your own home until you can sell. It means deliberately purchasing homes for the sole purpose of generating rental income.

Jim and Dana live in a mid-size college town where homes stay on the market for an average of 10 weeks. They ventured into the rental market nine years ago. "We started by purchasing three houses our first year and then added about one property a year after that for the next five years," Dana explains.

"Our plan has been to use as much of the rental income as possible to pay off the mortgage early. Once one property is paid for, its rent can go to pay off another. We started this venture before we needed the income, so by the time we do need it, most, if not all, of the properties will be paid for and the rental income will go to us and not the bank."

So why would you want to become a landlord?

Boost your income. Revenue from rental property has been compared to an inflation-adjusted annuity — since rents are almost sure to rise over time. Dana agrees. "This is a great retirement plan, which can provide income and fun activities," she says. "As you get older and less interested in maintaining these properties, you can sell them off one at a time to add to your income."

Enjoy tax benefits. You'll get more tax benefits with rental real estate than almost any other investment. Deductions include mortgage interest, depreciation, repairs, property-related travel, wages for contractors or repairmen, credit card interest for rental purchases, and insurance premiums.

Stay active. "We think that investing in rental property is a good way to keep active," says Jim. "The fix-up jobs — painting, mowing lawns, and raking leaves — provide opportunities to stay healthy in retirement plus occasions to help and interact with younger people."

Let your home earn extra cash

You have extra space in your home, but can't commit to a permanent roommate. Here are some fun and unusual ways you can use your home to bring in extra cash.

- Live in a popular tourist area? Rent out an extra bedroom — or your entire home — to vacationers for a single night or a weekend. Websites like *www.airbnb.com* will help you with this.

- Host an international student through your local college or university. Be aware that most high school exchange programs don't pay host families.

- If you live near a major stadium or other event location, let attendees park in your driveway — for a fee. If word of mouth doesn't bring in the business, consider advertising on a website like *www.craigslist.org*.

- An empty garage, basement, attic, or shed could equal monthly income if you rent out the space as storage for someone else. Advertise in a local paper or with an online broker like *www.StoreAtMyHouse.com*.

Smart advice from investment property owners

"Shopping for rental property is different from shopping for your own home," investment property owner Dana says. "A property does not have to be your dream home to be a good rental. And while you might justify overpaying for the perfect home for your family, rental property is an investment and must be a business decision, not an emotional one."

If you're looking to become a landlord, take your time on this very important investment.

Choose wisely for top income. Dana and her husband Jim are fairly picky when it comes to rental properties. "We look for homes in a neighborhood where the properties are well-maintained," she says. "We also avoid higher crime areas and select properties that are 10 to 15 minutes from our home. That way, it's not a burden to get to the property when the need arises."

Throughout their nine years owning rental homes, the couple has purchased properties through a real estate agent, individuals, and even auctions. Jim says the key is to know the property values before purchasing and not to overpay. "Looking up local tax values and visiting with a real estate agent who knows the area are good places to start learning about property values."

Do the math. As a landlord, you're responsible for property taxes, insurance, homeowner's association dues, repairs, and general maintenance in addition to any outstanding mortgage payment. Subtract all known monthly expenses from an average rent for the neighborhood. Pad it with a generous allowance for upkeep. Don't do the deal if you won't at least break even.

Take advantage of online calculators — like the one at *www.rental propertyreporter.com* — to decide if a property will have a good return on your investment.

Top tips for managing your own rentals

You could spend over $1,000 a year for a property manager who will collect your rent, screen applicants, and arrange for repairs. Or you could manage your rental property yourself.

If you can handle the job, no one will look after your investment like you will. But before you jump into property management, take some advice from seasoned investment property owners Jim and Dana.

Select tenants carefully. "We believe the key to being a successful landlord and property manager is to find good, long-term tenants that will take care of our investment," says Dana. This may leave the property vacant a little longer, she admits, but it's time well-spent. "After all, you are trusting a stranger with a property worth many tens of thousands of dollars."

When screening tenants, they always verify income. "We have found that a person or family should make at least three times the monthly rent to be able to comfortably afford the property," Dana says. "A tenant with money problems is not a happy tenant and that is bad for everyone involved."

In addition, these two experienced landlords never rent to anyone who needs a place today. "Better tenants plan ahead," Dana observes, "and poor tenants often rush the process to prevent you from checking them out thoroughly."

Repair it yourself. When asked if they have any tricks to keeping the cost of property management down, Jim says they do as much of the routine maintenance as possible. "The more you can do yourself, the more you can save — just know your limits in both time and abilities. If it takes you a month to complete a task that a professional could do in a couple of days, it might be worth it to hire the professional and get the property rented sooner."

Gather a team. Jim and Dana have also developed a network of skilled individuals to help out with things they can't or don't want to do — such as roofing, heating and air conditioning, and carpet repairs. Visit a local lumber yard or home improvement center for quality recommendations.

Put your money where it counts. Attention to certain areas is essential. Cleanliness, updated baths and kitchens, and curb appeal give a good first impression, support higher rents, and attract long-term tenants.

Do not allow pets. Even small, older pets can cause expensive problems. "It's hard to get enough extra pet deposit to cover the damage a pet can do," says Dana.

Prepare for vacancies. It's always possible your property will sit empty because of a slow market or because it needs repairs. Be sure you can afford this downtime.

Accept the commitment. "Rental property can tie you down a bit," Dana admits. "You are responsible for someone's home, so if the heat goes out on Christmas Eve and you are in Florida, you need to have a plan to take care of the problem. Service is important in keeping good tenants."

5 ways to save thousands on your mortgage

Most people dream of owning their home free and clear. Retiring without debt — especially a mortgage — is certainly a dream worth chasing. Here's what it can mean:

- The national average monthly payment for a 30-year mortgage is just over $1,000. Subtract that amount from your monthly living expenses, and your retirement dollars will go a lot farther.

- Full equity in your home means it is an asset you can borrow against in an emergency — for unexpected health care expenses, for example.

- If you ever decide to sell, any proceeds will be pure profit.

- One less major bill means less stress. And that can be priceless.

Shift into hurry-up mode on your mortgage payback and watch that balance shrink. Every extra dollar you pay reduces the principal of your loan, the total interest you'll pay, and the length of your loan.

There are several ways to do this. Consider them all, then crunch the numbers carefully. An easy way to work out your exact savings is to use an online calculator. Go to *www.bankrate.com* and click on "Calculators."

Sign up for the biweekly plan. Divide your monthly mortgage payment in half and pay that amount every two weeks. By following a weekly schedule instead of a monthly one, you end up making the equivalent of 13 monthly payments in a year. Check with your lender before you try this. Some won't accept half payments, and some charge a fee to process biweekly payments.

Make accelerated payments on your schedule. Anytime you can send a little something extra to your lender, do so. Perhaps you can add one-twelfth of a monthly payment to your regular amount — which will work out to one extra payment a year — or simply round up an $850 payment to $900 and send that every month. This method allows you to respond to your cash flow on a monthly basis.

Pay down your principal monthly. Talk to your lender about sending extra money every month that will go straight to paying back the loan principal. This will greatly reduce the amount of interest you'll pay long-term.

Send in a lump sum. When you have some extra cash, ask your lender to apply it all to your loan principal.

Refinance. Do this only at a lower interest rate and a shorter loan term — but continue paying at least the same monthly amount as you did before.

The final question is should you pay off your mortgage early? There can be drawbacks. Remember, your mortgage interest is tax-deductible. Depending on your situation, you could lose a deduction that's a little or a lot. You just don't want to get caught short from this back-door tax hike. So plan accordingly. Talk to a tax accountant and put extra money aside in case you owe more in taxes after paying off your mortgage. In addition:

- Don't become house-rich and cash-poor. That means don't deplete all your liquid savings just to pay off your mortgage.

- Always pay off higher interest debt, like credit cards, first.

- Funnel extra cash into investments if they are earning more than your mortgage interest is costing.

- Do not pull money out of retirement savings to pay off your mortgage.

- Think twice if you're planning to move in the next few years. Paying off your mortgage will tie up your money in property that may or may not sell quickly.

Slash expenses without living like a pauper

Over half your monthly expenses fall into just five categories. Shave a little off each and you could easily save some serious bucks. Read the stories listed below for smart ways to do just that.

Mortgage. Pay down the principal on your home loan faster by making biweekly payments. Find out how on page 283.

Groceries. Shop at special no-frills grocery stores called hard discounters. Go to page 179 for details.

Utilities. Use a programmable thermostat to automatically adjust your home's temperature down a few degrees in winter and up a few in summer. Read more energy-saving tips on page 210.

Health care. Ask your doctor if you really need every test or procedure he proposes. Learn what questions to ask on page 149.

Transportation. Squeeze every last mile out of your gas dollars. Find clever ways to do this on page 204.

Safeguard your home from con artists

Mortgage fraud is a growing crime targeting seniors and veterans especially hard. The stumbling economy coupled with tighter lending practices has made thousands of homeowners vulnerable. According to the FBI, suspicious activity involving mortgage fraud has increased over 1,000 percent in just eight years.

Beware these scams. Here are three top cons designed to cheat you out of your money and your home.

- Foreclosure rescue schemes. Frantic to avoid foreclosure? All you have to do is shell out an upfront fee of hundreds to thousands of dollars, sign over the title of your home, and even pay rent to continue living in your home. These swindlers take your money, never make the mortgage payments, and run — leaving you homeless.

- Reverse mortgage scams. Instead of giving you a loan against the equity in your home, the fraudulent company keeps the cash and you get evicted.

- Loan modification fraud. If you're delinquent in your mortgage payment, these scammers offer to renegotiate the terms of your loan with your lender — if you pay them a fee upfront, supposedly for preparing the documents. The con is that they don't arrange new financing leaving you facing foreclosure, get you an even worse deal, or slip in an ownership transfer document with the phony loan papers — which means you've unwittingly signed your home over to them.

Don't get hoodwinked. Protect yourself from unscrupulous people by being a smart, cautious consumer.

- Do not pay fees upfront to modify your loan. The Federal Trade Commission has made it illegal to do so.

- Don't let anyone pressure you into something you don't feel comfortable with or badger you into signing documents quickly.

- Ask questions. Just because a service has an official-sounding acronym doesn't mean it is legitimate.

- Read everything you sign. If you don't understand it, take the time to have an attorney or someone you trust look it over.

- Make sure any real estate and mortgage professional you intend to work with is legitimate. Check their licenses and ask for referrals.

- Be cautious of offers you receive in the mail or from cold calls.

- Don't sign any documents with blank spaces that can be filled in later.

- Be wary of glitzy advertisements promising the end of all your financial woes.

- Never put your property in someone else's name — even "temporarily."

- Talk directly to your lender when negotiating new loan terms.

For questions or more information, visit the Financial Fraud Enforcement Task Force online at *www.stopfraud.gov*.

Cash in on college town savings

Follow one simple rule to find the best places to retire. Look for a college town. These great cities offer a quality of life for seniors that others — even in the same state — just can't match.

Cut your cost of living. Affordable real estate is up for grabs in many college towns where a good number of students and school employees live on tight budgets. Plus, you can easily supplement your income by renting a room, garage space, or basement apartment to a college student or first-year teacher.

Like to eat out? Restaurants in college towns cater to those with limited funds.

Feed your brain for free. Want to brush up on your French? Or rediscover American history? Take advantage of tuition waivers for older adults, and sign up for classes. If the school in your area doesn't offer waivers, talk with a professor about auditing a class, or check into continuing education courses specifically for seniors.

Catch a concert. Senior adults can take advantage of free or discounted tickets to stellar concerts or star-studded plays. College campuses attract performers from all over the world including singers, authors, musicians, and lecturers. Students majoring in dance, music, and theater also offer quality productions.

Grab a game. Throw on your team jersey and head to the ball fields. Universities offer plenty of action from football games to swim meets to tennis matches for little to no cost. If pumping iron or jogging on a treadmill is more your speed, many schools boast state-of-the-art athletic facilities, which may be open to the public for a fee.

Take a stroll or hop on a shuttle. Free or discounted transportation is a staple in and around college towns. Schools make it cheap and easy for students and visitors to walk or shuttle across campus or to commute from nearby cities onto school grounds.

Enjoy high-quality health care. Many large universities partner with teaching hospitals, giving you immediate access to new medications, specialty treatments, and clinical trials.

Surf the Web for savings

Figure out how much it would cost to retire in cities across the U.S. and overseas with these helpful online tools.

- Scroll down to the cost-of-living calculator on *www.bankrate.com/calculators.aspx* to compare everything from the price of a home to a T-bone steak in more than 300 cities.

- Visit *www.basiceconomicsecurity.org/gateway.aspx* to see how much money you need to cover your basics. Click on the Elder Index tab and create a free account.

- Enter "cost of living" in the search bar on *www.find thedata.org* to find the average price of food, health care, housing, tax expenses, and transportation in more than 600 cities.

- Click on the Quick Check tab on *www.homeequity advisor.org* to see if you're better off staying in your current home or moving.

- Check the prices of millions of homes around the globe on *www.houses.com.*

- Find locations where your income goes further with the cost-of-living calculator on *www.salary.com.*

Retire abroad and live like royalty

Would you like to live comfortably for a lot less money, while having the adventure of a lifetime? Then retiring overseas may be just what you need. More and more retirees are living abroad to stretch their retirement dollars with added perks — they live like kings and queens. Popular destinations include Spain, Thailand, Colombia, Croatia, Ecuador, Malaysia, and Panama.

Spend less, savor more. In most retirement-friendly countries, the overall cost of living can range from $1,100 to $3,500 a month. Believe it or not, that includes everything from health care, housing, and utilities to groceries, dining out, and entertainment. A comfortable rental house alone can run just $400 to $1,000 a month.

Live a life of luxury. Dream of never doing housework again? In Lake Atitlan, Guatemala, housekeeping services run about $4 to $10 a day. Tired of yard work? In some countries you can hire a weekly greenskeeper for $50 a month. Maybe a swanky beach resort suits your retirement style. Then check out the coastal condos of Salinas, Ecuador, where a couple can retire for $1,500 a month, including dinner out most nights.

Clip health care costs. Outside the United States, complete health coverage can go for as little as $60 to $100 a month. Prescriptions often cost a fraction of those in America. And a dental checkup and cleaning runs about $17 in Chiang Mai, Thailand. The downside is Medicare does not cover medical expenses overseas.

Know before you go. It's important to spend time in the country you're considering and get a feel for the lifestyle. Here are some things you should do before you make a decision.

- Research the climate, health care, visas, and infrastructure.

- Find out if there are other English speakers in the area.

- Decide if you feel comfortable living far away from family and friends.

- Explore how quickly you can get back to the United States.

- Check crime stats by visiting *www.nationmaster.com.*

If you think the expatriate life is for you, these websites can help guide you to the best places to live out your dream:

- *www.expatexchange.com*

- *www.internationalliving.com*

- *www.liveandinvestoverseas.com*

Modular homes offer surprising benefits

Looking to build your retirement home on that dreamy little mountain or lake lot? Be sure to consider a modular home.

These are not mobile homes, but permanently placed residences that simply begin life a little differently.

Sections are built at a factory, then transported and assembled on your land. You can choose from hundreds of stock floor plans then customize to your heart's content.

Modular homes generally cost less to build than traditional homes, and insurance companies, banks, and appraisers treat them just as they do site-built homes. Other advantages — modular homes are usually completed quickly and can be very energy efficient.

You cannot buy a modular home directly from the manufacturer but must go through a local retailer. To learn more, visit the National Association of Home Builders' website at *www.nahb.org*, and search for "Modular Home Building Council."

Save $2,400 with DIY move

Moving is stressful. But it doesn't have to be expensive. Let's say you pack up your two-bedroom house and move 1,200 miles away. You could pay almost $5,500 for a full-service move — including materials and labor — or you could cut that cost almost in half by using the money-saving tips below.

Don't take it with you. The amount of belongings you move and how much everything weighs is one of the biggest factors in calculating the cost of your move. It's also something you have a lot of control over. Your new motto should be "downsize." Go from the contents of a two-bedroom house — at about 7,500 pounds — to what will fit in a two-bedroom apartment — about 5,000 pounds — and you've just saved over $1,500.

Avoid the summer rush. Moving companies usually charge a premium rate for moves during their busy season — anywhere from $200 to over $1,000, depending on the size of your home. Time it so you relocate between September and May. While you're at it, schedule to avoid any price hikes over weekends and holidays.

Supply the materials. Start saving boxes as soon as you know you're moving. Visit the local recycling center and area liquor stores, drugstores, supermarkets, and offices. Even hospitals and shoe stores get deliveries in sturdy boxes. Best of all, they are free. If you get desperate, individuals and even some moving companies sell used boxes and wrapping paper at a discount.

Just don't fork over good money for Bubble Wrap. Save newspapers and use your own linens and clothing to wrap delicate items. A moving company could charge $200 and up for packing materials.

Box it up. It might cost you $400 to $500 to have the movers pack your two-bedroom house. Start early, do it yourself, and save. Be sure you understand the liabilities of self-packing, however. Contact your homeowner's insurance provider for details.

Mail it yourself. Use the post office to ship books and magazines at a special, inexpensive rate.

WARNING

Don't be a victim of moving fraud

Protect your belongings and your money during a move.

- Gather the names of at least three moving companies through referrals. Call friends and realtors you trust. Don't use a broker.

- Check each out online. Search by name in the U.S. Department of Transportation's Safety and Fitness Electronic Records System at *www.safersys.org*.

- Choose local companies if possible.

- Get written estimates in person.

- Don't sign any releases or any agreements that have blanks.

- Video your belongings before they are packed and record as much of the packing process as possible.

9 quick tips to lower your rent

Everyone needs to make their housing dollars stretch further these days. Especially since almost half of all apartment-dwellers make less than $20,000 a year. Shave a few dollars — or even more — off your monthly rent with these smart ideas.

Negotiate. Do your homework by checking out rents for other properties in your area. Use classifieds and websites like *www.rentometer.com*, *www.apartmentfinder.com*, *www.trulia.com*, *www.zillow.com*, and *www.rent.com*. If you find lower rates, ask if your landlord is willing to meet or beat the competition.

Provide a reference. Show your landlord you've been a good tenant in the past, are a trustworthy employee, or have stable ties to the community.

Bring in referrals. Ask if you can receive a discounted rent for referring other tenants.

Supply your own credit report. Application fees can nickel and dime you to death — especially if you apply to multiple properties. If your prospective landlord charges to run a credit check on you, sidestep that cost by pulling your own credit report for free and bringing in a copy.

And while you're at it, take a good look at your credit score. Do what you can to raise it before applying and use that to negotiate a lower rent.

Sign your lease during the off-season. Everybody wants to move during the summer and that can drive rental prices up. Get on a winter cycle and you may be able to move in for less.

Commit to a longer lease. Lock in today's rate for two or three years and protect yourself from rent hikes.

Offer rent in advance. If you have the cash, pay two or three months' rent upfront in exchange for a lower rate.

Agree to extra services. Volunteer to do yardwork, minor repairs, painting, or other maintenance tasks for a cut in rent.

Ask for perks. Sometimes paying a little more in rent saves you in the long run if you also get another benefit — like free parking, utilities included, or free access to a gym.

Protect your money from phony landlords

Renters beware of housing scams that will take your deposit as well as your rent payment and leave you homeless.

Extremely attractive fake listings are posted online by fake property managers or fake owners. Once the scammers have your money, they disappear. Here's how you can protect yourself.

- Make sure the property is not listed for sale. Look up the address online or ask a realtor to help out with a title search.

- Check that the property is not in foreclosure. Freddie Mac's listings are at *www.homesteps.com*.

- Demand to meet the owner or agent in person, at the property, and establish that they have the key to the door.

- Contact the real estate company, if one is advertised, to verify the listing and the agent.

- Never submit an online lease application with personal credit information until you've investigated the recipient.

- Don't hand over any money until the lease is final.

- Question any deal that sounds too good to be true. Compare listings in the area.

- Never wire money or send a check to someone you don't know.

- Be wary of listings with missing details or bogus-sounding information.

- Watch out for agents who will accept renters with poor credit.

Phones & Internet

Low-cost ways to connect

Save money with the right cellphone plan

There used to be just one phone company. Now you have to choose a carrier and a plan when you get a new cellphone. Pick the wrong plan, and you could be wasting money big time — or end up with a shockingly huge bill at the end of the month.

Wireless plans come in three major varieties. Here's an easy guide to help you select the right plan and save a bundle.

Standard contract. People who use their cellphones a lot — to call, text, and browse the Internet through a data plan — can probably control the costs best with a traditional plan.

Look for one that gives you unlimited calling, texting, and data usage. You're probably looking at spending at least $50 to $60 each month.

Also think about where you'll do most of your calling. Will you travel a lot, or do you usually stick close to home? A regional plan can save you money if you don't travel much, while a nationwide plan may give you free long-distance and roaming.

Monthly no-contract option. This choice lets you pay less each month for services similar to those in a contract plan, but you'll probably pay more for the actual cellphone. It may be a good option if you're not dead set on keeping up with the latest model of phone.

Prepaid minutes. This option may be the cheapest way to have a cellphone. It's big in Europe, and it could be right for you, especially if you are a light user of your cellphone and don't need a data plan.

Here's how it works. You pay ahead of time for a bucket of minutes, then use them as you need them. It costs more to talk on a per-minute basis than with a standard contract. You can find plans for as low as $10 for 30 minutes of service, and those minutes remain valid for 90 days. Spend more for more minutes, and they can remain available for up to a year.

Wireless carriers are realizing how popular prepaid plans have become, offering a greater variety of phones and even smartphones with prepaid minutes.

When it's time to switch plans, use the calculator available at *www.myrateplan.com*. It compares your current plan with others, looking for a deal that may save you money. You can also see coverage maps for the major wireless carriers to be sure you'll get good service at home.

Say 'No' to cellphone insurance

Cellphone insurance rarely saves you money. With the average cost of new cellphones shrinking, you may be surprised to learn you can usually replace even a smartphone for much less than you would pay in monthly insurance fees and deductibles.

You can get insurance either through your cellphone carrier — Sprint, AT&T, or Verizon, for example — or through a third party. Although plan details vary slightly, the numbers, amazingly, aren't all that different.

Looking at three independent insurers and four major carriers, monthly fees range from $5 to $9, which means you'll spend anywhere from $60 to around $100 a year just in fees. Add in a deductible — from $50 to $200 — and you've spent from $100 to $300 to replace a damaged or lost phone. The worst news is your replacement phone could be a different model or had a previous owner.

Filing a claim early into your policy is certainly the most cost-effective. But that's the problem with accidents — you never know when they are going to happen.

Here's a bright idea. Take the money you would pay monthly for insurance and build up a cellphone replacement emergency fund.

Avoid bill shock with overage alerts

Ten wireless service providers, including four of the biggest — AT&T, Sprint, Verizon Wireless, and T-Mobile — have voluntarily agreed to send out alerts when you near limits on data, phone minutes, or text messages. That means no more expensive surprises on your monthly bill.

Fight fraudulent mobile charges

Look at your cellphone bill — carefully. Is there a small charge listed for "web hosting," "calling plan," "mail server," or even "special services"? Are unexplained fees inching your wireless bill higher and higher? If so, you may be the victim of cellular cramming.

This fraudulent practice has affected landline customers for years — costing them millions of dollars. Now that 90 percent of Americans own a mobile phone, the scammers have moved their focus to this very lucrative market.

The Federal Communications Commission (FCC) defines cramming as "the practice of placing unauthorized, misleading, or deceptive charges on your telephone bill." What these con artists are hoping is that you will be so confused by your phone bill you won't notice or question these extra fees. And, unfortunately, that is quite often the case.

Just think, if you saw an unexplained 99 cents on your bill, you might not consider it worth investigating. But if scammers have billed that charge to 10,000 customers, they are making quite a haul.

Cellphones are particularly vulnerable to this type of attack because many third-party charges are legitimate. Besides scrutinizing your monthly cellphone bill, here are some other steps you can take to protect yourself from mobile cramming.

- Safeguard you cellphone number just like you do a credit card.

- Find out if your carrier allows direct-to-phone bill charges. Ask what protective measures they have in place.

- See if you can block third-party billing charges — as long as you understand how this might limit your phone use.

- Keep a record of all services you've authorized with your cellphone, and make sure you understand if there will be recurring charges.

- Think twice before engaging in risky behavior like entering a contest using your cellphone number or responding to text messages from unknown senders.

- Act immediately if you suspect fraudulent charges. Call your carrier, demand a refund, and follow up by filing a complaint with the FCC online at *www.fcc.gov/complaints*. Just be aware that currently, wireless carriers have no legal obligation to reimburse you for cramming charges.

Cancel your contract without penalty

It's easy enough to sign up with a cellphone carrier and take your new phone home right away. Trouble comes if you want to switch to a new carrier before your contract time is up.

One survey found nearly half of all cellphone customers would consider switching carriers if they didn't have to pay an early-termination fee. These fees can run to $350 depending on how much time is left in your contract term.

But there are ways to get out of your cellphone contract early, without paying huge fees — although your mobile provider probably won't tell you how.

Have a really good reason. If you're moving out of the country or to a place the carrier doesn't cover, or if you are a soldier being deployed, you may be able to end your contract with no fees.

Ask nicely, and keep asking. When you make your case to your wireless provider, you'll probably talk to a customer service representative over the phone. Don't accept the "no" you'll get from the first call. Instead, call back, ask for an executive in charge, and escalate the issue — whatever it takes to get the attention you need. You can even use social media — Twitter and Facebook, for example — to voice your concerns and try to resolve the issue.

Try for a trade. As much as you dislike your carrier, there's someone else out there eager to join up. You can sell the remainder of your contract to one of those folks through websites like *www.celltrade usa.com* and *www.trademycellular.com*. You'll probably pay a fee of around $20 to $25, but that's much less than an early-termination fee.

Switch to a smaller company. Small carriers and those categorized as mobile virtual network operators (MVNO) may be so eager to get your business, they'll buy out your contract if you sign up for a new plan. MVNOs, like Boost Mobile and Virgin Mobile, are good services to try.

If you can't get out of your contract, lower your bill by cutting text messaging, switching to the smallest data allowance, and reducing your number of minutes.

How to use a smartphone with no plan

Ditch your cellphone service and still make calls — for a lot less. You've probably heard of Skype, the free app that lets you use your phone, computer, or TV to talk, video, and instant message other people on Skype. It's been around since 2003 and has finally picked up some competition. All of these apps work even if you have no cellphone plan.

Fring. Using Voice over Internet Protocol (VoIP), fring allows free video calls, voice calls, live chat, and text messaging with other fring users. You can even conference call or video chat up to four people at once. You can call other mobile or landline numbers in the continental United States by purchasing credits at about 1 cent a minute. Higher rates apply for other areas. Download the app for free at *www.fring.com*.

Tango. Download this free app to your smartphone, tablet or PC, and keep in touch with other Tango users. You can call, text, video chat, share photos, and more — all for free. Check it out online at *www.tango.me*.

Talkatone. This free app lets you call, text, chat, and share with friends and family even if they don't have Talkatone installed. It claims to turn your iPhone, iPod Touch, iPad, or Android device into a true Internet phone, using any data connection, Wi-Fi, or 3G/4G and your Facebook or Google account. Find out more at *www.talkatone.com*.

TextNow. Go to *www.textnow.com* and get your very own dedicated phone number, which allows you to send and receive unlimited texts as well as talk to other TextNow users for free. All incoming calls are free, but you'll have to purchase minute packs to make calls to people who are not TextNow users.

Talk for less with free Google Voice

If all you know about Google is its search engine, hang on to your hat — introducing Google Voice. This free service allows you to consolidate all telephone communication through one number. It doesn't matter what kind of phone or carrier you use. One number — either an existing number or a new Google Voice number — will ring all your phones, retrieve voice mails online, block and screen callers, and even place conference calls.

Google Voice can save you money in a number of ways.

- If you have limited minutes on your cellphone — simply answer your cell calls on a landline.

- Drop your texting plan and let Google Voice route all text messages through your email.

- Take advantage of the lower Google Voice international rates.

Find out more online at *www.google.com/googlevoice/about.html*.

Talk, text, and surf for free

A completely free wireless plan? It's not just wishful thinking. FreedomPop, a startup backed by one of the founders of Skype, offers the first 100 percent free smartphone service — with 200 free anytime minutes, 500 free text messages, and 500 megabytes (MBs) of free data.

Initially, this service is only available using one phone, the HTC Evo Design which sells for $99, but look for other Android handsets to join the program soon.

Check them out online at *www.freedompop.com* where you can also upgrade to a paid version with unlimited voice and texting or learn about their free Internet service.

---

4 ways to hang up on high phone bills

You may not be ready to cut the cord on your landline phone completely. After all, there are advantages to staying connected this way. A landline:

- allows the convenience of having multiple phones within your home.

- is not dependent on a charged battery.

- should always get service inside your house.

- cannot get lost or stolen.

- never runs out of minutes.

That said, you can still explore ways to trim your phone bill down to size.

Make sure you have a recent statement in front of you. Read it carefully and try to highlight fees and services in question. Then do some online homework. See if your current provider offers any specials on their website. Make note of their prices for different plans. That will give you ammunition when talking to a service representative. Also, know what the competition will charge for comparable plans. Now give your phone company a call.

Go back to basics. There are no-frills plans available from most providers that are seldom advertised. But if you ask, you can often get cheap phone service that includes unlimited incoming calls and outgoing local calls only.

Don't double up on services. Are you paying for voicemail on your home phone every month while you have an answering machine hooked up to your phone? That overlapping service could run $120 or more a year. What other "extras" are you paying for and what can you do without? By the way, if you don't have an answering machine, buy one for $15 to $20 and save that monthly fee.

Ask for credit. Whenever something goes wrong, call the phone company immediately and ask for credit. This could be an interruption in your service, dropped calls, or a misdialed long-distance number. All these little charges can add up.

Put a stop to cramming. Just as your cellphone bill can get loaded with sneaky and unauthorized fees — called cramming — so can your landline phone bill. In fact, about 20 million landline customers are crammed every year. Read the story *Fight fraudulent mobile charges* earlier in this chapter for tips to protect yourself.

'Naked' DSL saves landline fees

Digital Subscriber Line (DSL) service is a very high-speed Internet connection that traditionally uses the same wires as your landline phone.

Naked DSL simply means DSL without phone service. It's also called standalone or dry loop, and it can be an attractive option if you choose to discontinue your regular landline phone service but still want Internet.

Certain providers offer naked DSL, but only in certain areas. Many times choosing this option will save you money since you aren't forced to pay for a service you aren't using.

Cut your phone cord and save with VoIP

Cancel your landline phone service completely if you're paying more than $30 a month and switch to Voice over Internet Protocol or VoIP.

This developing technology lets you make telephone calls using a high-speed Internet connection, like DSL, instead of normal phone lines. Depending on the service you choose — there are currently close to two dozen VoIP providers — you can call from a traditional phone, a special VoIP phone, or your computer.

It's an easy switch. Most systems supply an adapter that links your existing phone to the Internet. Simply plug it in and start dialing. Monthly fees for VoIP service range from $4.99 to $29.99 a month. For that, you should get unlimited minutes, free long distance, and most of the calling features you are used to.

Read the fine print. Before you commit to a service, find out about hidden fees and tricky disclaimers. Ask these questions:

- Is there a setup or activation charge?
- Are there cancellation fees?

- Can I keep my current phone number for free?

- What is my term commitment?

- Am I limited to calling only numbers using the same service?

- What features — like voicemail, caller ID, call waiting, conference calling, call forwarding, call blocking, speed dial, and directory assistance — are included?

In addition, spotty customer service can be a deal-breaker. Call the provider's help line and ask the representative a few questions just to see how they respond.

Prepare for emergencies. An especially attractive VoIP feature is its portability. Whether you are moving to a different city or traveling on vacation, you can take your number and your service with you.

That means, however, that the voice server follows you based on the IP address of the network you are using, not a geographic location of your phone. This can impact 911 service. You must know your provider's policy on 911 calls and update them on your location as needed.

Choose a provider. Here are just some of the top-ranking Voice over Internet Protocol providers.

ITP *www.itpvoip.com*   Skype *www.skype.com*

Lingo *www.lingo.com*   ViaTalk *www.viatalk.com*

Net2Phone *www.net2phone.com* Vonage *www.vonage.com*

PhonePower *www.phonepower.com*

Check your speed for free

Just how fast is your high-speed Internet? You're paying for that speed, but are you getting your money's worth? Find out with an online speed test.

First, understand that the amount you pay for Internet through cable, DSL, or satellite is usually based on a specific download speed. For instance, one cable Internet provider may offer 3 megabits per second (Mbps) for $20 a month, 6 Mbps for $50, and 105 Mbps for $80. The different speed levels are often called tiers.

If you use a cellular carrier, your bill is based on the amount of data you transfer — but that's different.

To test your speed, you can use a testing service through your ISP or visit one of these websites:

- *www.speedtest.net*

- *www.speakeasy.net*

- CNET Bandwidth Meter at *cnet.com/internet-speed-test*

- Consumer Broadband Test at *www.broadband.gov/qualitytest*

To get a good gauge of your Internet speed, take several measurements at different times of the day on weekends and weekdays.

Cap your Internet costs

You'll read about strategies for lowering the cost of cable television in the *Hobbies, Pastimes & Entertainment* chapter. These same tactics can also help reduce how much you pay for high-speed Internet.

- Compare providers to negotiate a better deal.

- Threaten to disconnect your service.

- Buy your own modem.

- Check your bill every month for errors or added charges.

- Bundle services like phone, cable, and Internet.

Here are some more tips that may help you save on your Internet bill.

Downgrade your speed. First, do a speed test on your computer —
this measures how fast you can upload and download data. See *Check
your speed for free*. Then find out from your Internet Service Provider
(ISP) the exact speed you are paying for. If you're not getting that
speed, they either need to charge you less or fix the problem.

Experts say most people don't need more than 5 to 15 megabits per
second (Mbps). If the results of your speed test are higher, there may
be room to negotiate with your ISP. Ask if there is a lower speed tier
you could switch to — for less money.

Find a free provider. There are cheap and free ISPs all over the
country. Use a service like All Free ISP at *www.all-free-isp.com* to
find alternate providers in your area.

Switch to dial-up. This solution isn't for everyone — if you download large documents, view lots of pictures, game online, or have a
need for speed while you browse the Internet, then dial-up is not for
you. But for basic service at a rock-bottom price, it can't be beat.

Use hotspots instead. You could cancel Internet service altogether
and rely on free Wi-Fi hotspots to surf and browse — if you don't
mind relocating to a public space. Restaurants, museums, libraries,
and cafes commonly offer public networks. Just remember, security
should be priority one.

- Use a good firewall and keep it up to date.

- Use strong passwords.

- Enable your Web browser security.

- Disable file sharing on your computer.

- Hide folders with sensitive data by marking them as "private."

- Encrypt any files you plan on using via a public network.

- Manually select a Wi-Fi network rather than letting your
  computer automatically select the first one it finds.

- Look for secure hotspots that require a password.
- Don't stay logged in to any online accounts longer than necessary.
- Avoid risky transactions like banking and shopping.

How to save money on almost everything

Here are five simple things you can say to a salesman that might save you money on everything from cars to Internet service.

- Don't be shy. Ask if they can offer a lower rate or price.
- Find out if there are extras, bonus items, or benefits you can get for that price.
- Do your homework and let them know a competitor is offering a lower price.
- Ask to speak to a manager or someone with the authority to lower the price.
- Let them know you'd rather not switch to another provider, buy from another retailer, or cancel a service — but you will if you have to. The trick here is to leave the door open for a counteroffer.

If all else fails, try saying nothing for a minute or two. Sometimes an uncomfortable silence will prompt a seller to make another — better — offer.

Squirrel away $500 a year by tethering

Use your smartphone as a modem to connect your home computer to the Internet and eliminate your Internet bill altogether. This linking process is called tethering, and it makes your smartphone's Internet connection available to other devices, like your laptop, desktop, or tablet.

You'll still pay for your phone's data plan, but tethering allows you to drop Internet service through a cable, DSL, or satellite Internet Service Provider (ISP). According to the Federal Communications Commission (FCC), the average household pays $450 to $555 a year for broadband Internet. That makes tethering a smart option.

In order to tether, connect your phone to your other device wirelessly, through Wi-Fi or Bluetooth, or use a USB cable — a faster, more secure, and less battery-draining option — and then access your phone's Internet connection and data plan.

Talk to your carrier. Before tethering for the first time, ask your cellphone carrier these questions.

- Does my cellular plan allow tethering? What does it cost?

- Do I have or need a wireless data plan? What are my data usage limits? How close am I to that limit?

- What other requirements and costs are there?

Check your systems. Read your smartphone manual to learn whether your phone and your computer's current operating system support USB, Bluetooth, or Wi-Fi tethering. If not, download a third-party tethering app such as PdaNet or EasyTether.

Free versions of these apps may only be free for a limited time or have restricted abilities. Other third-party apps may only be available if your phone has been rooted or jailbroken, processes that remove certain security measures and may void your warranty.

Tethering works on devices running Windows Vista, Windows 7, and Windows 8. Before tethering, make sure your computer won't download large updates during tethering that might push you over your wireless plan's data limits.

Connect to your personal hotspot. The process for tethering varies depending on which carrier and operating system your phone uses. To learn about USB, Bluetooth, or Wi-Fi tethering for your specific phone, check your smartphone's manual, visit your carrier's website, or contact your carrier for help.

Shopping
Buy for less, sell for more

Save a bundle on classy clothes

Before you buy that new skirt or sweater, consider this. You can
find gently used, name-brand items for slashed prices, if you know
where to look.

Shop upscale for a low price. Pay a visit to the thrift store in the
nicest part of your town for designer duds at discount prices. "I had
a friend in New York who did this and would talk about all the
high-end clothing available there at normal Goodwill prices," says
Melody Henderson, a thrift store regular. "I've shopped the Goodwill in a nicer part of Atlanta and found the same thing — really
nice, barely worn leather shoes for a low price."

Many thrift stores even offer coupons, senior discounts, and special
bargain days. Never hesitate to ask.

Cut your costs at consignment stores. These shops tend to be
pickier about the items they accept for resale, and shoppers reap
the benefits by finding like-new clothes at rock-bottom prices.

"I found a pair of $500 Manolo Blahnik pumps at a consignment store for $20," says Olga Bonilla. "They looked like they had never been worn and they fit me perfectly."

Don't forget, you can also make money by consigning your own gently used clothing. Ask each store for its policies.

Find deals at the dry cleaners. What happens to apparel abandoned at the dry cleaners? It's got to go somewhere. While some cleaners donate unclaimed items to charity, many sell them. One New York establishment sets prices at $5 to $20 per item, depending on the quality and brand name. Check with your neighborhood dry cleaner for bargains like these.

Browse, click, and save with online shopping

Online shopping can save you time and money in many ways. While websites like Amazon and Overstock offer thousands of apparel promotions, other sites provide even more value-packed offers and coupons.

- Every day, *www.bradsdeals.com* sorts through thousands of coupons and promotions, and then posts 100 or so of the best ones. Look for deals such as 45 percent off Dooney & Bourke totes or wool sweaters from Jos. A. Bank for $23 with free shipping.

- You can find local and national fashion deals on *www.tippr.com*, like stainless steel Superman cufflinks for $12 or a chain-link tote handbag for $23.

- Go to *www.dealoftheday.com* to discover the best fashion buys from online retailers like Amazon and eBay in one place.

- If you prefer designer attire, join *www.gilt.com, www.hautelook.com, www.ideeli.com*, or *www.ruelala.com* for free. These sites sell BCBG, Kate Spade, Badgley Mischka, and more for up to 75 percent off retail.

- For free shipping codes and online coupons to stores like Kohl's, Sears, and 4,000 others, try *www.freeshipping.org.*

Another great way to save when you're out shopping is with smartphone apps. Shopkick is a free location-based reward app. You earn "kicks" when you check in at participating retailers — like Macy's, Target, or JCPenney — or scan certain barcodes. It then sends an alert to your phone with the best deals in that store. And Coupon Sherpa delivers an assortment of mobile coupons for thousands of merchants, such as J.Crew and Dick's Sporting Goods, directly to your phone. Download either app from iTunes or Google Play.

Cash in at outlet malls

Premium outlet malls claim to offer shoppers current styles at 25 to 80 percent off retail prices. And you can certainly find some good deals. Just be familiar with the retail price of the item you're considering before buying. Sometimes a piece of merchandise is cheaper when it's on sale at a regular retailer than at an outlet mall.

For added savings, check an outlet mall's welcome center for coupon books, and ask about AAA and AARP discounts. Or look online ahead of time. Many outlets post printable coupons on their websites.

To track down an outlet store or mall anywhere in the U.S., visit *www.outletlocator.com* for a complete listing.

Clean out your closet for cash

Consigning your clothes to make extra cash is not a new concept. But doing it via the Internet is. Online consignment stores pop up regularly, and offer more ways to cash in on garments you no longer wear. Each site operates a little differently, so make sure to read the fine print. One perk they all have in common — sellers receive free shipping labels or packages.

- *www.tradesy.com* — This site will accept items from affordably priced labels such as Gap and Banana Republic. Rather than ship your items to Tradesy, you upload photos onto its online catalog. If your clothing sells, the company will send you a free shipping packet to mail directly to the buyer. Tradesy keeps only 9 percent of the sale price.

- *www.liketwice.com* — Unlike most consignment stores, Twice will pay for your items up front. Mail in your garments and wait for them to make you an offer. Twice prefers high-end brands like Ann Taylor and Jones New York.

- *www.threadflip.com* — Threadflip accepts just about any brand from Nike to Chanel. Complete a short order form and send in your garments. The company will photograph and price your merchandise. You make 60 percent of the sale.

- *www.shoprdr.com* — Consign your luxury brand items like Fendi and Prada on Rodeo Drive Resale. Ship your outfits to them and they'll clean, photograph, and upload the information. The percentage you receive depends on the item.

- *www.recycleyourfashions.com* — List the items you want to consign on their online form and email it to Recycle Your Fashions. Upon approval, ship your items to them and earn 50 percent of the final selling price.

4 ways to stop wasting money

Impulse buying is a way of life for some folks — and an easy way to throw away thousands of dollars over time. Curb your urge to splurge with these tips.

- Shop with cash. If you carry credit cards, debit cards, or a checkbook, you're less likely to stick to your budget and more likely to spend extra money.

- When a website asks if you want it to store your credit card information for future use, decline the offer. Instead, enter your credit card number each time you make a purchase. This buys you a little extra time to reconsider.

- Wait 24 hours before finalizing a purchase, especially if the item costs more than you had planned. Give yourself time to think it over.

- Shop when your time is limited. The less time you have to shop, the less time you have to browse and buy impulsively.

Save $44 with beauty dupes and deals

Beat the high price of department store makeup by shopping for online deals and duplicate products, or dupes as they're known in the beauty world. You can stock up on eye shadow, lipstick, and foundation at a fraction of the price.

Look for drugstore doubles. Why pay high prices for prestige cosmetics when drugstores and mass retailers offer copycats for less? You can easily compare makeup lines online by searching for "drugstore dupes." For example, a Nars blush costs $28. But Milani sells a comparable blush for $9 at Walgreens — a savings of $19.

A beauty blogger on the popular Disney site *www.babble.com* takes pricey brands and stacks them side-by-side with e.l.f. products. Take Stila's liquid eyeliner — it costs $20. A similar eyeliner by e.l.f. sells for $1 to $4 at Target and Wal-Mart. You save about $19. In fact, most e.l.f. cosmetics sell for under $5.

Discover online deals. Mass retailers like Wal-Mart and Target offer beauty bargains online. Occasionally, these bargains include freebies. Go to *www.walmart.com* and type "Free Samples" in the search bar. Or try *www.targetsavers.com* and search for cosmetic coupons and discounts.

Also visit *www.cvs.com* and click on "Deals." You may find cosmetics on clearance like Aero Minerale Hydrating Mineral Foundation marked down 40 percent from $14.99 to $8.99, a savings of $6.

Join the club. Sign up for emails and text alerts from cosmetic companies. Earn rewards for free samples, and learn about special offers and giveaways.

Try *www.sephora.com* and click on "Beauty Insider." Or go to *www.ulta.com* and sign up for Ulta Rewards. You can also visit your favorite makeup manufacturer online.

WARNING

Save your money and your health

Mercury is toxic. Unfortunately, it's also an ingredient in skin lighteners and anti-aging products. These creams are man-ufactured abroad and sold illegally in the United States, often in Asian, Latino, African, or Middle Eastern shops. To protect yourself, follow these tips from the U.S. Food and Drug Administration.

- Don't buy skin care products without a label or a list of ingredients.

- Avoid products labeled in languages other than English.

- Look for the words "calomel," "mercury," "mercuric," "mercurio," or "mercurous chloride" on labels. If you see any of these, stop using the product immedi-ately. Wash the exposed area thoroughly and call your doctor. Or contact the Poison Control Center at 800-222-1222.

- Seal any creams that may contain mercury in a bag or leak-proof container. Ask your local environmen-tal agency how to dispose of it.

Cut down the high cost of haircuts

People need haircuts, but they don't need to pay extravagant prices for them. Slash your haircut costs with these slick ideas.

Go to an at-home stylist. With low overhead costs, a stylist who works from home can pass along her savings to you. Just make sure she is professionally trained.

Ask about free trims. Make your haircut last longer with a free trim for your bangs. Most salons offer free trims between full haircuts. And they only take a few minutes.

Try a trainee. A stylist-in-training can offer you a great haircut at a discounted price. They work under the supervision of an experienced stylist. Check with larger salons in your area, and ask about their trainees.

Save a few bucks at beauty school. Search for a cosmetology school near you, and ask about their prices. Trained teachers supervise students, and you reap the savings.

At one beauty school, a cut by a first-year student costs $12. And a cut with a second-year student is $15. Compared to the standard $60 for a wash, cut, and blow-dry at a salon, that's a savings of $45 to $48.

Keep it simple. If you sport a simple haircut, going to a chain or mall salon will save you a bundle. Most charge around $20 for a wash, cut, and dry. Or ask your stylist for a cut that will grow out well. You might be able to go three months without another cut.

Keep your color longer for less

Don't let the high price of hair coloring get you down. Try these simple at-home tips to extend your hair color for less.

- Try the product Just for Men. It costs half as much as women's products, and the color lasts twice as long.

- Make your color last longer with a clear glaze treatment. You can purchase these at a drugstore and do the treatment at home. Glazes help to seal in color.

- Color your own roots between highlight treatments.

"I had my roots done one time at a salon for $80," says Hannah Rivers. "Now I use a root touch-up I buy at the drugstore for around $6. I would rather splurge at the salon on highlights and save $74 by doing my own roots."

Talk your way to a cheaper gym membership

Joining a gym gives you access to oodles of expensive equipment, classes, maybe even a swimming pool. Don't pay top dollar just to belong when there are so many ways to get a better deal.

Get with a group. Ask your fellow employees about negotiating to get a group discount, say 10 to 20 percent off membership price. Gold's Gym offers a group discount to 10 or more coworkers who sign up together.

And Bally Total Fitness offers a 33 percent discount as a friends-and-family deal if you mention a friend or relative who is a member. If you're already a member of a gym, ask about getting a price reduction or free month for bringing in a friend to sign up.

Pay in advance. Signing a contract to pay a fee every month locks you in for a certain length of time. Instead, offer to pay in advance for several months. You may be able to get a discount of around 20 percent off, plus avoid an initiation fee.

If your gym won't make this deal, check out offers at warehouse clubs like Costco. Customers recently bought a two-year membership to

24-Hour Fitness for $320. That comes to $13 per month — well below the usual price of $37 a month paid in monthly installments.

Shop around, then negotiate. Don't start with the gym you want to join. First check out the facilities of similar gyms in town and get their prices. Use this information as a bargaining tool to get the price you want at the fitness center you're interested in.

During your negotiations, point out the features of an all-inclusive membership that you won't be using, such as free childcare or time in a tanning bed. Then offer to pay less for a membership that doesn't include those extras.

Negotiating may work better during the slow season, when gyms are starving for new members. You might have a harder time getting what you want around New Year's, when people make resolutions to get into shape. And some gyms have monthly goals for attracting new members, so try at the end of the month.

Save $250 buying used exercise bike

Never pay full retail price for gym equipment. You can score great deals on used equipment with just a little searching.

First you need to decide exactly what equipment you want. Test out various treadmills, stationary bikes, all-in-one weight machines, and more during a free trial week at your local gym.

Next, look for a similar model at a used sporting goods store, such as Play It Again Sports or 2nd Time Sports. These chains sell new and used equipment and clothing for nearly any activity you want to try. You can also find deals online from secondhand sellers through Craigslist and eBay.

For example, an Atlanta-area Craigslist seller recently offered a Schwinn Airdyne AD4 upright exercise bike "in perfect condition" for $499. That model sold new for $750, so some lucky buyer could easily save $250 buying used.

Get cash for your used gadgets

You just got a new laptop for Christmas, but you hate for your old laptop to just gather dust. You could place an ad in the newspaper or eBay, but why do all that work when someone else will do it for you.

Visit *www.wireflytradeins.com* to see what your old gadget is worth. They take laptops, monitors, e-readers, mice, tablets, HDTVs, cameras, camcorders, MP3 players, cellphones, and more — and they even take damaged or not working items. Search for your product by clicking on the photo. Next, choose the manufacturer. If you don't see your model number, click on the "Show All Models" button.

Click on your gadget when you find it, answer any questions you're asked, and you'll get a cash offer. If you accept the offer, click on "Accept" and print their shipping label. Wireflytradeins covers the cost of shipping your gadget to them. After they receive your gadget and appraise it, they'll send a confirmation email. You can expect payment two to four weeks later. Choose to be paid cash, receive payment through PayPal, or donate the money to charity.

Another site that pays for gadgets is NextWorth. NextWorth offers an online option for cash, or you can visit one of their 1,500 retail partners and get a gift certificate for the store where you trade in your gadget. Visit *www.nextworth.com* to find participating stores.

You can also try *www.amazon.com* where you can get an Amazon gift certificate in exchange for a wide array of gadgets, including a few desktops. Other good sites to check include *www.radioshack tradeandsave.com*, *www.gazelle.com*, and *www.gamestop.com*. Just be sure to read each site's explanations and Frequently Asked Questions carefully to make sure you get what you expect.

4 smart things to do with your old cellphone

Don't add to the 50 million tons of electronic waste disposed of each year. When it's time to replace your cellphone, consider these options.

Sell it. Many phones have resale value as long as they are in good condition. You can sell it yourself to another individual or use a website like *www.SellCell.com* to compare online buyers. Even go through a major carrier like Sprint, Verizon, T-Mobile, AT&T, or Apple. You may get money or a trade-in value for it.

Swap it. Visit the Amazon trade-in program at *www.amazon.com*. Click on "Help," then "Ordering" under "Topics," and you'll see "Amazon Trade-In Program." Search the website for your model to see how much it's worth. Amazon will pay for the shipping, and you get the credit.

Or visit Best Buy online at *www.bestbuy.com* and look under "Services" for "Trade-In Center." Find an estimate of your phone's value, mail it to their Center, and within seven days, you'll receive a gift card in the mail, good for anything in the store or online.

Recycle it. Manufacturers and retailers try to make it easy to keep used electronics out of landfills. Companies like Sprint, Samsung, Staples, Dell, LG, Nokia, and Best Buy all offer either in-store or mail-in recycling options.

Donate it. Cell Phones for Soldiers is a nonprofit organization that recycles millions of cellphones and uses the proceeds to purchase calling cards for U.S. troops stationed overseas. Find out more about this program at *www.cellphonesforsoldiers.com*.

Price compare for big savings

Before you make any big purchase, do a little research online, so you'll know what you should pay. Use these trusted price-comparison websites, even if you plan on purchasing locally.

- Bizrate.com. You'll find reviews of the product you're shopping for along with reliable price-comparison information.

- PriceGrabber.com. This site lets you compare current prices and see an item's price history over the past six months.

- Dealio.com. At this site, you can compare prices on a specific item and find coupons and deals for your purchase.

- Nextag.com. Along with price comparisons, this site lets you set up alerts so you'll know when the price drops on the item you want to buy.

Spend less for a computer

Here are a few bright ideas for saving money the next time you go computer shopping.

Buy refurbished. Instead of paying big bucks for a brand new, state-of-the-art computer system, look for a refurbished model. You could save anywhere from 5 to 30 percent off the retail price.

These not-quite-new or used computers have been restored to like-new working condition. Your best bet is to get them directly from manufacturers. In many cases, these are computers returned by customers, previously leased systems, or those used as store models. Here's where to find refurbished computers online. Search on the word "refurbished" or "used," and you should be able to locate the manufacturer's outlet store.

- Dell — *www.dell.com*

- HP — *www.hp.com*

- IBM — *www.ibm.com*

Don't pay for an extended warranty. The experts at *Consumer Reports*, as well as other respected shopping gurus, say extended warranties and service contracts on computers are a waste of money. Most products won't break during the covered period, and repair costs are usually less than the price of the contract. Put that money into a computer repair or replacement fund, instead.

Buy a USB hub. Just because you don't have enough USB ports on your computer to plug in all your peripherals — printers, scanners, keyboards, monitors, and more — doesn't mean you need a new, fancier computer. Spend as little as $5 for a USB hub that expands a single USB port into several.

Don't buy a system repair disc. This is something you can make at home for free — and you should, since it will help fix significant problems your computer might develop with its operating system. Just don't pay extra money at the store for one.

Don't pay retail for software

Hardware isn't the only expense you'll have when you're loading up your technology closet. Software can set you back more than a few pennies. If you can't find freeware from a trusted source like cnet.com, check out the prices on these websites:

- SoftwareMedia.com
- NewEgg.com
- BitsDuJour.com
- TheSoftwareClub.com

4 ways to help your computer last

You can't afford a new PC yet, but your old computer is outdated and painfully slow. Try tips like these to help speed up your computer and keep it alive for longer.

Become a power updater. Check weekly or monthly for the latest software updates, drivers, and patches for Windows and for each of your most crucial programs. If you can't set up automatic updating for a program, visit the support section of the manufacturer's website to get updates.

Create a Windows Restore Point before installing each update just in case anything goes wrong.

Defend your digital turf. Use security software to regularly scan for viruses, spyware, and other malware, and keep that security software up to date.

Offload files. Move the documents, pictures, video, and other files you've created from your internal hard drive to an external hard drive. This may ease the load on your computer.

Keep it simple. Your PC can only stand so many extra toolbars, gadgets, and other unwanted programs, so restrict the ability to install them. You can do this with tools like security software and parental controls.

Meanwhile, play it safe. Start thinking about how to get the best deal on a new computer, and be sure to back up your important files regularly on an external hard drive — just in case your computer suddenly gives out.

3 smart tricks to save printer ink

Ounce for ounce, printer ink is more expensive than gasoline, vodka, or Chanel No. 5 perfume, according to recent information from Nuesion.com and Ninemsn.com. Fortunately, you can start using even less ink with these tips.

Remove Web ads and more. When you print a Web page, you don't want to print the ads, banners, and other ink-wasters. To fix this, add an item called a bookmarklet to your Bookmarks toolbar. A bookmarklet is a tiny program in a bookmark that performs tasks that help you when surfing and searching the Web.

For example, a free bookmarklet called Readability sweeps away ads and other unwanted items so you're only left with what you want to print. You can even choose to delete all pictures or automatically create footnotes showing the URL for each link. Visit *www.readability.com* for this bookmarklet.

Other bookmarklets or programs let you choose specifically what to remove or may offer options that help squeeze more words into a page than Readability can. Check out these options.

- PrintWhatYouLike at *www.printwhatyoulike.com*

- PrintFriendly at *www.printfriendly.com*

- Printliminator at *www.css-tricks.com/examples/ThePrintliminator*

Change your settings. Many inkjet printers use more than just black ink to print black text and graphics. They print color ink underneath to make a darker black. When you print a document in black and white, set your printer to grayscale. That tells the printer to use only black ink to print in black, which can save a surprising amount of ink.

Make a digital copy. Instead of sending the document to your printer to convert to hard copy, make a PDF (portable document format) instead. A "Print to PDF" program sends a copy of the document to a digital file. The PDF looks like the printed file would, but it stays on your computer. Save the PDF somewhere.

on your computer and you can read the document whenever you want and print out a hard copy if you need it.

Because a PDF can be read on any computer that has the free Acrobat Reader program installed, you can also take the document with you on a flash drive or send it as an email attachment. Free PDF-creation programs include:

- CutePDF at *www.cutepdf.com*

- doPDF at *www.dopdf.com*

- Adobe Reader at *www.acrobat.com*

Save money with a Wi-Fi only tablet

Almost 90 percent of tablet owners connect to the Internet through Wi-Fi instead of a cellular service, one survey found. This may be a smart, budget-friendly decision.

Save when you buy. You can connect a tablet to the Internet in two ways, through a Wi-Fi connection or through a 3G or 4G cellular connection. Tablets that only feature Wi-Fi capability may cost up to $130 less than tablets that also offer a 3G/4G connection. Wi-Fi only tablets also tend to have a longer battery life, which will save replacement costs.

Don't pay to connect. Your Wi-Fi connection may come from a private home Wi-Fi network or a publicly available network, sometimes called a hotspot. You'll get Wi-Fi service only when you are within the range of one of these and connected to it.

At home, you probably already pay a monthly fee to your Internet Service Provider (ISP) for an Internet connection. If you also have a home Wi-Fi network, adding your tablet to that network won't cost anything. Many public Wi-Fi networks are free. To access others, you'll have to pay a fee — hourly, daily, weekly, or even monthly.

Connecting through a 3G/4G cellular service is different. A cellphone carrier — like Sprint, AT&T, or Verizon — provides your connection to the Internet, so it doesn't matter if you're in an area where Wi-Fi is available. But you will depend on a cellular signal, which can be spotty in some areas.

You'll pay a monthly fee for having your tablet on a cellular plan plus a flat rate for the amount of data you use while connected. Depending on your carrier and your choice of plans, a cellular connection can cost a little or a lot. Check all the options your carrier offers for your particular tablet.

Slash the price tag on home appliances

Never pay retail for an appliance. Search out these options, and pick up a stove or fridge for a steal.

Snatch a scratched appliance. If you want lots of value for a low price, check out a scratch-and-dent store. An appliance with a little wear and tear on the outside can still work just fine. To find a store near you, call your local appliance center or look for a Sears outlet.

Seek out reconditioned items. Look for dealers that specialize in "certified factory refurbished" appliances. Though often used, their merchandise must be in good working condition, and most carry warranties. Manufacturers are in the refurbished game, too. Oreck, for example, offers many factory reconditioned products on their website at savings of up to $100 off their regular prices.

Scan the classifieds. Find new and used appliances in print and online want ads, including Craigslist at *www.craigslist.org*. Builders and architects often list brand new items here at a fraction of the cost. But beware. Some sellers deal in stolen goods. Be ready to walk away if you're suspicious.

Snag a deal online. Believe it or not, Amazon provides a larger selection of appliances for less than brick-and-mortar retailers like

Sears and Home Depot. Another online retailer, Abt at *www.abt.com*, offers great prices. Look for free shipping deals, and don't be afraid to ask for a better price via email, live chat, or by calling customer service.

---

3 ways to pocket extra cash

- Skip the fancy features like eco-cycles and vent-blockage indicators on washers and dryers. None of them save you a significant amount of money, and many don't live up to their claims. Before buying, research reviews online and in *Consumer Reports* and *Consumers Digest* for the most cost-effective extras.

- Say no to extended warranties. Purchase items with a credit card that offers free warranty protection, instead. Many often double the manufacturer's warranty at no extra charge.

- Remember to mail in your rebate. Appliance rebates usually amount to a big chunk of change.

Bring new life to old appliances

Don't give up on an appliance when it is past its prime. Here are two bright ideas that may keep it part of the family for years to come.

Fix it yourself. When your blender's on the blink or your fridge is on the fritz, give an online search a shot. Describe what's wrong in the search bar, and try including and excluding the model number. You may find a simple fix, a recall, or an offer for a free repair. You can also call the manufacturer's help line for guidance in diagnosing and even fixing the problem. Some companies will walk you through a repair over the phone for free.

Give it a new look. Repaint an aging appliance yourself with Thomas' Liquid Stainless Steel. Various kits sell for $25 to $80 at *www.liquidstainlesssteel.com*. Rust-Oleum appliance paint — roll-on or spray — is available in various colors for $4 to $15 at Home Depot. Both are inexpensive ways to save a trustworthy item.

Wondering if it's time for a replacement? Here's the rule of thumb — if the repair will cost more than half the price of a new model, replace it. Another factor to consider is age. If the appliance is more than six to eight years old, it might be time to part ways.

Fight back against fraudulent contractors

Summer brings with it bright flowers, warm breezes, and corrupt contractors. Scam artists and unscrupulous repairmen cruise neighborhoods, most often in summer, looking for people to rip off. Don't become one of their victims.

Close the door on cold calls. Never, ever hire someone who shows up at your door looking for work. Ask friends, neighbors, and other trustworthy people for recommendations when you need something fixed. You can also look for highly rated repair people on websites like *www.angieslist.com*, *www.homeadvisor.com*, *www.redbeacon.com*, and *www.kudzu.com*.

Call at least three contractors and have each one give you a bid in writing. Have a neighbor or friend at home with you when interviewing contractors if you live alone. Ask them for at least three references, and call each one before making a choice.

Space out payments. Divide the total cost of the job into three or more payments and space them out. Give your contractor the first payment upfront but link the others to finishing specific stages of the project. On a bathroom remodel, for instance, you might agree to give him the next installment once he finishes tiling the shower. Don't release the final payment until all of the work is finished and has passed any required inspections.

Be careful about cash. Here's a common scam — someone pulls up in a truck and says he noticed a few shingles had peeled off your roof. He offers to fix them for you, but he'll need some cash to pick up the supplies. You hand him a few bills, and he leaves to buy materials. Except he never comes back.

It happens all too often. Resist the urge to hand a contractor cash to buy the supplies for your project. Contractors should be willing to purchase those themselves. If yours balks, offer to meet him at the store, buy what he needs, and have the store deliver the goods to your home on the day of the job.

Just say no to financing. Don't let a contractor "help" you arrange financing for your home improvement project. He may claim he knows someone who can get you a low-interest loan, but he may steer you to a friend of his who will sign you up for a high-interest home equity loan. Once his friend pays him a cut, you may never see your contractor again.

Fix it yourself for a fraction of the cost

You want an experienced professional to do electrical work or roof repair, but why not try your own hand at simple jobs? You'll save lots of money and learn something useful at the same time. Best of all, you can get the know-how you need for free.

Head to the hardware store. "Go to any home improvement or hardware store and start asking questions," advises single home-owner Melanie Drew. "That's how I learned almost everything I know about home repair." Local stores like Ace, as well as national chains such as Lowe's and Home Depot, hire experienced contractors to staff their aisles and help customers. "Grab someone," Melanie says. "Explain what you're trying to fix. Ask him to show you what you need and tell you how to do it."

Take a free class. Many home improvement stores offer free do-it-yourself classes on all types of projects. Some classes are even geared toward women. You can learn firsthand how to install a kitchen sink, tile a floor, or refinish cabinets. Call nearby stores to learn about upcoming workshops.

Watch an expert. Have a computer and an Internet connection? Let expert videos teach you how to replace a broken tile or fix a leaky faucet. Type a question into a search engine such as *www.google.com*, or into a website that specializes in videos such as *www.youtube.com*.

"I could not for the life of me figure out how to replace the leaky flush valve inside my toilet," says Melanie. "And the instructions on the replacement part didn't help." So she turned to YouTube. "I typed a phrase like 'replace flush valve Kohler Cimarron toilet' into the YouTube search box," she explains. "I found a video made by a plumber that showed me exactly what to do."

Online videos and how-to articles can also give you a feel for how easy or complex the job will be, helping you decide whether to tackle it yourself or hire a professional.

Hit the books. Don't forget your local library. Check out a do-it-yourself repair guide for a week or two. Can't find what you need at the library? Flip through the how-to books for sale at a home improvement store, or stand in the "Home improvement" section of any bookstore and read up on your project.

3 ways to cut the cost of any project

Forget about spending a fortune on brand-new fixtures, tools, and supplies. You can find almost everything you need for a home improvement project for less.

- Rent, don't buy, an expensive tool if you only need it one time. You could spend upward of $300 buying a pressure washer to clean your siding, or rent one for less than $70.

- Scan the barcode on lighting and other fixtures with a free application such as RedLaser, Amazon, or PriceGrabber. Download it to your smartphone and scan the item's barcode to see what it costs at other stores.

- Call local plumbers before you buy a new sink or toilet. They may have gently used ones they removed when clients upgraded their baths, and they may be willing to sell them at a deep discount. The same goes for cabinet makers and contractors who install kitchen cabinets.

Decorate with designer furniture for less

Have you ever entered a model home and dreamt of owning the designer decor? If your answer is yes, you can stop dreaming. Once a model home is sold, home stagers — the decorators that carefully pick and place each piece of furniture — sell their inventory at reduced prices.

While you can find used furniture deals at yard sales, thrift stores, and Craigslist, nothing beats these name-brand goods. To find out where to look, pull up a chair and check out these savvy shopping options that give you more bang for your buck.

First, check out the furniture in model homes in your area. If you spot a piece you can't live without, talk to the agent. He or she may be able tell you if the item will be for sale or up for auction once the model home is sold.

Another avenue for designer furnishings is a clearance center like CORT. The company, with more than 60 locations across the U.S., sells model home and previously rented furniture for a steal. You can save up to 70 percent off the retail price of bedroom suites, dining room sets, living room furniture, and individual pieces.

Model Home Furniture Clearance Center based in Montgomery County, Md., also sells furniture, accessories, and artwork from upscale model homes for up to 75 percent off the retail price.

You can find additional clearance centers across the country like Coaster Fine Furniture in Arizona and Jugo Designs in Michigan and California. Check your yellow pages or online for stores in your area. And make your dream for designer decor a reality.

WARNING

Don't let the bed bugs bite

Buying used furniture will save you a bundle. Getting rid of bed bugs will not. As you shop at yard sales and thrift stores, use these safety tips. And keep in mind, bed bugs will infest wood pieces, too, not just upholstery.

- Carry a flashlight, latex gloves, and magnifying glass with you.

- Run a credit card or index card through cracks, grooves, joints, and seams. With gloves on, inspect the edge of the card with your fingers. Look for tiny, six-legged oval bugs, molted skins, or dark red stains.

- Shine a light on nail and screw holes, and behind loose paint on a painted piece of furniture.

Update your decor with simple savings

A new rug or color can revitalize any room. Decorate your home with these cost-saving deals.

- Have a carpet remnant bound for a bargain area rug. Ask the carpet store to refer you to someone who can do the job.

- Look for home-decorating deals like the one Cassie Everett found on *www.groupon.com.* "I went on the Rugs USA website and found a colorful, outdoor rug for my porch for $174," says Cassie. "Then I purchased a $75 voucher for $170 worth of rugs on Groupon and saved 55 percent off the price of the rug."

- Create a custom color with leftover paint. Stick to similar shades, pour them into one container, and add a fresh coat to any room.

- To give kitchen and bathroom cabinets a facelift, paint them. Then, replace the old hardware with inexpensive brushed nickel fixtures.

Design your landscape for less

Beautify your yard with a quality plan for little or no cost.

- Call the colleges and universities near you, and ask if they have a landscape design or horticulture program. You may be able to hire a student designer at a reduced cost.

- Sketch out your own ideas. Hire a landscape designer to look over them and make suggestions or corrections. You'll spend a fraction of the cost of having a whole plan drawn from scratch.

- Snag free landscape designs from the Arbor Day Foundation at *www.arborday.org/trees/landscapedesign*. Plans range from a traditional knot garden to a flowering woods edge.

3 surprising ways to find free plants

It's easy to spend thousands of dollars cultivating a lush yard full of shrubs and flowers. It's also easier than you think to get that same yard for less.

Rescue. There's plenty of greenery looking for a good home — if you're not too picky about using a certain variety.

- Call a funeral home and offer to pick up plants left by families. You'll be doing the funeral director a favor.

- Stop by your local nursery and ask if you can carry away tired, sad plants that haven't been sold.

- When you see landscaping crews at work along the road or in a retail display, offer to cart away the plants being removed.

- Look for baby plants that sprout up in your garden all on their own that you can transplant.

Swap. Trading plants and seeds with other gardeners is a great way to add variety to your landscape without spending a dime. Contact your local Master Gardener Program or check online swap sites like *www.freecycle.org* and *www.craigslist.org*. Follow these basic rules at a plant or produce swap so other gardeners will be happy to share with you again next time.

- Alert the swap organizer that you are planning to come so she can make space.

- Find out if the swap has basic rules for participation. Some groups assign monetary values to different types of plants or produce to encourage fair trades.

- Prepare plants by potting them and labeling with genus and species names.

- Feel free to bring seeds, bulbs, and tubers to trade, but be sure they're in plastic bags with labels.

- Bring your own reusable bags or boxes to carry items home.

- Don't remove plants from another gardener's table without asking if he would like to make a trade.

Forage. Native plants, or the varieties that grow wild in your area, have a good chance of surviving a move to your yard. But follow these rules for foraging when you gather free-growing plants.

- Ask before you take plants or seeds from private property, even if it's clear the plants are being removed for construction.

- Don't take an entire group of wild plants. Leave a few so they can grow back.

- Never take a rare or endangered species.

- If you're gathering wildflower seeds, spread a few where you found them so they can continue growing.

Finally, be sure you have the knowledge to transplant successfully. If you don't know how to deal with a certain variety, you may kill it rather than save it.

Spend less to feel safe at home

Home security systems aren't only for the rich and famous. You don't have to spend a lot of money on one, and the few dollars you may spend can offset the terrible price of a theft or break-in.

According to the FBI, in 2010 there were 1.4 million home burglaries, with the average victim suffering a loss of more than $2,000.

Ask a company to install an alarm system, and you could pay a hefty $800 or more. Add to that the cost of monitoring — around $30 to $40 a month — and you could be throwing away a big chunk of your retirement budget.

But here's a cost-cutting idea which will still protect you and your home. Install your own alarm system for under $300. In fact, some home security products, like components of the GE Choice Alert Wireless Home Security System, run as low as $35. You can find many brands at home improvement stores like Lowe's and Home Depot, or online at *www.smarthome.com* or *www.home securitystore.com*.

When you install your own system, you have two monitoring options. You can pay a company like Alarm Relay about $9 a month plus a $35 start-up fee. Find the company online at *www.alarmrelay.com*. Or monitor the system yourself, and save the monthly fee entirely. This is simple and effective when you're at home, but requires you to control, monitor, and respond to the system via your computer or smartphone when you're away.

A home security system offers a couple of additional benefits. It will increase the value of your home and could save you up to 20 percent on home insurance.

Smart ways to save on personal safety

More than a third of adults over age 65 will fall every year, according to the Centers for Disease Control and Prevention. And a third of those falls will happen at home. But you can do something about your personal safety by checking into these value-packed solutions.

Carry a PERS. Personal Emergency Response Systems allow you to contact one or more preselected emergency numbers simply by pressing a button. Wear the transmitter around your neck or wrist, clip it to your belt, or keep it in your pocket. Charges for equipment and services usually include a setup fee — anywhere from $50 to $200 — and a monitoring fee of $30 to $60 a month.

When shopping for a PERS, look for a company that does not require a contract and offers free repairs on all equipment.

Set up security cameras. One way to keep an eye on an elderly parent is with indoor security cameras. Purchase two at a store like Home Depot, for instance, for just $250, and install them yourself. Then monitor your loved one for free from a computer, smartphone, or tablet. Compared to a company like Xfinity, which charges a whopping $399 installation fee and $49.95 a month for monitoring, DIY installation will save you a bundle.

Make a call. The truth is, just having a smartphone may save your life or the life of an older parent. Carry it with you at all times — whether you're in the kitchen or on the go — and you can call someone for assistance, even if you fall. Emergency response apps for iPhones and Androids can make this even easier by placing calls, sending texts, and dispatching emergency medical help with a single press of a button.

Travel

See the world on a shoestring budget

Relax with cut-rate hotel deals

Never pay full price for a hotel room. If you're willing to bid, barter, or simply do a little homework, you can reserve a hotel room for a reduced rate.

Solicit a senior discount. Some hotel chains offer discounts for AARP members or adults ages 60 and over. Before completing a reservation, ask.

Book off-season. You can find deals for a steal before or after peak travel season. But beware. Off-season travel can mean bad weather and no amenities. Do a little research in advance.

Reserve against type. Book a business hotel for weekend stays, or reserve a leisure hotel on weekdays. Typically, business hotels are empty over the weekend, and leisure hotels need customers during the week. Hotels will offer price breaks to fill their rooms.

Cut a deal. Check hotel rates online and call the company's 800 number. Then, call the hotel directly and barter for the best price.

Place a bid. To bid for a low rate on a hotel room, visit *www.price line.com*. The online forum *www.biddingfortravel.com* will give you ideas on how low you can go. If you prefer not to bid, check deals on *www.hotwire.com*. This site offers unsold hotel rooms for up to 55 percent off their regular rates. Another forum, *www.better bidding.com*, allows you to check out Hotwire and Priceline deals found by other customers.

Dodge extra fees. Always ask about fees before you book. Then negotiate for free or reduced fees, or look for a hotel that doesn't charge extra for Wi-Fi, parking, and other services.

Sign up for rewards. Loyalty programs are free, and membership can offset the cost of extra fees. Plus, hotels often treat members to room upgrades and other perks.

3 ways to cut costs off the beaten path

The destination sounds great. The cost of the hotel does not. Don't worry. With a little flexibility, you can still enjoy your stay.

Pay less next door. You can book a resort, relish its amenities, and dig a hole in your pocket. Or you can stay next door for a lot less.

For instance, save hundreds of dollars by reserving a room at the Comfort Suites in Nassau, Bahamas, instead of the hugely popular and pricey Atlantis. You'll still enjoy full use of the Atlantis resort's pools, water parks, and health spa — for free.

Stay nearby. Traveling to a major city? Compare hotel rates in the city with those of a small town nearby. You could save a bundle if you don't mind the drive.

Choose a cheaper locale. If you're looking at a particular vacation destination — beach, mountain, wine country — you can cut costs dramatically by not staying in tourist traps.

When Joe and Annie decided to take their eight-year-old son to Europe to explore medieval castles, they first looked at airfare and accommodations in England. Then they compared rates with Ireland.

"Ireland was significantly cheaper," said Annie. "And for a kid, a castle is a castle. We chose Ireland."

Pay a pittance for a home away from home

A hotel room may not be the best deal in town. For value-packed accommodations, explore these alternatives in the U.S. and abroad.

Swap houses and save. A home exchange is easy on the pocketbook. Exchanges are free, and an annual membership to *www.homeexchange.com* runs a little over $100.

Cozy up for free. Stay with locals in a guest room in their private homes. Just make sure the host meets your needs for privacy. Otherwise, you may end up on a couch. Join *www.couchsurfing.org* or *www.hospitalityclub.org* for free to find the right fit for you.

Be a guest for less. You could also stay in someone's guest room for a small fee. Check out *www.evergreenclub.com* for travelers ages 50 and over. Annual membership is $75, and rooms run from $20 for a single to $25 for a couple. This includes a hearty breakfast and sightseeing tips from your hosts.

Another option is *www.airbnb.com*. Here you will find mostly private rooms in host homes. The more adventurous can try castles, houseboats, tree houses, even train cabooses. Prices range from really cheap to sky-high.

Rent at remarkable prices. Find a fully furnished home, cabin, condo, or apartment, and rent it directly from the owner. Try *www.vrbo.com* to begin your search. Cut vacation costs by taking advantage of kitchens stocked with dishes, silverware, and cookware.

Think outside the box. Do you consider yourself open-minded? Then you may want to explore a few more unorthodox ways to save on lodging.

- Hostels — they're not just for the young crowd.

- Monasteries and convents — sparse, but clean and peaceful.

- University housing — revisit your college days with a dorm stay.

- Farm stays — rest and relaxation in rural surroundings.

Save $1,300 for your next vacation

If you think you can't afford a vacation, think again. The Yaycations Calculator will help you spend less throughout the year and save from hundreds to thousands of dollars. Here's how it works.

- Log on to *www.travelmuse.com*.

- Type in "Yaycations Calculator" in the search bar, and hit enter.

- Click on the "Yaycations Vacation Calculator" link, then click on "Start."

Choose from one of 20 categories, and consider what you're willing to do without for a year. Then plug in the numbers. For example, cutting out movies two weekends a month will save you $216. Foregoing your twice-a-week lattes will put $364 into your vacation budget. Not enough? Try cutting out casual dining once a week. Your savings — $1,300.

Once you've reached an amount you're happy with, click on the "Show me where I can go!" tab. TravelMuse will help you find a vacation that fits your budget.

Enjoy a value vacation in the great outdoors

Saving money on vacation is as easy as pitching a tent or hopping into your motor home. If you love the great outdoors, here are some ways to camp or RV for less.

Look for cheap gear. While camping itself can be inexpensive, the price of gear is not. Borrowing gear is one great way to save. You can also check for pre-owned items on eBay, Craigslist, and used sporting goods stores.

If you want to buy new, shopping off-season can help you save, or check out an outlet store like Columbia. To grab some real deals, log on to *www.buystand.com*. You can make an offer on a new item and see if a retailer will match your price.

Explore campsite rates. Fees for campsites can vary. While one national forest might offer sites for free, another may charge as much as $50 a night. Plus, some private campgrounds ask $20 or more a night.

The trick here is to do your homework in advance. Search for campgrounds at national parks and forests on *www.recreation.gov*, and check into free or discounted entrance passes. If you're age 62 or over, a $10 pass gets you and your spouse and children into any national park, monument, or recreation area for life. You can buy the pass at any national park.

To find campsites outside the national parks system, log on to *www.reserveamerica.com*.

Rev up your RV. To get the most out of your RV vacation without breaking the bank, give these tips a try.

- Ensure that your motor home is in optimal condition.

- Pack light to reduce the weight in the RV and save on fuel consumption.

- Drive 55 mph instead of 65.

- Bypass gas stations on the interstate, and drive into the closest town where it's cheaper. Or pay cash for gas at a truck stop.

Cruise your way to a low-cost getaway

Ocean cruise getaways can fit anyone's budget. Use these tips to help you escape to the high seas for a low price.

Book last minute. Cruise lines offer incredible last-minute deals when they don't fill up. This is great news for seniors with flexible schedules. Log on to the website of your favorite cruise line or sites like *www.lastminutecruises.com* to find the very lowest rates.

"If you prefer to book in advance and the rates drop, don't be afraid to ask your cruise line for the lower rate before your final payment is due," says Marie Ryan, a cruise aficionado from Georgia.

Pass on peak times of year. Avoid a cruise during high season, and you could save a bundle. Opt for a cruise during the school year instead of over the summer, winter and spring breaks, or any holidays.

Consider hurricane season. You can find remarkable deals if you're willing to sail the Atlantic between June 1 and Nov. 30 — aka hurricane season. Cruises are rarely canceled because of bad weather. "Cruise ships will avoid hurricanes by changing their ports of call or staying out to sea longer," says Marie. To find deals and storm updates, visit *www.cruisecritic.com* and type in "hurricane zone" in the search bar.

One thing to keep in mind — if your cruise is delayed, you may have to fork over extra money for a hotel. Paying for travel insurance may be a good investment. Look for a third-party insurance provider.

Bring family and friends. Most cruise lines will give away one free cabin for a group reservation depending on the number of passengers. Some will even offer additional perks to groups such as free photos, onboard credits, and discounts on group excursions. Ask your cruise line for details.

Reap benefits with repositioning cruises. You can find deeply discounted cruises by waiting for a ship to relocate during its off-season. These one-way cruises tend to be longer than most and require passengers to book flights home.

Look for savings for singles. Singles who cruise on their own must pay a supplement charge — a charge for one person occupying a cabin for two. To avoid this fee, ask about matching programs. These programs pair singles of the same sex and smoking preference in a cabin. Or try looking for a cruise line with new singles-only cabins. You can save up to 18 percent of what you'd pay for a double state-room with a supplement.

Talk to a travel agent. Cruise specialists can help you find the voyage that's right for you based on your budget and interests.

"Cruise lines, like people, have personalities," says Marie. "A travel agent can help you find a cruise for the family, a romantic getaway, or a party ship. Whatever it is you're looking for, a cruise professional can steer you in the right direction."

Five ways to save as you sail

Cruise lines often promote themselves as all-inclusive. The problem is, they're not. Find out what's included in your cruise and how to save on what isn't.

Feast for free. Most cruise fares include meals in the main dining room and buffet, along with room service. To save money, steer clear of special dining and snack options like specialty restaurants, Ben and Jerry's, and Starbucks.

"If you want to splurge one evening, some cruise lines offer discounts in their high-end restaurants on the first night of the voyage," says frequent cruiser Marie Ryan.

Trim your drink tab. Typically, milk, coffee, iced tea, and some juices are included. Sodas, water bottles, and alcohol are not. Ask about soda packages, or see if you can bring your own. In general, cruise lines restrict toting your own alcohol. But you can still save on cocktails by checking daily drink specials and skipping the fancy glasses.

Snap your own photos. Bring your own camera to avoid the ship's pricey photo services. And remember to pack plenty of batteries, memory cards, and a charger.

Get a grip on tips. Some cruise lines automatically add tips to your onboard account, but you can always adjust the amount.

"Cruise lines have different tipping policies," says Marie. "Make sure you know what the policies are by checking with the company online or asking your travel agent."

Cut excursion costs. Plan your own sightseeing tours and skip the ship's pre-planned trips. You'll save significantly. Just heed this warning from Marie.

"If you are on one of the cruise line's excursions and get back late, the ship will wait for you," she says. "But if you're on your own and have a problem returning, the ship will leave without you."

Pick up perks with loyalty programs

Like the airlines, cruise lines offer special programs for loyal passengers. These programs can add up the savings.

Amenities may include onboard credit and coupon books, discounts on staterooms and spa services, Internet minutes, laundry service, a bottle of wine, minibar setup, dinner for two at a specialty restaurant, members-only parties, and special fares.

Some companies will even throw in the ultimate perk — a complimentary cruise. Sign up online or on board to start reaping these benefits.

Fly the friendly skies with low fares

The high cost of air travel can take the fun out of any vacation. It doesn't have to. Soar into savings with these suggestions.

Be flexible. If you're up in the air about your travel plans, you're likely to find a great deal. Search for fares that fit your budget, then pick the dates and destination that's right for you. For tremendous savings, a little flexibility goes a long way.

Pick the best day to book. For cheap fares, plan to fly on Tuesday, Wednesday, or Saturday afternoon. Early morning and late night departures also cost less than daytime flights. Plus, you can pick up bargains by buying tickets between late August and early September or late December and the beginning of January.

Choose alternate airports. Cash in on extra savings if you fly into a nearby airport and not the biggest or closest one to your destination. Just make sure you consider time and transportation costs. Log on to *www.alternateairports.com* to search out airport options.

Sign up for alerts. Sign up for email alerts from your favorite airline and *www.airfarewatchdog.com*. You'll receive news about special sales and promo codes.

Compare rates and airlines. Call an airline directly before booking online. You can ask an agent to hold your reservation for 24 hours. Then, compare rates on *www.kayak.com* where you can quickly scan hundreds of travel sites for the cheapest airfares. Check budget airlines such as Southwest separately. Kayak doesn't include discount airliners.

If you're traveling throughout Europe, look into discount airliner Ryanair. Travel experts consider it the world's cheapest airline.

Free yourself from airline fees

Do airlines nickel and dime you with fees for every little extra? Yes. Can you do something about it? Absolutely. Glide past those pesky fees with these cost-cutting tips.

Bypass baggage fees. Consider shipping items to your destination instead of checking extra luggage. It may end up costing you less. If you must check a bag, keep these tips in mind.

- Pack as much as you can into the maximum-size carry-on bag allowable — no more than 45 inches overall. An example would be a bag 22 inches long, 14 inches wide, and 9 inches deep.

- Fly budget airlines that don't charge baggage fees.

- See if your airline offers a discount if you prepay for bags online.

- Check your airline's weight limits, then weigh your bags to avoid penalties.

Pack a snack. Don't pay astronomical prices for airline or airport food. Bring your own fruit, snacks, and sandwiches. You can also take an empty water bottle through security and refill it in the gate area.

Check on change fees. Most airlines charge a hefty fee to change your flight. Look for those with more reasonable fare plans. For instance, JetBlue's policy states that the earlier you adjust your itinerary, the lower the change fee.

Also, if the cost of your flight goes down, see if your carrier will refund the difference without charging a fee.

Park away from the airport. Airport parking is expensive. Off-site parking with a free shuttle to and from the airport terminal is your best bet. Compare rates at *www.bestparking.com* and *www.longtermparking.com*. Don't forget to search for discount coupons online, in mailers, and in local magazines.

Trip insurance pays off with peace of mind

Trip insurance may take a small slice out of your vacation budget. But it could save you thousands in the long run. Consider trip insurance if you're taking a cruise, a tour, or a trip that requires you to prepay thousands of dollars. Policies will cover you if your luggage is lost, you experience a medical emergency, or your trip is canceled.

Before you purchase a policy, check with your health and home insurance companies. Some policies will cover medical emergencies, and others will pay you for lost luggage.

If you find you need trip insurance, only purchase it from an independent company, not the trip's organizer. Start with *www.travelguard.com* and *www.allianztravelinsurance.com*. Or log on to *www.insuremytrip.com* or *www.squaremouth.com* to compare quotes from multiple providers.

Drive away with rental car deals

Renting a car can take a bite out of your vacation budget. But it doesn't have to. You can bite back with these cost-saving tips.

Benefit from off-brands. Small rental car companies can save you big bucks. Try Fox, Payless, and Sixt for starters. Their rates can be found on *www.autoslash.com, www.carrentals.com*, and *www.car rentalexpress.com*.

Pick the prepay option. You can save up to 20 percent on a rental car simply by choosing the "pay now" option. Just remember, if you need to cancel your reservation, you may be charged penalty fees.

Look into car sharing. If you need wheels for less than a day, try car sharing — renting a car by the hour. Smaller companies such as RelayRides and Getaround offer this service. So do larger agencies like Hertz, Avis, and Enterprise.

Check for hidden charges. Taxes and fees can turn a great rate into a great rip-off. Always ask about additional charges, or look for them on the company's online reservation page.

Compare rates online. Why search from one company's site to the next when aggregators will do the work for you? Try *www.vroom vroomvroom.com*, a site dedicated to car rentals. And don't forget Orbitz, Expedia, and Travelocity.

Don't buy insurance. Find out if your car insurance company or credit card cover your rental car. If they do, don't purchase additional insurance.

Consider airport alternatives. Rent away from an airport and cut costs by 30 percent or more. Just make sure the fee for the bus or taxi to the rental location is worth the savings.

Chris Darnowski learned this firsthand when she and her husband flew into Sacramento. "We couldn't find a weekly rental under $500 from the airport," she says. Her husband checked around and discovered a rental company in the city offering a rate of $350.

"Even with the cab ride it was much less than we would've paid for the airport rental," she says. "Plus they let us drop the car off at the airport when we returned. It was a great deal."

Travel cheaply with these deals on wheels

Nothing beats a bus ride for $1, especially when that ride spans multiple states. Even trains deliver passengers at popular prices. With deals like these, you can see more of the country for less money.

Hop on a bus. Let someone else do the driving while you relax with a good book. Or pull out your laptop and surf the Web. Many buses today offer free wireless service in addition to all the usual comforts.

- Without a doubt, Greyhound is the most recognizable name in bus transportation in North America — and the bus line with the most deals. For special Web-only fares to more than 3,800 locations, book your trip at *www.greyhound.com*. Or save up to 50 percent with Greyhound's advance purchase promotions. If you buy a full-price ticket, you can bring up to three friends or family members with you at half price. Greyhound offers seniors ages 62 and over a 5-percent discount, but you can't combine it with other offers. Call 800-231-2222 to ask about additional specials.

- Megabus is a low-cost, express bus service offering fares for as low as $1. In operation since 2006, the company serves more than 100 cities across the U.S. and Canada with luxury single- and double-decker buses, free Wi-Fi, at-seat plug ins, and panoramic windows. To snag the cheapest fares, book way in advance and be flexible with your schedule. Look for specials on *www.megabus.com*, or call 877-462-6342. One note — Megabus does not provide parking at any of its stops. When you make a reservation online or by phone, ask about available parking nearby.

- BoltBus, another value-packed bus line with free Wi-Fi and extra legroom, serves the Northeast and West Coast only. Each route sells at least one $1 seat. The earlier you book at *www.boltbus.com*, the greater your odds of grabbing a seat for a buck. Contact a reservationist at 877-265-8287 for details.

Ride the rails. If the idea of traveling by train appeals to you, Amtrak offers an array of economical excursions. You can save 25 percent off one-way coach fares with Amtrak SmartFares, available only on *www.amtrak.com* on Tuesday through Friday.

Veterans with a VetRewards Card and seniors over age 62 receive a 15-percent discount on most train tickets. Active duty military and AAA members get 10 percent off.

Like the airlines, you can earn reward points with bus and train lines. Check each company for details.

6 tips to sightseeing savings

You don't need to pay full price to a museum, amusement park, or sightseeing tour. Discount tickets to attractions like these abound online and in coupon books. To find deals, check out these options.

Pick up coupons upon arrival. When you check in to your hotel, check out the coupon racks, or ask your concierge about discounts. Also, make sure to stop by the city's visitor center or the Chamber of Commerce.

Snip costs with warehouse clubs. Did you know that BJ's and Costco provide travel deals? That's right. Club members can enjoy exclusive offers which may include discounts to attractions. Check with your club before leaving home.

Claim your senior or military discount. Ask and you shall receive — a discount that is. Seniors and military personnel can save a few bucks by simply asking about a price break at a museum, monument, or theme park.

Purchase a pass. A CityPASS bundles prepaid admission to the top attractions in 11 cities across North America. For example, Chicago's CityPASS is a booklet of tickets to the city's five must-see sights at 49 percent off the combined admission price. Check with your hotel or visit *www.citypass.com*.

Buy a book. An Entertainment book provides thousands of coupons for restaurants, attractions, and more in well over 100 North American cities. A book plus digital access usually runs about $30.

An online and digital membership is cheaper. Look for books at your vacation destination, or log on to *www.entertainment.com* to see what's available.

Scan websites. Always search an attraction's website before leaving home. Many offer 10 percent off admission if you order tickets online. Or you can visit *www.discountattractions.com*. With deals in more than 80 cities, it's worth a look.

Trim your foreign travel tab

You can afford a vacation abroad. Simply choose low-cost destinations like Asia, Eastern Europe, or Latin America. Then, tack on these value-packed vacation tips for extra savings.

Make smart money choices. As you travel, know where to get cash and when to use a credit card.

- Avoid using traveler's checks. You'll pay fees on both ends.

- Avoid changing money at airports and hotels where transaction rates are high. Change money at a local bank for a better rate.

- Ask your credit card company about their fees for international use, or sign up for a fee-free card.

- See if your bank is part of a fee-free bank alliance abroad. If so, use an ATM to get local currency.

- Use a credit card if you're uncomfortable with local currency and exchange rates. You will never pay the wrong amount with a credit card.

Request your VAT refund. Visitors from outside the European Union are entitled to a value-added tax (VAT) refund. As you shop, ask merchants if they participate in the VAT program before making a purchase.

Check into American hotel chains. Many American hotel chains honor their senior discount offers overseas. Don't hesitate to ask for it.

Sit back and enjoy the ride. Once you arrive at your destination, get around with these bargain rides.

- Rail passes include stops in multiple cities or countries within Europe, Japan, Canada, and Australia. See if a pass or point-to-point tickets work best for your budget.

- Buses provide cheap transport in Latin America. For instance, you can trek long distances across Costa Rica for less than $5.

- Tuk-tuks, three-wheeled motorized vehicles, provide cheap, quick rides across cities in southeast Asia and Latin America. Always agree on a fare with the driver before hopping in.

- In bike-friendly cities, renting a bike can provide hours of low-cost transportation.

Secrets to saving on meals

You're probably used to paying an extra 15 to 20 percent when you dine out at home. But before you throw those extra bills on the table in a foreign country, make sure you know the local customs. In some countries, tipping offends the locals. And in others, a 10-percent tip is more than plenty. Always look over your bill to see if it already includes a service charge.

To save on meals, pick up meats, cheeses, and bread at open air markets or local delis. Or eat your main meal mid-day. Many countries in Europe offer lunch for a low, set price with three courses, wine or beer, and coffee.

Hobbies, Pastimes & Entertainment

First-class fun at no-frills prices

5 smart ways to load your e-reader for free

Electronic readers — commonly called e-readers — are thinner, lighter, more powerful, and less expensive than ever. The problem comes when you start stocking your e-reader with digital books. The average price for one is just under $10. Here are a few ways you can read to your heart's content for pennies.

Check out the library. With distributors like OverDrive, you can go through your local library to download a copy of an e-book, choosing from hundreds, if not thousands, of titles — all without ever leaving home. Best of all, there are never any late fees. When your lending period is up, the book is automatically returned.

Borrow from friends. Some e-readers — the Amazon Kindle and the Barnes & Noble Nook, for instance — have programs that let friends swap e-books for up to 14 days. There are some restrictions, so be sure to check out the lending information on *www.amazon.com* and *www.barnesandnoble.com*.

Swap with strangers. It's fun to share with friends you've never met. Many organizations operate a lending or swapping service online. Most are free and only require you to register with a valid email address.

- *www.booklending.com*

- *ebookfling.com*

Access public domain. Thousands of e-books are free in the United States because their copyright has expired. These works are said to be in the public domain. You can download and share them all you want, for free. The most famous website for public domain works is Project Gutenberg at *www.gutenberg.org*. They currently offer over 42,000 free e-books.

Download from a third party. Several of the major online book-sellers — including Amazon, Barnes & Noble, Sony, and iTunes — also offer e-book titles for free. Once you are on their website, look for a "free" category or search by price.

Here are some other sites not affiliated with a major company that offer free downloads.

- *manybooks.net*

- *openlibrary.org*

- *www.pixelofink.com*

- *www.smashwords.com*

- *www.free-ebooks.net*

Save $180 a year on audiobooks

Nothing makes a long commute or plane ride go by faster than an audiobook. Listening to a classic or the latest bestseller is a welcome distraction and just plain fun. Whether you're using your laptop, tablet, MP3 player, e-reader, or smartphone, don't pay $30 for a single audiobook. At just one book a month, you could spend $360 in a year.

Be a smart consumer like Anna Carter, who has been listening to audiobooks for more than 10 years. She has found that a combination of sources works well and saves her money.

"I used to borrow CDs from the library," she says, "and I still can, but that technology is older and a lot more difficult to use. I'm lucky my library now offers a digital download service that works great. You are limited to the number you can check out and how long you can keep a title, but everything is free. I only wish they had more titles."

To fill in the gaps, she also has a membership to Audible, Amazon's provider of digital recordings. Based on a credit system, Audible offers memberships by the month or year. In addition to a certain number of audiobook downloads, Anna is also eligible for discounts, deals, and freebies.

"They even let you return any audiobook for full credit if you're not happy with it," Anna says.

One of the main reasons customers are dissatisfied with a recording is because of poor narration. "It can be a wonderful book, but if you have just an average narrator, it can really detract from the story," she says. "That's why I'll sometimes go onto Audible's website to read customer reviews on a certain title. If most people are happy with the narration, I may then try to check it out from the library or download it. That keeps me from wasting time and money on a poorly read story."

Check out Audible memberships at *www.audible.com*. Their cheapest is $14.95 a month or about $180 a year — that's still half what you could pay for one full-price recording a month. If the cost still sounds too high, consider splitting a membership with a housemate or family member. You'll share all account information, but you can download to multiple devices.

Rounding out Anna's listening choices is a subscription to Christian Audio's free download a month program. Find out all about it at *christianaudio.com*.

If you are interested in the classics or little-known titles, check out these websites that offer free audio downloads. Many will be narrated by volunteers.

- *www.openculture.com/freeaudiobooks*

- *www.gutenberg.org/wiki/Gutenberg:The_Audio_Books_Project*

- *www.booksshouldbefree.com*

- *librivox.org*

Take advantage of tool lending libraries

There's always another tool that would come in handy in your garden, but costs add up. If gardening is your hobby, save your money for plants and seeds, and borrow tools you won't use very often from a local tool lending library.

Some nonprofit tool lending libraries, like the North Portland Tool Library, lend tools for free to local residents. Others, referred to as "tool banks," charge a small fee and may lend only to charities and other groups. Ask local gardeners or do an Internet search to see if there's a tool lending library near you.

When it's time to trim your rhododendrons, you could spend around $46 to buy a new pruning lopper. That's great, but it'll sit in your garage for a year, getting dull and gathering dust. Borrow a lopper from a tool lending library and bank that $46 instead.

Bright ideas to cut your cable bill

Not much can spike your blood pressure like seeing your cable bill in the mailbox. People in the U.S. pay an average of $86 a month for basic TV service plus premium channels. That's more than you'd pay to fill a gas tank on a mini van. And according to a leading market research company, that number is only going up — to around $200 by the year 2020.

It might not be easy, but if you're determined, you can cut that bill down to size. Here's how.

Compare and negotiate. Sometimes you're stuck with only one telecom provider in your area — but make sure. A website like *www.whitefence.com* searches within your ZIP code for all offers. With that information, you're in a position of power. Let your provider know you've found competing offers. Ask if they will price match. If not, be willing to cancel service.

Schedule a disconnect. You've found a better offer with another company and your provider won't budge. Go ahead and set up a date and time to disconnect your service — a week or two away. You may be surprised at the deals you'll be offered from your current provider as the disconnect date gets closer. At this point, it may be smarter and easier to take their deal and cancel your new service.

This tactic will be more successful if you are a long-term customer who pays on time.

Change your lineup. Really examine your viewing habits. Do you regularly watch all 300 channels in your package? If not, compare package lineups and switch to a cheaper one with fewer channels. Also be aware that companies change their packages frequently.

"I stayed with a higher-priced cable plan for a year because the provider didn't offer a lower-tier package that included two or three of my favorite channels," says Melissa Ackerson, a longtime satellite cable customer. "When I checked later, I discovered they had changed their basic package to one that — incredibly — now included the channels I wanted to keep. I was able to lower my bill by $40 a month."

Cancel that DVR. When the digital video recorder (DVR) came on the scene in 1999, lives were changed forever. No more racing through dinner to view a favorite program. No more flipping channels to catch conflicting sitcoms. Today, more than half of all cable or satellite subscribers have these handy gadgets in their homes — but at a cost of anywhere from $6 to $20 a month.

Could you live without this convenience? If your cable company offers free video-on-demand as part of your package, you can use it to view recently aired shows, movies, and often previous seasons of popular programs. Or take advantage of streaming services that would make your DVR obsolete.

Decline free trials. These are tempting, but unless you are an excellent record-keeper, it's likely you'll forget to call and cancel this add-on when the free promotion expires.

Purchase your own modem. Renting one through your cable provider can add about $7 a month to your bill. Buy your own and you'll recoup your expenses within a year.

Inspect your bill. One month, Kerry Clark from Atlanta noticed her telecom bill had increased by $10. When she examined the charges, she saw her provider had added a package of Spanish channels to her programming without permission. "They removed the package immediately when I called," she said, "but it seemed quite sneaky. I'm just glad I noticed."

Of course, you should always start by calling your cable company and simply asking for a discount, promotion, or a lower rate. Be honest. Tell them your cable bill is too high and you'd like their help.

Although you may chafe at being tied to one provider, bundling — receiving TV, Internet, and phone service from a single company — is usually cheaper than shopping a la carte.

Watch TV for free

Would you like to say farewell to your cable or satellite television bill forever? Then take a step back in time and use an antenna.

No, not your grandma's antenna, but a digital antenna that can get you network programming in high-definition.

Some may look like the "rabbit ears" from the 1950s, while some look more like a science project, but inside there is pure 21st century technology that's a snap to use. Simply plug into your television, scan for channels, and go.

You'll spend anywhere from $10 to $80 on either a set-top or rooftop model. And as long as your TV was made after 2007, that's it. Older sets will need a digital converter box.

Your particular success will depend on how far you live from a broadcast tower, how many trees and buildings surround your home, and exactly where you place the antenna. Visit *www.AntennaWeb.org* and input your ZIP code to discover the correct antenna type for you.

Get the best deals on gift cards

Gift cards are perfect for friends, family members, coworkers, and — yourself. That's right, there are ways for you to actually make money and receive other benefits when you use the following tricks to purchase gift cards.

- A membership at Sam's Club, Costco, or BJ's Wholesale Club means you can buy gift cards from them at discounted prices. A $100 iTunes gift card, for example, sells online for $94.64 through Sam's Club.

- Use the loyalty points you've earned from a retailer, your bank, or credit card company to pay for gift cards. Even frequent flier card miles can often be redeemed this way.

- Purchase a gift card using a rewards credit card. Not only will you give a great gift, but you get to earn cash back or other perks. Read the fine print on your credit card to make sure gift cards qualify.

- Buy your cards from a retailer that offers you some incentive. Kroger, for example, lets you earn gas points from gift card purchases.

- Visit a website designed specifically to buy, sell, or swap gift cards — *swapagift.com*, CardCash *(cardcash.com)*, Cardpool *(www.cardpool.com)*, GiftCardRescue *(www.giftcardrescue.com)*, and Gift Card Granny *(www.giftcardgranny.com)* are good examples. After holidays like Christmas, Mother's Day, and Valentine's Day, these sites are swamped with good deals. If you're looking to sell a card, just remember you'll rarely get full value.

- Store loyalty programs allow you to earn points toward gift certificates with each purchase. Ace Hardware, DSW, and Speedway convenience stores are examples.

- Save when you purchase and use discounted gift cards yourself. For example, snagging a $50 Publix or Safeway card from a discounted seller for $45 means you just saved $5 on groceries.

How to be a frugal golfer

Jim Bishop, famous American journalist and author, once said, "Golf is played by 20 million mature American men whose wives think they are out having fun."

If golf is your idea of fun, but paying top dollar for equipment and tee times is not, try some of these money-saving strategies.

- Play a cheaper course. Search out public courses or join a discount club like Club 19 (*www.club19golf.com*) and pay less per round.

- Invest in a membership. Do the math to make sure you'll play enough to break even, then join in the off-season to get a deal.

- Find part-time work at a golf course so you're eligible for free rounds.

- Buy equipment in winter or whenever it's the off-season in your area.

- Look for used equipment from secondhand shops or from online sellers.

- Play with used or recycled golf balls but not refurbished balls, which are usually of lower quality.

- Schedule twilight or early morning tee times. These are often discounted.

- Look online for discounted tee times. Websites like *www.golfnow.com* and *teetimesavings.com* help you play more for less.

- Practice your putting and chipping for free on a public course.

- Pay less to play on nine-hole courses while still getting a good golf workout.

- Walk don't ride. You'll save a lot in cart fees.

- Bring your own food if the course permits, and always carry a water bottle.

- Don't subscribe to golf magazines. They are expensive and most are chock-full of tempting ads promoting high-priced equipment.

Have fun on a budget

You don't have to spend a lot to have fun. Here are some great ideas for a good time that won't break the bank.

- Host a book or magazine swap with friends.

- Audit a college course for free or sign up for a summer class at a reduced rate. Sometimes college classes offered in the early morning or on a secondary campus are cheaper.

- Take the grandkids to a minor league baseball game and rack up some major league savings. Tickets, parking, food, and souvenirs all come at bargain basement prices.

- Watch movies for free with an online service like Crackle. Go to *www.crackle.com*, create an account, and start watching.

- Find out if your local museums offer special "no admission" evenings.

- Check out a travel DVD from the library. Visit a place you've always wanted to go — for free.

Volunteer your way to free evenings out

The secret to a retirement filled with shows, concerts, sporting events, the ballet — even meals — without spending a dime on any of them? Give your time and energy as a volunteer. Helping others will help you enjoy some nice perks in your retirement years.

It's easy to get started. If you enjoy attending local venues — like a theater, concert hall, or sports stadium — simply call their main office and ask for information about volunteering.

Or check the newspaper for articles or advertisements recruiting volunteers for local festivals or events. You can attend the event for free and often get a free meal as well. Just ask 62-year-old Linda Thompson, who volunteers with the Great Georgia Air Show.

"While I'm working, I get to enjoy the festivities along with a free meal coupon. Plus, I get a T-shirt. It's a fun way to spend a weekend."

Other volunteer opportunities include national and state parks, film and music festivals, local colleges and universities, and race events and other competitions. You can choose to do something on a regular basis or simply volunteer for a single event whenever the mood strikes you.

If you have a computer, search these websites to match up your interests with the many volunteer options available.

- *www.volunteermatch.org*
- *www.serve.gov*
- *www.dosomething.org*
- *www.volunteer.gov*

5 ways to see a movie for less

You'll shell out $15 to see a movie at the theater in some cities. If that price seems excessive, try one of these easy ways to enjoy great movies without going bankrupt.

Get in early. A matinee showing is usually about 25 percent cheaper than a movie that starts after 6 p.m. But have a snack before you go, so you don't end up blowing your savings on high-priced drinks and food.

Watch at home. Keep an eye on cable TV listings for a movie you want to see. Record it early in the week, then save it to watch on weekend movie night.

Borrow for free. Look for movie DVDs you can borrow for free from the public library or a collection at church.

Be patient. If you can wait just a few months, you'll probably be able to catch that blockbuster for a dollar or two at a local discount theater, sometimes called a "late run" theater.

Find discounts. Membership in clubs and organizations has its rewards, including cheap tickets.

- Ask about discount tickets at a warehouse club like Sam's Club or Costco.

- Look for a loyalty program at your local theater chain.

- Ask for a senior discount at the box office.

Save $18 on concert tickets with group deals

Harness the power of group purchasing, and you can score deals on tickets to concerts, special events, travel, meals, and more.

You can sign up to receive email offers for local events, or simply check the website of group discounters like Groupon, LivingSocial, and Google Offers to see what's available in your area. Buying a ticket or voucher here usually saves you 50 percent or more.

For example, a recent Groupon deal in the Dallas area offered two tickets to an upcoming symphony concert for just $18. That's half off the regular price.

Be sure to check the rules, limitations, and expiration dates for any group deal you consider buying. But even if a voucher expires, you may still be able to get back what you spent. First, ask the ticket office or restaurant for a refund up to the amount you paid. If they won't refund your money, contact Groupon or LivingSocial.

Index

R

Rabbit ears. *See* Antenna
Ramsey, Dave 13
Readability 323
Real estate
  in college towns 287
  selling a house 269-274
  websites 274, 275
Rebalancing, stock 41
Rebates 326
Recipe substitutions 185
Recreational vehicle (RV) 341
Recycling, electronics 319
Refinancing, mortgage 283
Refund, tax 88, 90
Refurbished products 320, 325
Relocating. *See* Moving
Remodeling, home 136
Rental cars 347-348
Rental property, owning
  278-282
Renting 292-294
Replacement cost, for homes
  261-262
Research, donating to 119
Residuary clause 111
Restaurants, savings on 189-193
Restricted application, for
  Social Security 231
Retirement
  balancing nest egg 44-46
  calculating costs 50, 288
  college towns and 287
  health care and 148
  living abroad 289
  money mistakes and 46
  part-time jobs 239-240

Social Security and 225,
  233-234
taxes and 114
transitioning to 235-236
women and 54
working from home 240-242
Retirement date fund. *See*
  Target date fund
Reverse mortgage 276
  scams 285
Revocable living trust. *See*
  Living trust
Rewards cards 69-71
Risk tolerance 42
Roth IRA 33-35

S

Safe deposit box 112, 116
Safety. *See* Security
Sales cycles 175-176
Sam's Club. *See* Warehouse club
Saver's tax credit 32
Savings accounts 61-62
Scams. *See also* Fraud
  coupon 189
  debt assistance 10
  email 80
  foreclosure 285
  health insurance 132
  home repair 327-328
  medical 126-128, 133
  property tax 106
  rental 294
  reverse mortgage 285
  Social Security 232
  tax 88-90
  work-at-home 242